CW01502458

Contents

How to Think Like a Realist

How to Think Like a Realist

A Methodology for Social Science

Ray Pawson

Emeritus Professor of Social Research Methodology, University of Leeds, UK

Edward Elgar
PUBLISHING

Cheltenham, UK • Northampton, MA, USA

Published by
Edward Elgar Publishing Limited
The Lypiatts
15 Lansdown Road
Cheltenham
Glos GL50 2JA
UK

Edward Elgar Publishing, Inc.
William Pratt House
9 Dewey Court
Northampton
Massachusetts 01060
USA

Paperback edition 2024

A catalogue record for this book
is available from the British Library

Library of Congress Control Number: 2024932698

This book is available electronically in the **Elgar**online
Sociology, Social Policy and Education subject collection
http://doi.org/10.4337/9781035321100

ISBN 978 1 0353 2109 4 (cased)
ISBN 978 1 0353 2110 0 (eBook)
ISBN 978 1 0353 5480 1 (paperback)

Printed and bound by CPI Group (UK) Ltd, Croydon, CR0 4YY

To Wendy

Frontispiece: Newton

Figures

Tables

Boxes

About the author

'And what do you do then?' It's the inevitable question – be it delivered by a taxi driver, a medical practitioner, a fellow traveller, a wedding guest, a waiting room incumbent, etc. Blessedly, I am not a logistics engineer, a cloud architect, an internal communications officer, a social responsibility manager, or a chicken-sexer. Thank goodness, I don't work in the reviled professions like stock trading, politics, or real estate. Nevertheless, I always have trouble with *that* question.

Since we are started on the topic, my professional title is Emeritus Professor of Social Research Methodology. Not that I usually begin any chit-chat with the formal role; the 'emeritus' bit is tricky enough but as far as Joe Public is concerned being a 'methodologist' sounds a bit like membership of some obscure religious sect. Accordingly, my job *self*-description heads for safer ground and thus often I stump up with 'academic' or 'prof', though that inevitably leads to a second inquiry, 'What field?' To which I used to say sociology, where I started but which field, since I started, has dwindled into cultural commentary. Later on, I tried 'social policy' to which the persistent still pester – 'Which field?' I struggled in this respect because I've never stuck to a particular policy domain. I'm no expert in educational policy, environmental policy, health policy, criminal justice policy, monetary policy – or any other you may care to name. I did have a soft spot for penal policy thanks to my dealings with Reginald Hacksaw Molloy (but that's another story).

So how should I explain what methodologists do? Occasionally I stumble on: 'Erm, I research the way we do research, I research how we might improve social inquiry.' But to no avail. 'Research on research – what on earth is that?' By now the cabby has wished he hadn't asked, and the wedding guest has gone off for a Prosecco refill. And I'm thinking, why don't I brush up on animal husbandry and just pretend to be a chicken-sexer? Clearly, I'm never going to be able to explain myself. I reckon you'll just have to read the book.

Preface

Shall we for ever make new books, as apothecaries make new mixtures, by pouring only out of one vessel into another? (Laurence Sterne, *The Life and Opinions of Tristram Shandy, Gentleman*)

Now there is a formidable challenge. This is my fifth (and final) book and as already noted, I have filled the previous ones with ideas about improving research in social science and in policy evaluation (Pawson, 1989, 2006, 2013; Pawson and Tilley, 1997). Stubbornly and persistently, I have been concerned with the development of a 'realist' methodology for the conduct of social inquiry. So why another effort? Why is this old apothecary striving to concoct a new mixture out of the old ingredients?

There are several reasons. The first is that learning never stops. This applies to you and me and whomsoever has attempted to put pen to paper. Thus, whilst I believe that there is a dogged consistency and a sense of development in these books and dozens of my other scribblings, there is still 'room for improvement' as my school reports used to say. Some of my earliest realist pronouncements were oversimple, some have been misinterpreted, some made assumptions that were never properly explored, some failed to grasp problems that only emerged in the aftermath of inquiry. I aim to tidy up many such loose ends.

The second spur to authorship is, quite literally, to reclaim history. Realist methodology is blossoming, and realist studies are burgeoning. This is no flash in the pan. Accordingly, in the main body of the text, I try to explicate the ideas and the influence of dozens of other realist-inspired authors stretching back through time and across disciplines. This mission has never been more pressing. Sociology, nowadays, is an overexcited, self-absorbed teenager. It only has eyes for contemporary issues and 'neglected topics'. Citations identify contemporaries rather than progenitors. Interestingly, this unhappy phenomenon carries a name – 'scholarly forgetting' (Lamers et al., 2020). Perhaps the greatest student of the oblivion of ideas was Robert K Merton. He explored a number of potent mechanisms such as the 'Matthew effect', 'obliteration by incorporation', and 'cryptomnesia' that explain the uneven intellectual survival of concepts and of their author's reputations (Merton, 1968a). By contrast, I aim to give methodological insight credit wherever it is due and whenever it was uttered. Fittingly, Merton will feature as the progenitor of key realist ideas.

The third motivation for putting fingers to keyboard is to offer a rebuttal, albeit a necessarily modest one, on the challenge for social science in a 'post-truth' world. Realism sits proudly in the Enlightenment tradition, which can be traced back to Diderot and D'Alemberts's Encyclopédie (1751–66) and forward again to 20th century efforts to sustain an 'evidence-based' approach to policymaking and much else besides (Fowler, 2003). But then what happened as the century turned? President Bombast and Prime Minister Bluster were elected to populist acclaim. Experts are ignored. Technocrats are berated. Feelings have taken over and a new emotional politics has become normalised. Next, we have had the return of plague and petulance. Medical science, the very pinnacle of the evidence movement, the embodiment of analytical inquiry, was feeble in its initial attempts to quell the Covid-19 pandemic using public health controls (Pawson, 2023). And even the eventual triumph of the vaccination programme was denied by vehement 'anti-vaxxers'. Were this not enough, along came the Ukrainian bloodbath and the threat of World War III. Once again truth vanished. Simultaneously the conflict was seen by Russia as 'liberation' and by most of the rest of the world as 'genocide'. Realism is a way of thinking. It cannot, of course, engineer the political conquest of post-truth beliefs and movements. But it can make us think more closely about how to sustain the parlous pursuit of rational argument. It helps to know what truth is.

My fourth and main objective is revealed in the structure of the text, which journeys across physical science and clinical science, before landing squarely in social science. The coverage here represents a commitment to the 'unity of science' (Oppenheim and Putnam, 1958). This heroic proposition claims that there are core explanatory principles which underpin science in all it guises, and the book makes tiny, tentative steps in tracing the common realist tenets. Perforce, I am also committed to the 'unity of social science'. This is another brave mission, given hints already dropped about the recent, raging fragmentation of the constituent disciplines. I am unable to move mountains in this respect but what I want to show is that realist principles convert widely into realist practice. They find their way into all manner of empirical research, regardless of whether the evidence base is rooted in quantitative, qualitative, comparative, historical, evaluative, or textual inquiry. Realism embodies and relies upon methodological pluralism.

NOTE ON THE FRONTISPIECE

Before we enter the text, may I add an explanation of the frontispiece. It is taken from a photo of Eduardo Paolozzi's 1995 sculpture *Newton*, which stands in the plaza of the British Library on the Euston Road in London. It draws on a famous 1795 print by William Blake. The ancient print and the modernist public art both represent an intellectual battle – similar to one that will resound through this book. Newton is commonly regarded as a pioneer of Enlightenment science. Yet Blake despised him for the complete omission of a spiritual dimension from his theories, hence his scoffing depiction of the cold obsessive, oblivious to the glories of nature. For those of you unable to view Blake's print in the Tate Gallery, there is smudgy reproduction of it on the cover of my 1989 book. Paolozzi is somewhat kinder. His Newton is a picture of concentration and dedication, though he is bolted together as though he were a machine. Both artists use the symbolism of the compass, which according to a well-known art historian (and spy), 'represents the imposition of order on the world by means of measurement and the resulting destruction of human imagination' (Blunt, 1938). This book delivers a thundering counterhypothesis, with Newton as an emblem – it is only through imaginative theorising that we can begin to gather evidence on how the world is ordered and how to gain a measure of it.

STRUCTURE AND CONTENT

I have never been a fan of the 8000-word book chapter, less still the rapidly diminishing word limit that applies in modern journal papers. My topic, methodology, needs more room to breathe. Accordingly, you will find no chapters here, rather a book in three substantial parts. Worry not, dear reader, you are not about to be faced with indigestible 30,000+ word lumps of text. Each part is broken down into a dozen or so smaller 'episodes', each one describing an important contribution to the topic under discussion, each one providing a methodological keepsake that, hopefully, will be useful in and of itself.

The three major parts of the book address the classic methodological questions of social science, namely, (i) Causality, (ii) Objectivity, and (iii) Generality.

i.   Social inquiry begins habitually with the 'why?' question. Why did things turn out like that? Why are they patterned in this way? Why does change occur? Why do policies succeed (and often fail)? Why are certain beliefs so prevalent? To such brainteasers social science is expected to provide answers. And responses invariably begin, 'because …'. A chain of thinking about social causation is thus set in motion. Understanding how we infer, establish, and choose between causal explanations remains at the heart of social inquiry.

ii. Most but not all social inquiry has a concern for objectivity, hoping to construct sound explanation rather than concoct personal opinion. Such concerns are expressed via lofty ideals about 'truth seeking' and more workaday concerns about the 'reliability' and 'validity' of particular pieces of evidence. Yet we know that we cannot simply believe the evidence of our eyes – because sensory observation depends on who is doing the sensing. We now occupy a world of 'facts' and 'alternative facts', 'news' and 'fake news'. The battle for objectivity, the quest for trustworthy evidence, has never been more important.

iii. Assuming that we can master the issues of causality and objectivity, we than have to consider the matter of where our explanations apply. Empirical investigation is normally fixed in space and time, yet social science aspires to generality. Generalisation is the process of extending a specific explanation of a specific instance to a wider or universal set. It is no easy task. How do we choose a case study so that it that informs a wider set of cases? How can a small sample be made to speak to a wider population? How can we increase the scope of an explanation?

Each one of the issues has spawned a massive literature both philosophical and practical. It has also prompted debate, sometimes rather scholarly, sometimes nearer fisticuffs. On each topic, as my book title suggests, I will be pursuing a realist resolution to these ancient methodological puzzles. I will indeed be explaining 'how to think like a realist'. Rather than offering an initial summary or synopsis here, my understanding of realist inquiry builds through the book, episode by episode. Realist thinking requires a deep immersion in all aspects of inquiry and I seek to provide scores of practical pointers rather than an abstract blueprint.

To this end I should point out that my three classic topics remain classic because there is and never will be complete agreement on their meaning and realisation. Despite the habitual use of the appellation 'social science', many of my colleagues would reject any claim to follow science, dismiss any interest in causality, deny any need for objectivity, and scorn the possibility of generalisation. They are beyond hope. I don't seek to convert them. But in following their chosen paths these various tribes – constructivists, post-modernists, emancipators, critics, essayists, relativists, and so on – have found time to say why causality, objectivity, and generality are false idols. So, in defending the science in social science, their criticisms also need to be overturned. Whilst I will always seek to 'accentuate the positive' in realist inquiry, be aware that a few of the 'episodes' in the following narrative will also aim to 'eliminate the negative'!

The book has a short Afterword, shortened yet further here: *Realism provides the optimal methodology for social science, providing objective and generalisable causal explanations. Causality is understood through the action of generative mechanisms. Objectivity is approached by adjudicating between contending theories. Generality is captured in middle-range theories. Realism embodies the science in social science. But it is imperfect.*

ACKNOWLEDGEMENTS

As always, I want to acknowledge help, encouragement (and challenge) from colleagues whose ideas permeate this book. In my academic lifetime realist inquiry has transformed from maverick outsider to domesticated insider. This, with the help of a dedicated handful and then a coach load and now a community of scholars. No longer is it possible to name all names. You will, dear friends, recognise your own contributions in what follows.

FINAL THOUGHT

Fittingly, it goes to Merton who supplies this elegant response to Tristram Shandy's satirical challenge raised in the epigraph to this Preface:

> Re-reading an older work through new spectacles allows contemporary sociologists to find fresh perceptions that were blurred in the course of firsthand research and, as a result, to consolidate the old, half-formed insight with newly developing inquiry. (1968b, p. 37)

PART I

How to think about causality

Introduction to Part I

Everyone thinks about causality as soon as they pose the question ... 'Why?' Children are causal pedants. Why must I do this and not that? To which patient parents reply 'because' ... before embarking on a causal explanation of the positive and negative outcomes of particular behaviours. Physicists are long-serving purveyors of causal explanations, beginning perhaps with the answer to the question what caused this apple to fall on my head (answer gravitational attraction) and moving to explanations of the causal forces underlying all physical aspects of the universe (answer string theory). Medics are causal warriors and patients are causal worriers. Treatments are scrutinised meticulously to ascertain whether they will work, and patients hope fervently that causal efficacy applies to them. Whether they are working retrospectively (why did events turn out like this?), in real time (why does this happen?), or prospectively (what would happen if this was attempted?) social science researchers endlessly confront causal questions. Given the ubiquity of causal analysis across these and many other domains of inquiry, it is no surprise that philosophy has taken to the issue. Perhaps more printing ink has been splashed on understanding the nature of causation than on any other epistemological puzzle.

Part I of the book traces one particular pathway through this tumult, following the ideas that have emerged in proposing the merits and the utility of a 'generative model of causation'. Realists think generatively. They investigate a pattern of events, be it in physical science, clinical science, or social science and begin with some simple questions. How was it generated? What brought it into existence? What are the underlying mechanisms that created it? These three motifs, easy to utter, will consume the first 30,000+ words of the book.

These days everyone likes to say that they are on a 'journey' through life. So here follows an anecdotal and selective attempt to reconstruct my academic journey in getting to grips with the idea of generative causation. It is anecdotal in the sense that it depends on my deeply unreliable and distinctly non-chronological memory of encounters with diverse authors and proliferating narratives. It is selective, both in the obvious sense of scratching the surface of a gargantuan literature but also by way of compressing important contributions from several learned colleagues. They will have the consolation of being able to correct my simplifications.

The tale is told in recollections, in relatively short 'episodes'. Each one concludes with a boxed summary on 'lessons learned' in an attempt to provide a digestible, self-contained synopsis of the key features of generative thinking. The instalments are as follows:

Episode 1: The oldest maxim: correlation does not equal causation

Episode 2: Harré's distinction between successionist and generative causation

Episode 3: Stinchcombe's challenge to students (and the rest of us)

Episode 4: Newer maxims: contingency clouds causation; mechanisms are not variables

Episode 5: Generative thinking in pharmaceutical inquiry: the drug development pipeline

Episode 6: Provisos: the transience of causal relationships and the influence of context

Episode 7: Mechanisms, contexts, and demi-regularities in social science

Episode 8: Causation and change: Coleman's boat and the Caucus race

Episode 9: Causation in complex systems: boundary conditions and stopping rules

Episode 10: Generative thinking in sociology I: Goldthorpe on social mobility

Episode 11: Generative thinking in sociology II: Boudon on educational inequality

Episode 12: Generative thinking in programme evaluation: Pawson in prison.

Episode 13: Generative thinking in comparative historical research: whether protest movements?

Episode 14: Generative thinking in qualitative longitudinal inquiry: following young fathers

Episode 15: Generative thinking in legislative analysis: Megan's Law

Episode 16: Interlude

There is a logic to this playlist and a brief overview may be of assistance. Forewarned is forearmed. Episode 1 presents a mystery story about a causal outcome of activity on the surgeon's table. Solve it, dear reader, and you have started on the road to generative thinking. Methodology has the habit of throwing up fundamental disagreements, none more so than in disputes about how to establish causation. Episode 2 presents the contending parties via Harré's distinction between 'successionist' and 'generative' accounts of causality in science. Part I as a whole is an active combatant in the dispute; I gradually clear the ground for the latter by pointing out profound deficiencies in the former. Episode 3 borrows an idea from Stinchcombe to provide the first ingredient of and the first challenge to generative thinking in social science. Good theory is the bedrock to causal analysis, but social theory can be prolific, providing a superabundance of starting points. Episode 4 examines some elementary forms of data analysis in social science – contingency tables and multiple correlation. Rather than closing in on causation they rely on unspoken and unresearched assumptions about generative mechanisms.

Episode 5 provides a critique of the gold-standard application of the successionist paradigm – the clinical randomised controlled trial (RCT) in pharmaceutical inquiry. I commit successionist blasphemy. RCTs do not establish causation. That is established prior to clinical trials on the basis of many years of basic biological research on the drug's mechanism of action. Episode 6 introduces discussion of the durability of causal relationships. Even in physical and clinical science there are no causal 'laws'. Discovering where empirical relationships do and do not hold is another key to causal analysis. Generative thinking is always needed to explain the provisos.

Episode 7 provides the pivot of Part I. The basic ingredients of generative explanation in social science, namely, 'mechanisms', 'contexts', and 'outcomes', are explained. Mechanisms reside in human agency. Contexts refer to pre-existing social structures. Outcomes are the patterns that result from the way agents respond to structures. The basic causal blueprint is thus revealed … as is an enormous practical challenge for empirical research. The potential candidates for the role of mechanisms and contexts in social explanation are multitudinous. The outcome patterns that ensue proliferate accordingly and will only ever be 'demi-regularities'. Episode 8 goes on to show that causal forces in the social world generate constant self-transformation. Change is ceaseless. Causal explanation in social science needs to incorporate a time dimension. Episode 9 highlights the challenge of complexity and provides the final requirement of generative analysis. The causal propensities that drive change in the social world are beyond number. The social world is patterned and repatterned endlessly and unpredictably. Empirical inquiry cannot follow every sequence, every cause and consequence. There have to be 'stopping rules'.

Having detailed the realist toolkit for causal explanation, starting with initial theoretical hunches and ending in the careful explication of stopping rules, Episodes 10 to 15 go on provide six exemplary case studies of realist research. These put empirical flesh on methodological bones and are chosen to cover diverse substantive topics, to roam from the micro to the macro, and to incorporate the full repertoire of research methods – quantitative, qualitative, evaluative, and comparative. Episode 10 reconsiders the quantitative research on social mobility of one of the pioneers of generative causal analysis, John H Goldthorpe. Episode 11 returns to another foundational thinker, Raymond Boudon, and examines his generative models of transformations in educational inequality. Episode 12 reprises my own attempts to think generatively about social policies and programmes using the method of realist evaluation. Episode 13 examines the generative mechanisms uncovered in cross-national, comparative research on protest movements. Episode 14 takes us to qualitative longitudinal research uncovering the causal process involved when individuals reason their way through crisis. Episode 15 argues that deciphering complex causal structures requires cumulative bodies of research and provides an example from a realist synthesis on legislative interventions.

Episode 16 provides a brief summary and sets the scene for Parts II and III.

Episode 1. The oldest maxim: correlation does not equal causation

I cannot recall whether this famous phrase was part of my undergraduate methodology training or whether it just belongs to the everyday wisdom of the chattering classes. Either way, it makes for an essential departure point on the journey towards a generative model of causation. The maxim states that even strong associations between X and Y cannot be taken to imply that X causes Y. All sorts of fanciful examples are used to illustrate the mistake. For instance, it is said, and it has been shown (Matthews, 2000), that there is a strong correlation between the number of storks nesting in a region and the birth rate in that region. Attributing causal powers to these flying midwives commits the ecological fallacy, mistakenly assuming that relationships that hold at the collective level also hold for individuals. The correlation is usually credited to storks' fondness for peaceful, countryside habitats and to the preference for larger families that obtains in rural communities. Maybe? Though I still yearn for the day when we find evidence that kindly, individual storks deliver cherished, individual babies (Figure 1.1).

Source: https://www.publicdomainpictures.net/en/view-image.php?image=57449&picture=stork-with-baby-silhouette.

Figure 1.1   *Rare pictorial evidence*

Let me refrain from whimsey to make the important point. The mistake, correlation = causation, continues to be made. Take this headline from the *Guardian* (January 2022), 'Women 32% more likely to die after operation by male surgeon, study reveals'. Causality and blame(!) are implied in this little banner. Thank goodness the story was not picked up by the Daily Muckraker, where the headline might have read – 'Macho killer surgeons stalk our operating theatres'. But what is the real causal story in this case – who or what bears responsibility?

The study in question has an impeccable pedigree, namely, *JAMA Surgery* (Wallis et al., 2021). Its own conclusions read rather more benignly as follows:

> This large, population-based study demonstrates a small but significant increase in rates of adverse postoperative outcomes, defined as the composite of death, complications, or readmission in the 30 days following surgery when there is a sex discordance between surgeons and patients. This is driven by worse outcomes among female patients treated by male surgeons.

The 32 per cent difference as reported above caused some public consternation. It doesn't sound like a 'small' risk. Accordingly, the first point to clarify is the difference between the absolute risk and relative risk. The absolute risk of a particular medical outcome (e.g., an adverse postoperative outcome) relates to the chances of it happening in the whole treated population over a specific time period. So, if we take the most drastic outcome from the 'composite' in the Wallis study, patient advice websites go out of their way to reduce fear of operative deaths by specifying absolute risk levels as follows: 'The risk of dying in the operating theatre under anaesthetic is extremely small. For a healthy person having planned surgery, around 1 person may die for every 100,000 general anaesthetics given' (Hares, 2017).

Relative risk is used to compare outcomes across different groups of participants. In the present case the research concentrates *only* on the small fraction that experience adverse reactions and then compares risks according to whether the surgery is performed – male-on-male, female-on-female, female-on-male, and male-on-female. The reported 32 per cent disparity in death rates occurs in the latter group *as compared with* the other permutations. It is a difference within a difference.

Having located the specific nature of this particular 'correlation' we need to return to the matter of causation. This first thing to say is that, statistically speaking, the association turns out to be a sturdy beast. This is a sophisticated study in a pre-eminent journal and so all manner of covariates are examined. The overall difference in adverse reactions (deaths + complication + readmissions) is measured at 15 per cent to the detriment of the male-on-female dyad. This association varies somewhat *but holds* if controls are applied to all manner of patient characteristics, surgeon characteristics, surgical volumes, and hospital types. Although, for instance, women surgeons treated younger patents with fewer comorbidities, the relative risk for this specific sub-group still disfavours male-on-female operations. Importantly, nine different surgical specialties were examined producing somewhat different magnitudes of relative risk, but again all demonstrate the sex-discordance effect.

We are left with a small but highly persistent statistical residue – but does it permit a causal inference? Does it permit us to say that male surgeon/female patient sex discordance (X) is the cause of adverse outcomes (Y)? Interestingly and crucially, the paper's authors recognise that something important is missing. Accordingly, the main conclusion quoted above has a further final sentence, which reads as follows: 'Further work should seek the underlying mechanism' (Wallis et al., 2021, E1). What is missing, blessedly from the point of view of this book, is the generative account. The authors point out that this requires further 'sociological work' on 'patient-physician relationships, communication and trust'.

I don't propose to undertake this assignment here, other than to point out that these generative dynamics are elusive and cannot be represented as variables. For instance, ascribing causal powers to the 'sex discordance' between two key individuals misses an important point that surgery is practised in large teams often consisting of a surgeon, anaesthesiologist, physician assistant, nurse anaesthetist, operating room nurse, surgical technician, resident students, and robots (Randell et al., 2017). Before that a multidisciplinary team consisting, perhaps, of surgeons, specialist doctors, nurses, pharmacists, social workers, and patient representatives will have decided to recommend surgery as an optimal form of treatment. More research is needed on whether, how, and why male assumptions about the female patients permeate (or survive) in these complex communications and interactions.

Explaining the observed relationship also requires further work on risk taking and risk management during surgery. Wallis et al. (2021, E8) concede that many of their measures are not 'granular' enough to explore further hypotheses. It may be that within each surgical category senior male surgeons perform more cases with a higher level of complexity and attendant risk. It may also be the case that well-established male surgeons are more risk tolerant or more prepared to live with the consequence of error than their female counterparts. The lack of diversity in surgery has been criticised in official reportage (Kennedy, 2021). Preparedness for risk taking is subject to frank autobiographical discussion (Marsh, 2014). The 'alpha-male surgeon' it seems is alive and well. There is, however, still an empirical puzzle left untouched to explain why his penchant for risk taking should be concentrated on women patients.

Yet further explanatory hypotheses could be raised from the patient perspective. Is there a male/female difference in tolerance to trauma? Is there a gender difference in the willingness to report complications after treatment? These, I suspect, provide promising leads. But I curtail conjectures here with the first realist maxim in our search for the kernel of causality. We need to understand the mechanism!

KEY LESSONS

The key lesson from Episode 1 can be summarised with an adapted maxim: correlations raise more questions than they answer. Attributing causality, moreover, depends on providing answers to these surplus, unanswered questions. Correlational studies cannot say why a causal relationship occurs; the explanation is smuggled in tacitly. In the example considered here, one notes that the realist concept of the 'underlying mechanism' is raised and recognised in a clinical study framed by statistical methods. But its manifestation is still shady; many different hypotheses about potential mechanisms related to surgical history, its culture, its practitioners, and its patients remain unseen and unresolved.

Episode 2. Harré's distinction between successionist and generative causation

I think my first formal encounter with the idea of generative causation may have occurred in reading a chapter in Rom Harré's *The Philosophies of Science* (1972). As its title declares, the book is about the physical sciences, so we have work to do in adapting key concepts for social science.

Harré's task in chapter 4 is to prise apart the 'two great metaphysical theories of causation', which he refers to as the 'successionist' and the 'generative' perspectives. Well-used synonyms for the former include the 'constant conjunction', 'frequentist', and 'regularity' models – though I should also squirrel in my favourite, namely, 'Humean bondage' (Hitchcock, 2003). Generative causation is also spoken of via other terms such as 'underlying mechanisms', 'realist causation', 'process tracing', and 'relational realism'. 'Mechanism' remains the watchword and to begin, a little terminological clarification is required. The word mechanism in ordinary English usage means a mechanical contrivance, such as the levers and cogs that allow you to change gears on your bike. Harré notes that the term mechanism in causal explanation has a wider meaning – 'any kind of connection through which causes are effective'. Sometimes the term mechanismic is used to convey the broader meaning (but if you use it, you may find it offends your spell-checker).

Harré (1972) locates the difference between the two causal metatheories in terms of how they perceive observed relationships, as follows:

> Both start from the fact that some sequences of events are recognised as causal sequences and some are regarded as random or accidental sequences … In the generative theory the cause is supposed to have the power to generate the effect and is connected to it … In the successionist theory a cause is what usually comes before an event or state, and which comes to be called its cause because we acquire a psychological propensity to expect that kind of effect after the cause.

Historically, the successionist understanding was the earlier arrival, occurring centuries before the advent of the modern apparatus of science and statistics. It is usually associated with the philosopher David Hume's (1748 [2007]) ideas on 'necessary connexion', and it deals with the everyday or human understanding of causation. We can update Hume's examples with some commonplace encounters. We know from experience that sexual intercourse causes babies, that excess alcohol causes hangovers, and that a good joke will cause laughter. More esoterically, but still well within the domain of practical experience, we know that applying dock leaves to nettle rash causes a reduction in irritation. For this experiential perspective, there is nothing further to know or to add in establishing such causal connections. 'According to Hume, the great successionist, when we perceive a regular succession between one kind of happening and another kind many times then we form a mental habit and come to expect the one on the occurrence of the other' (Harré, 1972).

The successionist account is refined in modern thinking by using methods which replace the 'mental habit' with the techniques of statistical or experimental control. Accordingly, the core method for establishing the causal connection between X and Y remains with observation, that is to say, making repeated empirical findings that the one always follows the other. But the definitive connection, the constancy of conjunction is then established by applying additional steps. There is a need to ensure that the observed outcome Y is not spurious, so that it is indeed X and not any other event or happening Z that is the 'real cause'. At this point I will defer description of the huge variety of experimental and statistical controls that have been applied to this end. The goal here is simply to confirm that positing and then establishing strong and stable sequences of events remains the basic logic of successionist causation.

This brings us to the contrast with generative logic: 'The generative theory holds that there is a real connection between causes and their effects, and that in many cases this can be identified with a causal mechanism which on being stimulated by the cause produces the effect' (Harré, 1972). You have been forewarned. Mechanisms have pride of place in generative explanations. Mechanisms explain *why* the observed successions arise. They replace the 'mental habit' in a totally different way – namely, with a theoretical rationale for connecting up the stimulus of X and the genesis of Y. Harré's example of this is the famous association between tobacco smoking and cancer. He argues that the causal account is prefigured *but is not complete* if we rely only on studies which reveal the 'external pattern', namely, in this instance the higher rates of cancer in heavy smokers. The pioneering account here is Doll and Hill's (1964) ingenious empirical comparison of significant difference in cancer rates in 'smokers' and 'never-smokers' amongst 40,000 UK doctors. The generative account demands more and that more comprises knowledge of 'internal cause'. In this example, what is required is an understanding of the biology of the cancer cell. How do the compounds in tobacco smoke act on the body? How do they create mutations in the genes that usually protect us from cancer? Such studies were years in the making. The definitive account here may be found in a report from the Centers for Disease Control and Prevention (2010), though you might need a PhD in biology to understand the details.

This little example of how observation on external association is buttressed by knowledge of the mechanisms of internal connections repeats itself through natural science. The same investigatory couplet applies even at the level of the so-called 'laws' of physics. In the modern school classroom, it is quite possible to replicate early experiments on the 'gas laws', evoking the observational evidence of the constant conjunction between the temperature, pressure, and volume of a gas. But the question of why raising the temperature of a gas raises its pressures is only answered in kinetic theory. This model describes a gas as a large number of identical sub-microscopic particles undergoing elastic collisions between themselves and the walls of their container. Raising its temperature increases the speed of the collisions resulting in increased pressure on the container. There is much more to be said about the vast explanatory power of kinetic theory in respect of its ability to account for many other gaseous properties such as viscosity, thermal conductivity, mass diffusivity, Brownian motion, etc. For a primer one can do no better than to consult the entry in *Wikipedia* (n.d.). Understanding the action of underlying mechanisms underpins not one but many different observational outcomes.

This example of excitable microscopic particles forefronts another of Harré's doctrines on generative causal explanation. This pertains to what he calls the 'internal constitutions' of materials and things. The way that things are made up gives them a causal propensity:

> A material which is said to be inflammable, explosive, poisonous or sweet, is described thus because it is likely to burn when ignited, to explode when detonated, to cause sickness and death when ingested, or to taste sweet when placed on the tongue. But to say of such materials as petrol, dynamite, strychnine, or sugar, that they are respectively inflammable, explosive, poisonous and sweet is to say more than just what they will do or effect under certain circumstances: it is to say that they are of such a nature that they will do these things under the appropriate circumstances. To be an inflammable, the substance must have such a chemical and physical constitution that it will burn when ignited. (1972)

I quote this passage at length in order to consider its applicability to social science. The thesis is that the way entities are composed gives them 'abilities', 'propensities', 'tendencies', 'liabilities', or the favourite summary term, 'causal powers'. So far so good. It is not difficult to transfer this thesis to social entities. So, courts have the power to convict offenders, surgical teams have the ability to treat conditions (and produce adverse reactions), capitalist economies have the tendency to exploit workers, teenagers have a liability to be highly temperamental, and so on. The basic imagery seems to apply rather well. One obvious practical problem is that in any social episode rather a lot of 'entities' gather, all of which and all of whom have causal powers. In the physical world, we can isolate our stick of dynamite and ponder its causal powers. But to return to a favourite example, we might say that human and social entities such as surgeons, surgical teams, robots, operating theatres, hospitals, regional trusts, and national health services all have causal powers. At face value, it would seem possible to trace a particular outcome (e.g., adverse effects) to all of them. We return to the problem of overlapping social entities throughout Part I.

In social science, moreover, not only do we face an overabundance of entities with causal powers, but we also confront Harré's second stipulation, namely, that we must also investigate the 'appropriate circumstances' in which these propensities will be released. On first glance, this is a cause for celebration, for what is sociology other than the investigation of behavioural differences produced in different collectives – dictatorships versus democracies, traditional versus bureaucratic organisations, urban and rural communities, extended versus nuclear families, and so on. So far so good. But if we return to the list of entities in the previous paragraph, we see that many of them also perform as key circumstances necessary for the mechanism to operate. The surgeon's propensities are limited by the rest of her team, the facilities in the theatre, the hospital's resources, and so on. In the social world, the copious entities that possess causal powers are encircled by an abundance of external conditions that shape these propensities. Here, we have our first glimpse of the potential never-ending complexity that confronts causal explanation in social science. Be patient dear reader, we need to spend time in the quagmire to glimpse an escape route.

KEY LESSONS

Key concepts and foundational lessons are learned in Episode 2. Harré introduces three 'constituents' of causal explanation, namely, observational regularities, generative mechanisms, and necessary circumstances. Beside these, the elucidation of many specific properties of the generative approach are compelling and have rich, potential applications – causal powers, connectedness, internal composition, beneficial and limiting conditions, underlying and unseen mechanisms, etc. The basic apparatus of generative causal explanation is uncovered. The practicalities of applying it to social research remain to be addressed.

Episode 3. Stinchcombe's challenge to students (and the rest of us)

I vaguely remember that Arthur Stinchcombe was a visiting professor during my undergraduate days at Essex University. I still have a copy of his book *Constructing Social Theories* (1968). Theory teaching in those days consisted of a heavy dose of the classics and then a romp around the emerging contemporary paradigms. Plainly, theorising was something that went on in the heads of major intellectuals. Stinchcombe's book belongs on a different planet. It is about substantive theories and how to build them. Social theorising, he maintains, is a 'practical activity'. Thus begins his tale: 'The reason for having theories of social phenomena is to explain the pattern in observation in the world.' And the rest of the book presents a range of strategies to pursue this explanatory aim.

There is relatively little usage of the specific term 'generative mechanism' in this particular book. This terminology is preferred in a later and sadly ignored work, *The Logic of Social Research* (2005). In the earlier work, Stinchcombe expresses his realist inclinations in terms of the quest for sociological explanation. The key principle is raised in a famous passage from the introduction of the 1968 book: 'A student who has difficulty in thinking of at least three sensible explanations for any correlation that he is really interested in should probably choose another profession.' I've always considered that this challenge is too easy – why only three? If we take a familiar observational pattern such as the finding that girls have overtaken boys in UK school educational attainment, it is easy to spout dozens of potential explanations, dozens of competing mechanisms, which span changes in: the domestic division of labour, classroom culture, social media pressures, role models, curriculum innovation, the feminisation of teaching, labour and workforce requirements, family and household structures, and women's political emancipation. Pathetically, I've stopped at nine here, but the reader will grasp the point. As we have already seen, this potential for explanatory proliferation applies in the totally distinct arena of adverse surgical outcomes. And the same would go for my field of interest, namely, policy evaluation where I like to issue a sterner Stinchcombian challenge to newcomers: 'A would-be evaluator who has difficulty thinking of at least six sensible explanations of why a programme might succeed and six sensible explanations for why it might fail should probably choose another profession.'

If we read on, however, we see that Stinchcombe too has much higher expectations of his tyro sociologists (1968). Consider his full student assignment: 'Choose any relation between two or more variable in which you are interested; invent at least three theories not known to be false, which might explain these relations: choosing appropriate indicators, derive at least three different empirical consequences from each theory, such that the factual consequences distinguish among the theories.'

Now that's more like it! Stinchcombe wants us to do far more than dream up a loosely stated theory, give it a label, and claim that it accounts for a particular observational pattern (as, shamefacedly, I've done in each of my nine 'explanations' in the example above on girls' educational gains). He requires us to articulate each theory in much more depth and this involves specifying the particular indicators (I would prefer 'evidence') that would support the said theory. These indicators, moreover, must be different for each theory, otherwise we are back to square one with a proliferation of vague, plausible hunches accounting for broad, aggregate trends.

To return to the same simplistic hunches. If we suspect that the feminisation of the teaching workforce enhanced girls' educational performance, we might engage in some classroom ethnography to inspect whether the new cohort of female teachers interact differentially with girls and boys. If we suspect that changing workforce requirements opens up new opportunities for well-educated girls and closes some traditional opportunism for boys, we need to specify those roles and track recruitment patterns into them. If we suspect that curriculum innovation might have inspired womanly ambition, we need a content analysis of change in textbooks, teaching plans, governmental guidance, and so on. I leave the reader to plot research designs for the further theories.

Different theories should have different consequences, otherwise it is impossible to adjudicate between them. This may sound obvious, but it is a problem that applies with even more force within a different tradition of sociological explanation, which might be termed 'monocausal structuralism'. I will return to a fuller analysis of this curse in due course. For now, a simple example will suffice. A given structural force is said to permeate society and thus cause a wide variety of social inequalities. The same vague abstraction is forwarded to account for a welter of empirical outcomes. For instance, it is often and is easily said that differences in pay rates, occupational recruitment patterns, mental health problems, voting preferences, housework contributions, language usage, leisure preferences, toy purchases, criminal activities, pillion passenger riding, and dozens of other walks of life are 'gendered'.

Indeed they are, but under Stinchcombe's challenge this is repeated assertion and not an explanation. His aspiring sociologist should be able to think of
several different explanations of why occupational access is gendered, several
different reasons why leisure activities are gendered, several different hypotheses on why crime patterns are gendered, not to mention the several theories on
why adverse surgical outcomes are gendered. The candidate theories, moreover, will differ markedly from issue to issue. Under monocausal structuralism,
the task of identifying and then sifting and sorting between proliferating explanations remains untended. Realist explanation is founded on the idea that there
are always competing explanations. The first requirement is to derive different
empirical consequences from each one – 'such that the factual consequences
distinguish among the theories'. In this way, for each walk of life, we can build
more precise theories of how, why, and in what way it is 'gendered'.

KEY LESSONS

The crucial lesson from Episode 3 is that causal explanation is instigat-
ed by theories, and the way in which theory is constructed is crucial to
explanatory success. Sociological explanations are notoriously imprecise.
The same ambiguous theory may be drafted in to sketch over a multitude of
assorted observations. Alternative causal explanations often lie unexplored
and untested. The solution lies in better crafted theory rather than more
sophisticated research techniques. Good theories stipulate precise empirical
consequences, and this is the crucial first step in being able to corroborate
them and adjudicate between them.

Episode 4. Newer maxims: contingency clouds causation; mechanisms are not variables

This episode returns to practical issues of data analysis. In all forms of empirical social research, data are pummelled to see if they reveal a pattern. In Episode 1, we saw that the most basic pattern of all, namely, correlation, reveals little about causation. In this episode we pursue the issue in more depth by considering two other elementary forms of data analysis – contingency tables and multiple correlation. Both of these belong to the 'successionist' tradition in causal analysis and, as we shall see, they display characteristic weaknesses.

There is an old folk song which suggests that we 'all live in little boxes'. This is the initial issue of this particular episode – though it refuses the next line of the ditty, which suggests that they 'all look just the same'. The boxes we inhabit are the classifications, categories, castes, subdivisions, groups, ranks, and pigeonholes into which life is organised. They are all pervasive and, to quote another formidable intellectual, they stretch to infinity and beyond. These boxes replicate the everyday organisation of our everyday lives. Every single human activity – from the checklist in your new-born health record, to the types of school you attend, to the type of housing tenure you call home, to the occupation you follow, to the band for your income tax return, to the diseases that may kill you – carries a set of labels. Social science does, of course, create its own indicators and measures but in empirical work these academic neologisms are dominated by the classifications used in the routine play of daily life.

Causal analysis begins with the recognition that life is patterned, and social research habitually detects these pattens using the framework provided by these mundane classifications. We hypothesise that there will be significant linkages between one form of behaviour and another, and we begin investigation of the associations using cross-classifications of these everyday characteristics, often displaying the linkages in the form of 'contingency tables'. Let us take the example of voting behaviour and the simplest possible rendition of the simplest possible causal hypotheses, namely, that people vote on the basis of economic self-interest. To test the proposition, we need to classify people

Table 4.1   A basic contingency table

	Economic class	
Voting intention	Rich	Poor
Right	350	150
Left	150	350

Table 4.2   Perfect association

	Economic class	
Voting intention	Rich	Poor
Right	500	0
Left	0	500

Table 4.3   No association

	Economic class	
Voting intention	Rich	Poor
Right	250	250
Left	250	250

by economic class and by voting preference. Let us proceed with the crudest possible binary classifications, dividing the population by class, rich and poor, and voting intentions by left- and right-wing parties. Data collection proceeds (sample 1000) and this might provide an imaginary contingency table, taking the shape of Table 4.1.

What does this analysis tell us about causation? Can we infer that class interests 'determine' voting behaviour? Clearly not, but we might be happy to claim that they 'influence' voting behaviour. What is more, we can measure the strength of this influence. Table 4.1 falls short of perfect association, as in Table 4.2, but it is also unlike Table 4.3, which shows zero association. We can then apply one of a number of statistical coefficients (chi-square, Pearson's r, Cramer's V, etc.) that calculate the strength of the association displayed in Table 4.1. Seeking to establish the strength and durability of association, recall, is crucial in successionist thinking.

What does such a measure of 'imperfect implication' in Table 4.1 tell us about causality? If we apply Stinchcombe's test at this point the answer is … very little. He requires we sift and sort several explanations for a particular correlation – and this example is essentially devoid of explanation. It could be argued that the idea of 'economic self-interest' is visible in the overall pattern. But we certainly have no explanation for the fact that 30 per cent of the population vote against these purported interests. The reason for the exceptions is, of course, that we all live in many, many little boxes and that the folks in any particular box in the table live their lives under scores and scores of other categories, some of which may override their economic class and any trace of financial self-interest. I invite the reader to invent the biographies of the relatively rich left-wing voter and the relatively poor right-wing voter. For that matter you might like to think of the many other experiences, apart from their relative wealth or poverty that might have encouraged the 'orthodox' voting pattern. Scores of experiences, completely absent from the table, dictate the configuration of the table. Contingency tables are the little chunk of the iceberg above water, the gliding swan without its furiously paddling legs.

CONTINGENCY CLOUDS CAUSATION

Thus far, my critiques of successionism as it features in social science data analysis have been applied to simple bivariate examples (stork frequency 'causes' birth rates, sex discordance 'causes' adverse surgical outcomes, economic class 'causes' voting intentions). An obvious rebuttal might be to charge me with oversimplification because all modern variable analysis is, of course, multivariate. My rejoinder, about to be explained, asserts that multivariate analysis is also successionist. Vital underlying mechanisms, the real causes, remain unconsidered and undetected. There are myriad methods of multivariate analysis – multivariate regression, path analysis, causal modelling, analysis of variance, factor analysis, cluster analysis, canonical correlation analysis, and so on. Coverage of their respective logics is impossible here, so let us take the first simple step and introduce into analysis a third variable, known as a mediator (Figure 4.1).

The top row of Figure 4.1 begins with a simple correlation. X, the so-called independent variable, is found to be in constant association with the dependent variable, Y. The relationship between the two is measurable, strong, and stable – and by Humean decree X might initially be declared to be the cause of Y. However, no other variables have been examined to this point, so it must be contemplated that other influences may also have a significant causal impact on Y. One such variable is called a mediator (Z in Figure 4.1). In this scenario, the independent variable is not considered a direct cause of the dependent variable but rather the causal influence works through a third variable – the mediator, or the intermediate cause. Causation is still established by statistical association or constant conjunction. The mediator variable (Z) is considered the causal product of the independent variable (X) and a causal precursor of the dependent variable (Y).

The second row of Figure 4.1 describes slightly different scenarios. Complete mediation happens when it is discovered that the entire causal relationship between X and Y runs through the mediator, Z. The mediator replaces what appeared to be a direct cause as shown on the middle left of the figure. Partial mediation happens when Z reduces the relationship between the X and Y variables. In this case the observed strength of the relationship between X and Y diminishes, but not to a full extent, the causal pathway being described on the right of the figure. Multivariate analysis builds on this same logic introducing further variables and partial correlations, which trace out and measure the relative strength of the causal pathways linking a variety of independent variables to the key outcome of interest.

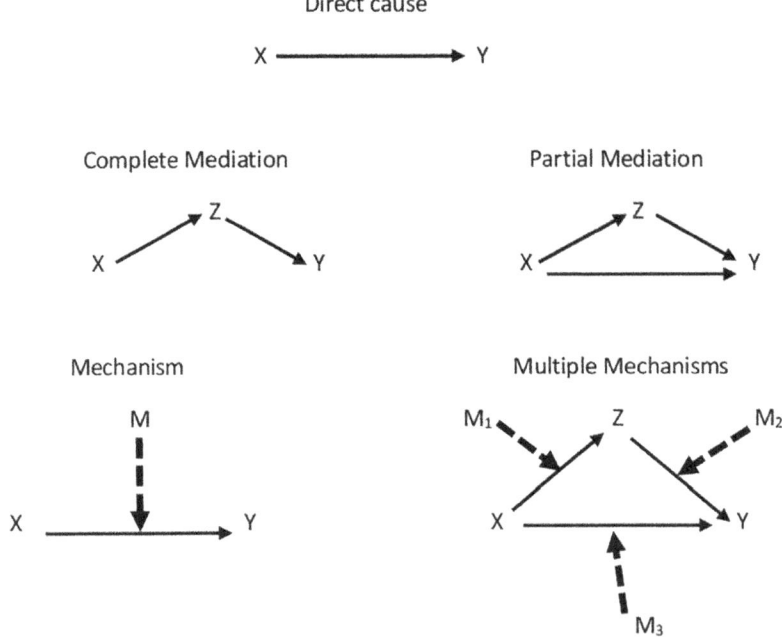

Figure 4.1   Mediators and mechanisms

For the realist, all of this is stuff and nonsense. Variables do not cause anything. People's actions bring about the observed patterns in the social world. Each relationship (XY, XZ, ZY, etc.) is forged in the reasoning, resources, and rivalry between groups of people. Social mechanisms bring about, form, create, produce, originate, constitute the observed regularity. This generative capacity is portrayed in Figure 4.1 (bottom left) with a mechanism arrow (M) that drives to the centre of the association. The mechanism is depicted as explaining the relationship. This representation enables us to see the difference between a mediator and a mechanism, a confusion that appears routinely in the literature. Adding more variables creates an explanatory lacuna. Each partial correlation still needs explanation. Each additional arrow in a multivariate model faces the Stinchcombe test. Whole swathes of action remain unattended; more and more explanatory material is left unconsidered. This tension is illustrated bottom right in Figure 4.1. As more interrelationships are brought under consideration, each one requires explanation by the corresponding mechanism.

Let us consider an empirical example. Suppose X is marital status and Y is suicide rate. There is such a correlation in the real world: single people are more likely to commit suicide than those in a marriage. But it is a nonsense to say that marital status causes suicide. The relationship (XY) is bought about by the difference in companionship, responsibilities, support, and obligations between single and multiple person households. Different groups have different levels of connectedness in these respects and, as Durkheim (1897 [1951]) famously taught us, it is different levels of cohesion and solidarity that are signified in the correlation.

Let us travel onwards to multivariate analysis, in which we might explore whether it is possible to detect the influence of a mediator. A candidate variable, namely, having children (Z), might be added to the causal model. Let us suppose that we can detect partial mediation as in Figure 4.1 – does this improve causal explanation? Not so says realism: marriage doesn't *cause* children; children don't *cause or prevent* suicide. What we actually confront are three associations (M_1, M_2, M_3), which all require generative explanation. To explain why married couples produce more children than singletons $(X{\rightarrow}Z)$ is not too taxing, but again it is the various mechanisms (M_1) around emotional fulfilment, building ties, the urge to nurture, and carrying on the family name, that come with marriage rather than marital status as such that explains procreation. Explaining why having children causes gross fatigue but seldom suicide $(Z{\rightarrow}Y)$ depends on the presence of another set of mechanisms (M_2) ascribable to the paramount need to *be there* in order to provide safety and support, and to pass on self-esteem and moral values. The third association $(X{\rightarrow}Y)$ I leave to Durkheimian mechanisms (M_3). The example is highly specific, but its lessons are entirely generalisable. For every single correlation and partial correlation, every single direct and indirect cause mapped in multivariate analysis, we need a knowledge of their underlying generative mechanisms to complete the explanation.

A couple of final points are necessary to complete the episode. The first is to say that both Figure 4.1 and the worked example simplify the task of generative explanation. In the text, I have merely suggested and given approximate shape to some potential mechanisms that might generate the observed correlations. In Figure 4.1, I draw one mechanism per correlation. But remember that Stinchcombe's rule of thumb still applies. Several alternative explanations or rival mechanisms might well furnish plausible hypotheses for each linkage. Empirical work always needs to be continued in excavating the further evidence that will decide between them.

Second, and with great emphasis, I must point out that none of the above suggests that the quantitative search for patterns can be ignored in realist thinking. Quite the contrary, as we shall see in Episodes 10, 11, and 12. The social world is full of regularities, and they need to be quantified in associations, correlations, multiple regressions, and so on. The difference with the successionist orthodoxy as stressed above is the expectation that ever deeper statistical manipulation can establish causation. For the realist, the statistical patterns are merely the little chunk of the iceberg above water, the gliding swan without its furiously paddling legs. For a much superior and less theatrical way of expressing this idea I refer readers to Abbott (1998) and Byrne (2002), who argue that patterns uncovered in statistical sociology never speak for themselves and are better thought of as 'traces' of the complex social interactions that lay beneath them. Inquiry might well be prompted by the discovery of interesting empirical regularities and puzzling statistical traces, but it is never complete without an understanding of the mechanisms that generate them.

KEY LESSONS

Episode 4 extends the critique of the successionist paradigm in causal analysis. Not only does correlation not equal causation, but its various extensions by way of contingency tables, partial correlation, mediator analysis, multivariate analysis, and so on are not, in themselves, able to establish causality. These methods portray the outer traces of complex social interactions. They rely upon and seem plausible because of implicit and unspoken assumptions about the corresponding underlying generative mechanism. Realist analysis requires that these underlying processes are brought to the surface.

Episode 5. Generative thinking in pharmaceutical inquiry: the drug development pipeline

Although Part I seeks to affirm the credentials of the generative theory of causation, to this day one finds that successionist practice keeps raising its pesky head. In the previous episode I argued that research needs sound understanding of both association and mechanism to complete causal explanation. This obligation raises an interesting question about how to order and balance the two components. In actual inquiry, which comes first – the observed regularity or the underlying mechanism?

In this episode I present a beguiling case study to help with this puzzle. Pharmaceutical investigation is causal inquiry incarnate. It is organised around a brutally simple causal question – does this drug work? The conventional (and proudly successionist) answer to this question is that we know they work because they have faced and have overcome the sternest possible empirical test – namely, the randomised controlled trial (RCT). For newcomers to this method, any number of primers will provide the complete background to the premise and the promise of randomisation (e.g., Berger et al., 2021). Here, I begin with a succinct account of the basic affinity with successionist logic.

X is the drug treatment and Y is the condition that it seeks to alleviate. Researchers identify a population suffering from the illness and then randomise them into two equivalent groups – the treatment group and the control group. The treatment group receives the drug, and the control group receives a placebo. Because of randomisation the two groups have exactly the same composition. Any difference in clinical outcomes between the two groups must be due to their one difference, namely, the application of the treatment. Because the influence of all other factors Z has been eliminated by randomisation, we have secured the association – the application of X must be the cause of Y.

This inference is hardened by supplementary controls. Both groups receive an identical looking pill, the control group receiving an inert placebo, rather than no treatment. Accordingly, patients do not know their group affiliation (treatment or control) and this ensures that the actual treatment rather than hopes for the treatment provides the causal influence. Desirability bias is eliminated. The practitioners offering the treatment and the researchers investigating it are also 'blinded', so any implicit preferences in favour of the treatment cannot influence the conduct of a trial, nor its interpretation. Yet further controls are sometimes applied. For instance, a fair trial of a drug remedy requires that participants complete its full course, and even 'treatment compliance' may be put to scrutiny in more scrupulous versions of the RCT. We arrive at the methodological point. Every step of the above causal logic is based on procedural uniformity. There is nothing further to know or to add in establishing the causal connection. A constant relationship between cause and effect is established and verified by meticulous, controlled observation. The successionist account is vindicated.

Or is it? The generative model requires much more and that more is illustrated in Figure 5.1. The figure provides a description of the full sequence of research strategies that go into the production of a pharmaceutical drug, often known as the 'developmental pipeline'. At a glance we can see that many research strategies are applied. The RCT as described above is only one of them (stage 7). Moreover, the whole process often consumes a decade or more. So, what is its function? In the text that follows I spell out the explanatory role of each component and this reveals that the pipeline is in fact a striking exemplification of the generative model of causation.

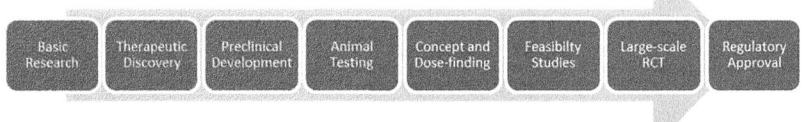

Figure 5.1   The drug development pipeline

STAGE 1: BASIC RESEARCH

Drug development begins in basic research seeking understanding of derailments in the basic biological, chemical, and genetic systems that initiate a disease. The objective is to raise hypotheses on potential biological, chemical, and genetic mechanisms of action that could reverse these malfunctions sufficiently to halt or slow the development of the disease. Note that the key term 'mechanism of action' is routinely used in basic pharmaceutical research and that it carries exactly the meaning described in previous episodes. Its mechanism of action provides the drug with the power, the ability, the propensity to treat the condition.

Let me offer a simplified example. Your body, bless it, contains about 37,500,000,000,000 cells in constant interaction, sending tiny signals back and forth, thus preserving all normal bodily functions. Failure to maintain these normal channels, malfunctions in the signalling system, can result in significant disease. Drugs work by introducing new mechanisms that 'reset' the signalling channels. As early as 1901, Langley introduced the notion that drugs work by generating a chemical switch that has the capacity to turn on and turn off this molecular interchange. For a full historical account, see Maehle (2004).

In order to discern these underlying generative mechanisms stage one research is conducted in vitro (colloquially known as 'test tube experiments'). Cells or biological molecules are studied outside their normal biological context, namely, in a solution or in an artificial culture medium. Evidence on the disconnection and potential repair of cell connection is collected through medical microscopy and medical imaging, themselves venerable disciplines (Wethered, 1898). The primary advantage of such 'in vitro work' is that it simplifies the system under study so that the laboratory researcher can focus on those small number of mechanisms that might break normal cell interactions and those that might go on to restore equilibrium.

STAGE 2: THERAPEUTIC DISCOVERY

Specific drugs are not developed in stage 1. Basic research provides fundamental hypotheses, but no more than hypotheses, about the molecular mechanism of action that will need to reside in a drug that is yet to be fully developed. Therapeutic discovery really gets underway in a separate, internally complex stage – referred to variously as 'assay development', 'high-throughput screening' or more simply 'searching for compounds' (Corr and Williams, 2009). The requisite biological process underlying the therapy has been identified. Chemists then have to sort, sift, and synthesise the specific compound to deliver that process in the most effective fashion. This is a challenging task because compounds can be refined with thousands of small variations in their molecular structure.

Patients are not directly involved at this stage. Testing is performed on blood samples and biopsy materials from patients whose type and stage of condition fulfils the tentative expectations about the cellular failure. A shortlist of potential drugs that might repair the malfunction is analysed through a test procedure known as the 'assay' and a 'candidate drug' that best fits the function is selected. The intended function of the compound's mechanism of action is already understood; the assay provides a further filter to improve the potency and selectivity of that action.

STAGE 3: PRECLINICAL DEVELOPMENT

Success up to this point has only been achieved in the laboratory. Once the best performing candidate compound is selected, further preclinical studies are undertaken to research optimal means for the delivery, or what pharmacologists call the *presentation* of the treatment. Drugs need to be transported into the anatomy with great precision. They need to be absorbed, distributed, and held long enough at the site of action to have the intended effect. Drugs also need to be transported away from the body with equal efficiency – 'one of the main reasons we can use drugs as therapy, without poisoning the patient, is that the body is generally very good at inactivating and getting rid of them' (McGavock, 2011). An entire discipline is devoted to investigating drug throughput – namely, human pharmacokinetics. It is often defined as the study of 'what the body does to drugs'. The main components of this process have come to be labelled with the acronym ADME (Absorption, Distribution, Metabolism, Excretion). Empirical work at this stage involves a small group of healthy volunteers to research whether the drug is effectively absorbed, properly distributed, remains at its site of action long enough to produce an effect, and is excreted efficiently (oh joy). I add the methodological rider here that, several years into the research, it still focuses on understanding and exemplifying the causal mechanism.

STAGE 4: ANIMAL TESTING

Animal testing remains a conventional if controversial stage in the drug development pipeline. The primary purpose is to contribute to safety studies. Does the drug, in prolonged doses, cause cancer, genetic alterations, or foetal abnormalities? Animals are also used to make the first foray into the question of effectiveness. The rationale for the use of so-called 'model organisms' is the evolutionary principle that all organisms share some degree of relatedness and genetic similarity due to common ancestry. The basic premise, simply stated, is that if the drug is safe and shows signs of effectiveness in the animal species, the same might apply to humans. Clearly, we are a million miles from any application to social research here. I mention it because this phase marks the entry of contextual considerations in clinical research – for whom and in what circumstance does the causal connection apply?

STAGE 5: PROOF OF CONCEPT AND DOSE-FINDING STUDIES

Humans enter here and so this stage is often referred to as a stage I trial. It has two functions. Safety studies continue here, which use healthy volunteers (usually students and others who welcome the customary fee). The purpose is to find a drug dosage that maximises the requisite biologic activity but minimises the toxic risk. Dose-finding uses a research strategy known as 'dose escalation', basically trial and error to find the optimal dosage. Note, methodologically, that attention remains on refining the mechanism of action. The therapeutic theory is identified, it is then embodied in a compound, the compound is then tested for its presentational (pharmacokinetic) properties, and the developing treatment is further distilled to provide an optimal dosage.

The term proof of concept also crops up in the literature here. The drug is administered, for the first time to a very small group of patients (again volunteers) with the condition targeted by the medication. The idea is to detect some immediate biological signals of its action. This is not a full clinical trial of treatment efficacy but may use blood tests or biopsy materials from these patients to detect that the expected cellular modifications are underway – has there been a useful amount of positive change?

STAGE 6: FEASIBILITY STUDIES

This is the final preparatory stage, a methodological 'dress rehearsal' for the following large-scale clinical trial. Researchers check the practicability of many important working assumptions on which that inquiry will be based: which patients will be included and which will be excluded, how will they be recruited, what numbers are required for statistically significant results, will patients be willing to be randomised, will clinicians be willing to recruit subjects, what are the proposed outcome measures, how will compliance be assessed, how long should the trial last, what is the optimal time interval for measuring outcomes? Small-scale pilot exercises are sometimes employed to help settle such issues (sometimes called stage II trails). Decisions are finalised, which then permits ...

STAGE 7: RANDOMISED CONTROLLED TRIAL

The candidate drug is tested in large patient populations with the specific disease. The method utilised in what are often termed phase III trials is, of course, the randomised, placebo-controlled, triple-blinded clinical trial, already described at the beginning of this episode. According to that logic, the

RCT provides certainty and finality. The method is said to sit at the pinnacle of the 'hierarchy of evidence' (Burns et al., 2011). Applying the procedure, by itself, authenticates the causal inference. It provides certain knowledge on whether the drug works. To rephrase Harré's pithy characterisation – once implemented, there is nothing further to know or to add in establishing such causal connections.

Or is there? Against this view sits the pipeline model presented above. It turns out the theory that 'drug X is effective in treating condition Y' rests on a sea of more specific theories which are tested over a dozen years or so, in vitro, in animals, in healthy volunteers and in real patients, using a huge medley of research methods. The RCT is a large-scale exemplification of this prior knowledge, and it cannot be performed without such knowledge. The role of the trial is thus corroborative – to demonstrate the treatment works sufficiently well under conditions determined by previous research. Discovering the mechanism of action tells us *why* the drug works and the further stages of inquiry provide further explanation of *how* and *when* to deliver it and *for whom* it may be effective. Causal attribution is thus established prior to rather than during the RCT.

I conclude that RCT, despite endless claims to the contrary, does not establish causality. What it does is to provide a robust measure of treatment efficacy in circumstances predetermined well before the trial. There is a massive gulf between this interpretation and the claim that the RCT sits at the pinnacle of the hierarchy of evidence. Which interpretation is correct? More effort and expenditure is applied in pharmaceutical research than in any other domain and deciphering its first principles is crucial. We go in search of the answer in the next stage of the pipeline.

STAGE 8: REGULATORY APPROVAL

Pharmaceutical drugs may not be supplied and sold without formal governmental approval. Powerful national agencies control this process such as the US Food and Drug Administration (FDA) and the UK Medicines and Healthcare Products Regulatory Agency (MHRA). Experts in a particular clinical field are drawn together to consider evidence provided by the drug companies and their researchers on all aspects of safety and efficacy as above. The 64K$ question for this episode is: what type of evidence is used in this formal decision making? A paper by Thaul (2012) provides the direct answer. '[Licensing] requires "substantial evidence" of drug safety and effectiveness. FDA has interpreted this term to mean that the manufacturer must provide at least two adequate and well controlled Phase III clinical studies, each providing convincing evidence of effectiveness.' Put this way (a mere two studies!) makes the requirement sound rather trifling but I should point out 'adequacy' in this respect means massive, coordinated international trials replicating findings for thousands of patients.

So, in terms of licensing and regulation does this rudimentary evidential requirement mean that successionist logic rules the roost? This is no trick question; the answer is yes! The following long quotation comes from an overview of FDA evidentiary standard produced by one of its most distinguished advisers – Russell 'Rusty' Katz. The terminology here is perhaps surprising. It certainly mirrors the methodological controversy under discussion in Part I. The message, however, could not be clearer.

> Although there is considerable information available both on the (presumed) mechanism of action of the drug under review, and the pathophysiology of disease under study, this information is typically secondary in drug approval. The Agency's primary regulatory philosophy can best be characterized as empiricist, one formal definition of which is the '… thesis that all knowledge of non-analytic [non-definitional] truths … is justified by experience.' Simply put, the Agency adopts an empirical approach to the fundamental regulatory questions of safety and effectiveness. Theories about mechanism of action of a drug or disease mechanisms play important parts in drug development and approval, but they are entirely subsidiary to the fundamental questions that must be answered in the course of drug approval; namely, is a drug effective, and is it safe in use. These questions can only be answered (within the limits of experimental error and statistical uncertainty) by direct examination of the question in a well-designed and conducted clinical experiment. (Katz, 2004)

So there we have it. Pharmacological science employs a generative theory of causation but pharmacological regulation is successionist. There are intriguing economic, sociological, and political questions about why the regulatory authorities prefer evidence derived from tightly marshalled efficacy studies. Alas, there is no space here to pursue the devilish influence of Big Pharma on evidence construction (Borchers, 2007: Bothwell et al., 2016) and we reach the methodological conclusion of this section.

KEY LESSONS

Episode 5 has an audacious mission – to dismiss the successionist account of causality in its proudest incarnation, the randomised controlled trial. Examined closely, the pharmaceutical drug development pipeline reveals that causation is established prior to the clinical RCT on the basis of evidence on the drug's mechanism of action. Extensive basic science reveals the underlying cellular processes in the drug's action upon a disease, and this knowledge informs all aspects of the trial, which is then able to provide a measure of its efficacy (only the latter being of concern in drug approval). What are the implications for social research? We need to extend the bold thesis established here that understanding mechanisms is the taproot of causal explanation. But it is also clear that, unlike in vitro work in medicine, we cannot isolate social mechanisms in separate, prior forms of inquiry. How is it possible to maintain the centrality of mechanism explanation within the standard forms of social inquiry?

Episode 6. Provisos: the transience of causal relationships and the influence of context

All causal claims come with provisos: they are never unconditional. Recall that Harré stipulated three 'constituents' of causal explanation, namely, observational regularities, generative mechanisms, and necessary circumstances. The third stands in equal importance. Gunpowder has the propensity to explode – but will only do so in the right circumstances. Chemotherapy has the capacity to slow cancer – but only in the right circumstances. Social distancing has the capacity to slow the spread of Covid – but only in the right circumstances. Thus far I have built up a picture of how mechanisms generate causal patterns but have had relatively little to say about the circumstances, the contexts, the scope conditions that regulate the firing of the mechanism. Such provisos come in all shapes and sizes, in all disciplines and all sciences – physical, clinical, and social. This episode draws together some key examples from the former pair in order to pave the way for an exploration of context in social research in the following episodes.

At school we learn that there are 'laws of nature' and this makes them sound universal – if X then *always* Y. Alas, this is a convenient little lie. The truth of the matter is expressed in the withering title of a paper by Scriven (1961), 'The key property of physical laws: inaccuracy'. In other words, one can always find specific circumstances in which any law will fail. Let us return to the previous example of the gas laws and a version that I learnt at school, namely: for a fixed mass of gas, the pressure gas is directly proportional to its temperature when volume is constant – symbolically $P \propto T$ (V constant). The first proviso is contained within the law, namely, that it applies to a fixed mass of gas and not, for instance, to the shifting air in the room in which you are now sitting. But the main exception which can be observed under simple experimental conditions is that proportionality fails at low temperature and at high pressure.

For a contextual explanation we need a generative theory. Kinetic theory understands a gas as a large number of tiny particles zipping around in an otherwise empty space, undergoing occasional elastic collisions between themselves and the walls of their container. Raising its temperature increases the speed of the collisions resulting in increased pressure on the container … and the proportional law is obeyed. One of the assumptions here is that the size of individual molecules is considerably smaller than the distance between them and so in an 'ideal gas' there is no intermolecular attraction. But at low temperature or high pressure the volume occupied by the gas is relatively small, so the intermolecular distance between the molecules decreases. The attractive force between them becomes significant and the $P \propto T$ (V constant) law breaks down. For a more detailed but still distinctly school-level exposition, see Lincoln (2020). The 'failure' of the law is important to science because it serves to simulate and guide the quest for further, fuller explanations. The gas laws do not lay in ruination. They are protected in two ways. The first is to assert that the laws apply to an 'ideal gas' and pertain in the theoretical condition with no significant intermolecular attraction between particles. The second is to track empirically the specific conditions, which specify the tipping points of high pressure and low temperature where the law holds and where it fails.

The influence of context on causation is also a perpetual dilemma in clinical science, with its daily reminders that treatments do not work for everyone.

> The history of medicine is replete with examples of treatments once common practice but now known not to work – or worse, cause harm … Leeches and bloodletting were used for thousands of years for almost everything. Attempts to show that they were ineffective were resisted with great passion by the medical profession. (Doust and Del Mar, 2004)

The temptation is to say, 'Well that was then' – but the truth remains that therapeutic effectiveness is only ever partial. To see why, consider the following quotation from Kent and Kitsios (2009):

> Determining the 'true' treatment effect of a given therapy is a bit like determining the 'true' weight of a liter of water. Those who answer that a liter of water weighs a kilogram are either assuming an implicit 'on planet earth, at sea level, at four degrees Celsius' or confusing the intrinsic property of mass with the extrinsic property of weight. Like weight, treatment effect is an extrinsic property, emerging only through an interaction between the intervention, the patient, and the circumstances in which it is being measured. Adjust the context and a different effect emerges – just as a liter of water weighs a little over a third of a kilogram on Mars.

Almost without exception, there are patients who experience greater and lesser benefits *within* the treated population. In clinical terms this is referred to as heterogeneity of treatment outcomes (HTE). As we have seen, Phase III efficacy trials have strict inclusion and exclusion criteria. Yet even *within* these very carefully delimited populations there is always mixed success in respect of the key clinical outcomes. The following quotations describe HTE and the dilemma it creates:

> Mounting evidence suggests that there is frequently considerable variation in the risk of the outcome of interest in clinical trial populations. These differences in risk will often cause clinically important heterogeneity in treatment effects (HTE) across the trial population, such that the balance between treatment risks and benefits may differ substantially between large identifiable patient subgroups. (Kent et al., 2010)

> When HTE is present, the modest benefit ascribed to many treatments can be misleading because modest average effects may reflect a mixture of substantial benefits for some, little benefit for many and harm to a few. (Kravitz et al., 2004)

This discovery has prompted more and more sophisticated ways of analysing trial data. HTE analysis, so to speak, deconstructs the orthodox measure of average treatment effect. As Varadhan and Seeger (2013) put it, 'The main goals of HTE analysis are to estimate treatment effects in clinically relevant subgroups and to predict whether an individual might benefit from a treatment.' I proceed no further into the technicalities of HTE detection. The important methodological consequence for this episode is that it demonstrates that clinical outcomes are strongly context dependent. Within the carefully preselected trial population there will still be outcome variation in terms of age, sex, disease etiology and severity, presence of comorbidities, concomitant exposures, and genetic variants (McCarthy et al., 2005). The consequence is that pharmaceutical inquiry is endlessly driven back to the drawing board. What is it about a particular sub-group that it 'clinically relevant'? Why might these patients have a different response to treatment? How might the treatment be modified to target these differences?

These questions trigger a return to basic science and to theory. What was described as the drug development pipeline in Figure 5.1 needs to be reimagined as an everlasting cycle of inquiry as in Figure 6.1. Under the contextual exceptions uncovered in HTE analysis, there is return to the pipeline. Phase one is repeated under the question – why might drug receptors be different in the sub-group in question? Phase two then contemplates how the existing compound might be reformulated to accommodate biologic/genetic differences. Phase three tackles how the new drug's presentational properties might be modified. And so on. In short, causal attribution is never finally established in the clinical sciences. Claims that the RCT is the final arbiter are misplaced. Causal attribution is a perpetual process. Successive investigations build knowledge of how the mechanism of action in a drug brings about subtly different outcomes in different contexts. The mechanism is then modified to increase the footprint of effectiveness. And so on.

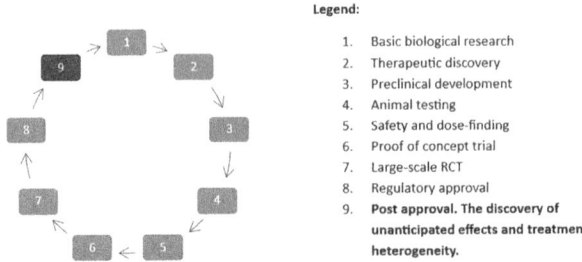

Legend:

1. Basic biological research
2. Therapeutic discovery
3. Preclinical development
4. Animal testing
5. Safety and dose-finding
6. Proof of concept trial
7. Large-scale RCT
8. Regulatory approval
9. **Post approval. The discovery of unanticipated effects and treatment heterogeneity.**

Figure 6.1   The everlasting cycle of therapeutic development

Drawing parallels across to social research is always difficult and it is the task that will occupy the remainder of Part I. The regularities uncovered in social science are much more fleeting and short-lived. They appear and disappear from location to location and from one time period to the next. Understanding contextual provisos becomes even more important and we should carry forward a couple of immediate lessons from the present examples. From the gas laws example, we see that theoretical models (i.e., kinetic theory) guide explanations of the contexts under which empirical regularities break down. We should foster exactly the same need for building theories that explain the differential influence of context in empirical social research. Theories are often expressed as 'ideal types', and this mode of abstraction is also useful in social science.

From the example on HTE, there are two lessons about dealing with the very large number of contextual differences that may shape causal outcomes. The first is that it takes many cycles of investigation to make inroads in the task. Can social science investigation duplicate this successive structure? The second is the residual and inevitable need to prioritise in the investigation of relevant contexts. There is perhaps a small clue in this respect in a phrase used earlier to describe where to seek HTE, namely, the idea that we concentrate on 'clinically relevant' sub-groups. In social research there may be a parallel in concentrating on contextual constraints that have policy or practice relevance.

KEY LESSONS

Episode 6 moves us further away from the constant conjunction model of causality. In physics, it transpires that its so-called laws only apply in certain circumstances. In clinical work treatments are judged efficacious in the knowledge that they only apply to some patients with some conditions. The search for pattern, however, remains at the heart of empirical investigation. Research continues apace without the assumptions that there is one true relationship to be uncovered. The expectation is that regularities will only apply in certain contexts and mapping the exceptions is itself a vital empirical objective. A progressive cycle of research ensues with the task of explaining a wider and wider range of heterogeneous outcomes. This methodological strategy can be incorporated into social science – though, as we shall see, the problem of heterogeneity looms even larger.

Episode 7. Mechanisms, contexts, and demi-regularities in social science

From this point on, I concentrate on pinning down the application of the generative model of causation in social science. Once again, I return to Harré's triumvirate of generative causal concepts to map out the method. To begin with mechanisms. What are they? How should we understand the nature of generative mechanisms in social science? Perversely, it is a question that can be answered in a couple of sentences. Generative mechanisms reside in human agency. People's choices shape the social world.

Alas, methodological matters are never so simple, and the concept of agency has been picked apart and argued over relentlessly in the sociological literature (Emirbayer and Mische, 1998). Let us begin with individual agents and consider how their decisions might be considered to have causal powers. People choose, people decide, people plan, people create, people react, people guess, people select, people blunder, people rectify, people judge, people discriminate, people repudiate, people negotiate, people hate, people love, and so on. These are all verbs, and you will remember from school that verbs are 'doing words' and doing all of these things has self-evident consequences for shaping social outcomes.

Of course, it is not only individuals that have agency. People gather together in a huge number of groups ranging the micro to the macro – friends, families, neighbourhoods, districts, regions, organisations, institutions, foundations, administrations, governments, states, alliances, and global federations. These collective agents make choices. They have causal liabilities, tendencies, and powers by the bucket load. Collectives govern, collectives make laws, collectives design policies, collectives administer, collectives regulate, collectives audit, collectives allocate resources, collectives forge ties, collectives provide work, collectives create algorithms, collectives communicate, collectives dissemble, collectives compete, collectives wage wars, and so on. Yet more doing words and the various doings listed have an obvious and formidable influence in shaping the social world.

We have a starting point. At first approximation one can thus say that agency, both individual and collective, constitutes society's basic causal mechanism. But even from the string of examples above we also recognise that such choice mechanisms are (i) plural, (ii) interactive, (iii) contested, and (iv) emergent.

(i) Individuals make dozens of decisions per day, so do organisations. Which ones are pertinent, and which ones bear investigation? Which come to fruition, and which fall by the wayside? (ii) These multiple decisions interact in various ways. A complex plan may 'come together'. Conversely, a person's or an organisation's ambition to achieve X may be thwarted by an earlier choice to commit to Y. (iii) There are always multiple decision makers. Rival viewpoints are visible in every collective from the family to the United Nations. The agency of one set of members may influence, encourage, dissuade, perpetuate, harm, inhibit the thinking of others. (iv) Put all of these dynamics together and we see that agency is in constant evolution. Individuals dissent and their disagreement causes some of them to change their minds. Similarly, collectives disagree, collectives monitor other collectives, collectives obliterate other collectives, and collectives design new collectives. Collective agents change their ideas and change the world.

Accordingly, although I bestow upon 'agency' the role of primary causal mechanism in shaping societal outcomes, it is plain to see that it is an unruly beast. When it comes to the design of real examples of social inquiry there is a need to prioritise. All actions are potentially interrelated, including those caused by the folkloric flap of a butterfly's wing. The very first step in empirical inquiry is thus to pinpoint which agents and which of these features of agency are under investigation.

Before we enter such discussion, it is vital to excavate further the second fundamental in Harré's generative model of causation, variously described as the conditions, the contexts, the circumstances that regulate the action of mechanisms. The basic idea can be expressed as follows – although individuals and collectives have causal powers, they are not always realised. Whether these wishes, ambitions, decisions, plans, goals, prototypes, projections, manifestos, and policies come to fruition depends on context.

Hundreds of social scientists have been keen to describe these contextual constraints on agency. Just as with mechanisms, key contextual forces range from the macro to the micro and here I settle for brief glimpses using some well-known examples. I begin with perhaps the most celebrated expression of the concept: 'Men make their own history, but they do not make it as they please; they do not make it under self-selected circumstances, but under circumstances existing already given and transmitted from the past. The tradition of all dead generations weighs like a nightmare on the brains of the living' (Marx, 1852).

In terms of major societal shifts such as revolutions, it is power structures transmitted from the past that determine whether revolutionary zeal becomes transformative action. In his 1852 essay Marx relates the political events that led to the downfall of the French Second Republic (1848–52). Marx spends the majority of the text discussing the relative power of *pre-existing* factions –

parliament, various political parties, bourgeoisie, monarchy, army, proletariat, and so on. Louis Bonaparte's quest for power took on all the trappings of his uncle Napoléon's rise to power. Yet it ends in self-destruction and, for Marx, a betrayal of the proletariat. The younger cousin's efforts are swallowed up by factions from the previous regime. Marx thus describes Louis Bonapart's efforts to make history as a 'fabric scrap' rather than the 'whole cloth'. In short, circumstances transmitted from the past stunt political agency.

For my next example I move down the layers of contextual constraint to the level of communities. Another stirring quotation makes the point for us. 'People make choices, but they cannot choose the choices available to them. Nor can they be sure what chain of events will follow from their choices, including choices made by others. People blunder and fail, just as they often get what they want' (Felson, 1986). Felson's discussion catapults us from attempted revolution to attempted crime. In terms of agency, the choices are clear. If a crime occurs, the victim failed to get what he or she wanted. If a crime does not occur, the potential victim succeeded but not the offender. What actually happens depends significantly on community context. Felson goes on to provide an illustrative contrast, which I abridge as follows:

> A tight community – where people know people, property, and their linkages – offers little opportunity for common exploitative crime. The Israeli kibbutz, where crime rates are low because there is not much to steal and nowhere to go with it, is a case in point ... The dispersion of kinship and friendship over a wider metropolitan space and the automobilization of the population make more difficult [this] kind of informal control.

In short, circumstances located in the community shape criminal agency.

A third example moves the influence of context down to the level of interpersonal relationships. People make choices which are heavily influenced by their peers and associates. This simple idea is the basis for reference group theory (Hyman, 1960; Merton, 1968b), which investigates how the individual takes the values or standards of other peers as a comparative frame of reference. Two individuals facing similar issues may well use different reference groups in appraising themselves. Merton (1968b) illustrated these paradoxical influences on personal choice with dozens of examples from Stouffer et al.'s *American Soldier* (1949). How well did new recruits take to being drafted? Short answer – with surprising inconsistency. It turned out that married recruits resented both unmarried recruits and married civilians, feeling that they had been called upon to make much higher levels of sacrifice. Black draftees from the South perceived an increase in wealth and dignity, not experienced by Black recruits from the North. Further examples extend to all walks of life. Cancer patients in lower-class social networks have more fatalistic attitudes than those with middle-class reference groups (Beeken et al., 2011). Different population groups (e.g., rural versus urban, youth versus elderly, and men versus women) experience the same objective labour status differently. In each case there is tendency to make comparisons with immediate peers rather that more distant networks (Verme, 2017). In short, circumstances located in everyday loyalties and associations shape human agency.

The list of potential contextual constraints on individual and collective agency is huge. I will not extend examples here and simply reiterate that they range from: an individual's past experiences, to their daily contacts with other agents, to the patterns of association in different communities, to the life chances offered by different institutions, to the laws and controls set by state institutions, to the powers that reside in history, and so on. All of these contexts pre-exist and limit agency. And, just as with agency, contextual influences are also: (i) plural, (ii) interactive, (iii) contested, and (iv) emergent. Take even the simplest example like consumer choice. An individual's decision to buy X may be influenced simultaneously by previous purchases, alternative options, budgetary constraints, the preferences of peers, availability and pricing, regulations on heath and safely, taxation levels, environmental considerations, intergovernmental trade restrictions, and so on. In the same manner, a manufacturer's decision to produce X at price Y will be shaped by dozens of evolving contexts.

Finally in this episode, I turn to the causal products of the action of mechanisms acting in contexts. In natural science, Harré terms these 'patterns', 'regularities', 'sequences', 'connections' (but not laws). In medical science, they are 'outcomes' or 'effects' of treatments. What is the nature of the patterns or outcomes generated by the action of social mechanisms acting in social contexts? How should we understand the product of choice mechanisms acting under contextual constraint? From the above analysis, it should be clear that social patterns are rather febrile, hard to establish, difficult to pin down. They are produced by the action of scores of potential mechanisms acting under the influence of scores of constraining contexts. Human agency generates social regularities only for human agency to modify them.

This paradoxical consequence of agency is both the spur to and the curse of social inquiry. It is ever present, never so well expressed as in Archer's (1995) famous conundrum:

> Society is that which nobody wants, in the forms that they encounter it, for it is an unintended consequence. Its constitution could be expressed as a riddle. What is it that relies on people's concepts but which they never fully know? What is it that depends on people's actions but never corresponds to the actions of even the most powerful? What is it that has no form without us, yet which forms us as we seek its transformation? And what is it that never satisfies the precise designs of anyone yet because of this always motivates its attempted reconstitution.

Few could match the brilliance of this quotation but perhaps the point is that we all experience these dynamics, even the most powerful of us. Here is Donald Rumsfeld, then US Secretary of Defense, reflecting on the reasons for policy failure: 'There are known knowns, things we know that we know; and there are known unknowns, things that we know we don't know. But there are also unknown unknowns, things we do not know we don't know.' This utterance is sometimes regarded as gobbledygook, but it has a surprising resemblance to the work of another master of sociology, namely, Merton (1936), in his essay on the unanticipated consequences of purposive social action. Our choices are often self-defeating because they are based in ignorance, error, short-termism, and dogmatism.

Unknowns lurk. Unintended consequences proliferate. Ideas clash. Contest and change are the norm. But none of this means that we face complete disorder. The world transforms but not into blue cheese. We make our way through daily life knowing what institutions deliver – education, transport, jobs, healthcare, etc. And when they fail to deliver, we can generally come up with an explanation – underfunding, labour disputes, international competition, pandemic upsurge, and so on. We know that social movements, grand designs, and policy projections often fall short – but that retrospectively we may be able to trace the unacknowledged, unconsidered influences that led to their failings.

We can begin to live with this impermanence simply by naming it. Lawson (1997) coined the term 'demi-regularity' to indicate that the patterns observed in all social inquiry are space and time dependent, that the conditions that give rise to these relationships are visible and open to public challenge, and thus are always liable to modification. They must therefore be assumed to be potentially short-lived or borrowing from the French – *demi*. Demi-regularities become the third realist anchorage for empirical social inquiry. Their lack of durability is no cause for abandoning causal analysis in human inquiry but the very topic for causal inquiry in social science. A crucial task of social research is not only to locate such punctuated patterns but to provide explanations for their relative permanence/impermanence. This introduces the need for a time dimension in generative explanation, which is the topic for the next episode.

KEY LESSONS

Episode 7 provides us with an initial menu of the ingredients to trace and research generative causation in the social world. Mechanisms reside in human agency, the choices and decisions made by individuals and by collectives. These choices are not always realised. They are supported or thwarted under different contextual conditions. Contexts range from the micro (the individual's authority, past experiences, and networks) to the macro (society's customs, laws, and history). Contexts predate mechanisms – some of these constraints have been transmitted from actions of the long-dead. The action of mechanisms in contexts creates demi-regularities. These are the semi-permanent patterns through which individuals make sense of the social world, the discovery and scrutiny of which provides basic empirical traces for social research.

Episode 8. Causation and change: Coleman's boat and the Caucus race

All scientific investigation utilises explanations relating mechanisms and contexts to empirical patterns. In this episode we confront a further challenge to this simple principle as it applies in social science. It is a challenge with many hard lessons. We have encountered the basic problem already. Societies transform incessantly. New ideas emerge endlessly. Change is the norm.

The physical world, whilst evolving in many respects, does so imperceptibly. Regularities, patterns, associations abound. We know, however, not to term these uniformities as 'constants' or as 'universal laws' (recall Episode 6). When exceptions to physical uniformities are discovered, theories are enlarged to account for them (recall the partial failure of the gas laws). Counter instances are gradually incorporated, and we can say in broad terms that in the physical and natural sciences the discovery of decay, entropy, evolution, and inconsistency does not overwhelm understanding.

In clinical science, empirical research gradually masters how the mechanisms of action within treatments are able to control the dysfunctions that generate disease. But medicine faces a constant stream of exceptions to this rule – everything from cellular mutation to changing health beliefs create heterogeneous outcomes. A permanent cycle of therapeutic development ensues (recall Figure 6.1), providing a knowledge base which is able to keep reasonable pace with most biological and human adaptation. In broad terms, adaptation and change does not overwhelm causal understanding.

Gradual change is not a feature of the social world. Its forms, its patterns, its configurations are demi-regularities. They apply there and not here. Just as significantly, they apply then and not now. You and I can live with this – life trundles on, things certainly change, but we only need to cope with a particular change when it turns up. But what about the big picture – how is social science able to incorporate incessant change into its explanations? Human agency is not only reactive but also proactive. We do not only choose from a menu of choices but choose to change the menu. As a result, change is ceaseless.

This property, self-generated change, is known as 'morphogenesis'. Dozens of social theorists have tried to capture the nature of this unruly beast. Some of the most notable contributions include Berger and Luckman (1966), Bhaskar (1979), Giddens (1984), and Archer (1995). My first and still preferred encounter with these ideas, however, came in a paper by Coleman (1986) and took the shape, according to your visual predilections, of a boat or sometimes a bathtub. A superb visual overview of the idea may be consulted in Stoltz (2014); a masterly narrative account may be found in Ylikoski (2016). My rendition of the idea takes shape in Figure 8.1, which represents the dynamic of change as it unfolds from one time period to the next.

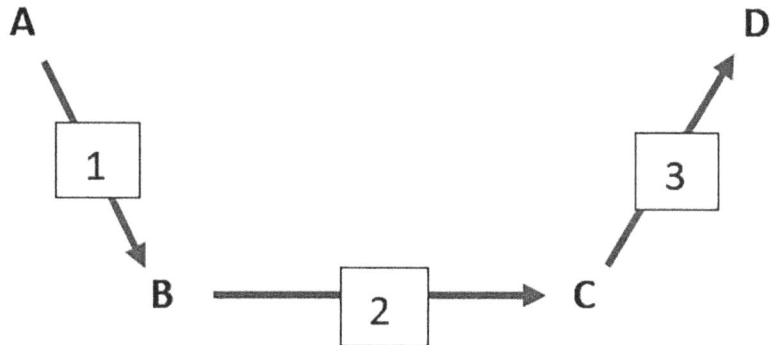

Figure 8.1   Causality in Coleman's boat

This and similar accounts of morphogenesis represent highly sophisticated accounts of how the social world goes round. We need examples to breathe life into the model and what I would stress is its utility in describing social change in many different forms, on totally different scales, at quite different tempos, with different degrees of permanence and reversibility. The following three pocket examples provide examples of the changing anatomy of morphogenesis.

Most applications belong in comparative historical sociology, character-ised splendidly by Tilly's description as the study of *Big Structures, Large Processes, Huge Comparisons* (1984). A grossly simplified example of social change at this macro level might go as follows. We begin in a traditional indus-trial society (node A). This system has a powerful influence on the positions and life chances available in the class/occupational structure (mechanism 1). That workforce (node B) is variously pleased, indifferent to, and oppressed by their economic opportunities. Accordingly, some groups seek to modify their existing economic opportunities and life chances (mechanism 2). Some with technical expertise may see opportunities for changing modes of production, some entrepreneurs may see advantages in outsourcing work abroad, some organisations may seek to protect and provide benefits for the disadvantaged. These reactions lead to the consolidation of new social groupings, such as technocrats, global investors, trade unions, and welfare agencies (the emerging agents at node C). Their actions and those of multivarious other agents (mechanism 3) transform the workforce creating new openings and closing others. So begins (at node D) the development of high-tech/service/welfare economies often captured in the term 'post-industrialised' society (Bell, 1974; Smart, 2010).

There we have a prime example of a big structure and some large processes. The human capacity for innovation and self-protection drives change and continues to drive change. It is important to register, however, that the boat model is not intended to portray linear historical transitions. In any substantial social change, one can say that there are many different trajectories and thus a potentially huge number of comparisons. Consider for a mere second the sketch above of the transition from industrial to post-industrial society. It is perfectly obvious that my simplified example is indeed a gross simplification because it omits scores, nay hundreds, of potential agents and agencies that steer the course of social change. If we begin at the macro nodes, it is clear that it is not only the economic order that shapes inequality of opportunity in industrialised countries. Political regimes, administrative assemblies, trade unions, professional associations, educational structures, immigration systems, health and social care services, demographic capacities, climatic conditions, and geography all have a role. All have causal powers. Then, at the micro level, we have a mass of different agents embedded in these structures and seeking to change them. Above, I have identified a measly three – technocrats, global investors, and welfare unions. I invite the reader to consider the mass of humanity pressing for societal shifts. Real social change involves not so much a boat as a flotilla of vessels.

Also note that the play of social time is non-linear and non-reproducible (Adam, 1994). The change that happens in a particular time and place depends on what has happened at other times and places. History appears to unfold to a given script only to stop unfolding. For an example, let us return again to the transition from industrial to post-industrial society. This transformation occurs at a quite different pace across nations because the capabilities and power differentials between the aforementioned competing groups varies considerably from nation to nation, time period to time period. Time sequencing itself is also important. The potential advantages that accrue from, say, installing an economy based on financing and services dwindle significantly when many others have arrived there previously (Randall Wray, 2009). The deindustrialisation of some nations also depends, perversely, on the capacity of other nations to industrialise in order to manufacture the goods that service economies have outsourced (Mees, 2016).

Pry deeply into the boat model and one sees its immediate application and also its profound challenge. The causal processes that drive social change overlap, interact, compete, coalesce, and emerge. They may even go into reverse. One is reminded of the Caucus race in *Alice in Wonderland*, when everyone runs when they like and leaves off when they fancy, so that it is not easy to see when the race is over and to know who had won (Figure 8.2). Not easy but essential. We return in a moment to consider causation in Wonderland … but first another voyage.

Source: https://en.m.wikipedia.org/wiki/File:Alice_par_John_Tenniel_09.png.

Figure 8.2   The Caucus race

The boat model also provides a fine template for describing change at the meso level. Consider its application to perpetual change in public policy. I use the example of crime prevention. The macro agent at this institutional level (node

A) is the law enforcement apparatus – the criminal law and the enforcement agencies, police, prisons, probation, etc. The causal powers in this infrastructure contain but do not obliterate crime (mechanism 1); some goes unpunished, some goes unnoticed. Particular groups of micro-actors (node B) are variously pleased, disappointed, indifferent to, or oppressed by the current preventive powers. Public opinion under the influence of the popular press and occasional moral panics may urge for higher levels of control. Law enforcement agencies are always inclined to push for greater resources. Treasury officials may balk at the potential costs. Industry might press the case for technological solutions. The criminal fraternity (big and small) may seek to remain invisible or find ways of circumventing the suite of current measures. According to the political climate, there is a realignment of these influential voices (node C). Negotiations at this level (mechanism 3) result in reform, leading to a changing pattern of resources which then constitute the next manifestation of the criminal justice infrastructure (node D). The cycles continue.

The boat model, once again, describes the grand contours but not specific trajectories. Crime prevention continues to reshape and to change focus. Criminal activity may fall, it may be displaced, it might oscillate, it may be relabelled. Let me sketch just three pathways. In certain time periods and for certain types of crime, the above causal sequences provide a virtuous circle. A Home Office report (Morgan et al., 2016) demonstrates that vehicle crime in the UK had fallen by 80 per cent in the previous ten years. Alliances between the police, manufacturers, and purchasers provide for a new generation of electronic immobilisers, which were sturdy enough to fox potential offenders and to promote a steady, long-term decline in car crime. A more detailed exploration of the 'crime drop' follows in Episode 22.

Other changes are sudden and sweeping. They can be caused by serendipitous changes in the public imagination. Crime prevention agencies (node A) first introduced CCTV in a few town centre locations as a crime prevention device. Cameras are unthinking bits of glass, metal, and electronics. Their effectiveness depends on how people use and respond to them. Initial research (Tilley, 1993) demonstrated a distinctly marginal impact on crime rates (node B). This mattered not one jot, for every single private and public organisation and very many households were captivated by their super-visionary potential (node C). A tipping point was achieved and there are now over 5 million CCTV cameras in use in the UK. You never walk alone. What began as a crime prevention measure transformed into the surveillance society (node D).

Another variation introduces the idea of high tempo, reversable change caused by the action of countervailing mechanisms. It is referred to rather cleverly in the crime prevention literature using the metaphor of the 'arms-race' (Ekblom, 1997). In the face of unacceptably high crime rates, criminal justice agencies (node A) generate a suite of prevention measures (e.g., police patrols,

CCTV, alarm systems, etc.) designed to limit criminal opportunities. Certain key agents, namely, offenders (node B), are initially deterred but eventually respond (node C) by seeking countermeasures which bypass the initial measures, and which over a period of time often see crime rebound to former rates (node D). Law enforcement then installs a further wave of prevention interventions (e.g., electronic surveillance, target hardening, etc.) designed to counter the counter tactics. But offenders eventually adapt seeking new ways of countermanding the second-wave measures. They may find a way around the novel devices or shift to different opportunities (see Lasky et al., 2017 for empirical examples). A new phase of the 'arms-race' ensues, with enforcement agencies responding in periods three, four, five, etc. with yet further revisions in the situational measures … which sooner or later may be thwarted. Crime rates fluctuate but in the long term may remain disappointingly static.

These three pathways are perhaps sufficient to tell an emerging story. The boat model provides a broad template for describing all social change but cannot decide or determine the exact contribution of specific trajectories. For a final example of its broad applicability, I turn to the micro level and the issue of family composition. Individuals make the babies but the causal forces impinging on family arrangements are legion. I sketch this example using Lewis Carrol rather than James Coleman as the inspiration. Alice arrives at the Caucus race: 'A queer looking party is assembled on the bank.'

What do they have to say about the determinants of family size?

- *Cheshire Cat*: The major explanatory factor is the historical shift from extended to nuclear families, this prompted by the dwindling need to use children as an economic resource.
- *White Rabbit*: Don't forget the importance of contraception providing some real choice on family size.
- *Mad Hatter*: What about cultural and religious imperatives? They drive in and out of the picture, prescribing ideals and proscribing planning.
- *Queen of Hearts*: Never forget the gender division of labour – we no longer operate with the model of male breadwinners and female carers.
- *Mouse*: Government policy plays a part, providing child benefits and care facilities, counterbalancing the increasing cost of providing for children.
- *Gryphon*: Newer family forms must be taken into consideration – families with same-sex partners, intentional single-mother families, donor conception families, surrogacy families, communal families, and so on.
- *Caterpillar*: What about the influences of 'influencers'?
- *Thackery Earwicket* … and the 'bank of mum and dad'.

The Dodo's verdict on the Caucus race was that 'everyone has won and all must have prizes'. The verdict from the point of view of causal explanation is that morphogenetic analysis does add a distinct twist to the generative model and that this modification should be reflected in the basic research question. With Harré, I have characterised generative causation in physical science as the analysis of mechanisms, contexts, and regularities (MCR). In clinical research the focus, quite properly, is on mechanisms, contexts, and outcomes (MCO). In social research, it might be wise to begin with the shorthand mechanisms, contexts, and change (MCC). There is a clear need to incorporate a time dimension. Since change is the norm, causal explanation requires a focus on transformation rather than stability, on becoming rather than being. Rather than seeking to explain survey style correlations whereby variable X lies in constant association with variable Y, it is preferable to ask, 'How did that pattern emerge?', 'What made it come about?', 'How durable is it?', 'Why may it go on to change further?', 'Is it reversable?', 'Why does change occur here but not there?', 'Why did it occur then but not now?'

There is no single formula for posing and researching these questions. With this in mind, my pocket illustrations ranged across macro, meso, and micro change, all of them with internal variations. At the core of all of them there is a generative causal explanation of the emerging trajectories. For many pieces of empirical work, the basic mechanism, context, demi-regularity formulation (Episode 7) will be adequate to initiate the research design. Thereafter, depending on the substantive issue, it will be necessary to stipulate the time dimensions involved; the repertoire, sequencing, and interaction of the mechanism to be explored; the range of contexts to be compared; and the array of evidence needed to trace the subsequent outcomes patterns. Causal forces in the social world are real and powerful. But they are also reactive, adaptive, interactive, competitive, collapsible, and historical. To repeat, there is no single design template to cover all causal configurations. Accordingly, the basic causal claim attached to any piece of empirical work needs to be understood and its boundaries stipulated with great exactitude. The remaining episodes will provide detailed illustrations of a wide spectrum of such designs.

The final (and frustrating) upshot of the arrival of morphogenesis in realist thinking is to acknowledge that it heaps yet further complexity on the conduct of empirical research. What is true of all social change and what is not really depicted in the boat model is the oceanic clamour of mechanisms, contexts, and outcome patterns actually involved. Real social change involves not so much a boat as a flotilla of vessels – some sinking and others awaiting in the boat yard. Put this all together and we arrive at a basic summary statement of the causal structures confronting social science research: *Heterogeneous mechanisms, acting in heterogeneous contexts, generate heterogeneous outcome patterns, which all go on to change heterogeneously.* It is time to face the proliferating excess of the potential ingredients of generative explanation. Research design needs precision in identifying the causal configurations to be explored, but it needs equal exactitude in justifying what will be omitted. I turn to the issue in the next episode.

KEY LESSONS

Lessons learnt aboard the boat. Episode 8 reveals that causal analysis in social science should incorporate a time dimension. We need more verbs, less nouns. Since change is the norm, causal explanation should have a capacity to explain transformation rather than stability, to understand becoming rather than being. Change is ubiquitous – language transforms, individuals change their minds, groups alter their affiliations, organisations adapt to survive, nations stumble from crisis to crisis, international alliances twist from mutual benefit to one-sided exploitation. None of these features are beyond explanation, for change itself is patterned. Rather than seeking social uniformities and trying to explain fixed patterns, generative causal analysis needs to explain the drivers, the reach, the tempo, and the boundaries of social change.

Episode 9. Causation in complex systems: boundary conditions and stopping rules

A key motivation in Part I has been to show that key concepts used in generative causal analysis in the physical and clinical sciences can be transplanted into social science. The donations went smoothly enough with little sign of rejection – save for a rather large elephant that kept appearing and reappearing in the room, going under the name of complexity. The fecundity and thus the potential complexity of causal forces in social research was first raised in Episode 3 via Stinchcombe's challenge about the relative ease of supplying different explanations for any correlation. Thereafter, the description of social mechanisms, social contexts, and social demi-regularities in Episode 7 all emphasised that the potential candidates for these roles were multitudinous. Then came the discussion of morphogenesis in the previous episode, emphasising the time dependence and thus the endless interchangeability of the countless relationships between contexts, mechanisms, and outcomes patterns. That, dear social scientist, is the big picture, the big moving picture – and it follows that no empirical inquiry can hope to capture the totality of causal connections that create the real world.

So how does empirical research proceed in the foreknowledge that it will be incomplete, that it will track only a portion of the conceivable causal forces responsible for any given event or action? A huge methodological prize fight has arisen on this conundrum, much of it revolving around the difference between 'closed systems' and 'open systems' inquiry (Buckley, 2007). The former systems are said to contain stable, empirically identifiable causal relationships, whilst in the latter fleeting causal connections spiral away in an unpredictable state of impermanence … and when it comes to their investigation, never the twain shall meet. I don the gloves here, arguing: (i) that there are no perpetually open systems and no completely closed systems, but only partially open/closed systems, and (ii) it is only under the actions of researchers that systems become sufficiently closed to permit valid and reliable causal inferences.

Science, taken as a whole, investigates a heterogeneous medley of 'systems'. Social systems are not the same as planetary systems, which are not the same as molecular systems, which are not the same as human cellular systems, which are not the same as evolutionary systems, which are not the same as environmental systems ... and so on. It is tempting, indeed perfectly reasonable, to contrast these in terms of their *relative* stability. I do so here, making four such comparisons in four paragraphs. They are chosen to understand the nature of closure. What are its determinants? What qualifies as an open system and what qualifies as a closed system? Are there any completely closed and any completely open systems?

Perhaps hands are being raised for the candidature of planetary systems as supreme exemplification of the former. I have surprising news for you. The Earth's orbit and axis orientations are constantly changing because they are being deformed by the gravitational attractions of other distant bodies (Krajick, 2019).

> If you could measure the average distance from the Earth to the Sun over the course of an entire year, you'd discover something unsettling. With each passing year that you made that measurement, you'd find the Earth was a little bit farther away from the Sun – about 1.5 centimetres (0.6 inches) more distant – than the year prior. For billions of years, Earth has been migrating outward in its orbit, a trend that should continue for billions of years to come. (Siegel, 2020)

Even more shocking is the further revelation in Siegel's piece that in the long run this trend will be reversed, and we will eventually crash into the sun. Don't be alarmed. The underlying processes are well understood, and Armageddon will take an eternity or two. It transpires that even our closest candidate for closed system status undergoes minute irregularities and long-term transformations.

The physical world, whilst evolving in many respects, does so imperceptibly. Regularities, patterns, associations abound. We know by now not to term these uniformities as 'constants' or as 'universal laws' (recall Episode 6). When exceptions to physical uniformities are discovered, theories are enlarged to account for them (recall the partial failure of the gas laws). Counter instances are gradually incorporated. Even more damaging to the idea that physical systems are closed is the concept and the measurable property of entropy. The essential idea is that all physical objects and systems exist in a state of impermanence and disorder. In any natural process there is an inherent tendency towards the dissipation of useful energy. Liquids cool, ice melts, iron rusts, clouds transform, and so on. Many of these changes are irreversible. Without venturing further into the field of thermodynamics (Atkins, 2010), one can paraphrase the first law by saying that whilst the amount of energy in the total system remains constant all of its components are in a state of entropy, decay, evolution, and thus openness. But such change does not overwhelm understanding.

Next, consider cellular systems. A glance at the face in my mirror reveals that they are most definitely not closed – cells continue to die and degrade.

The whole system, cellular society, is generated by a process of cellular communication within the body, as cells release and receive hormones and other signalling molecules. This vast network of communication is fragile. Cells may fail to send out a signal at the optimal time, the sequence of signals may not be synchronised, the transmitted signal may fail to reach its intended target, the receiving cell may not respond, or it might overrespond in the absence of a signal (Genetic Science Learning Center, 2020). Such breakdowns often result in disease. Enter pharmaceutical inquiry, with the purpose of identifying where and how the cellular system has malfunctioned and then seeking to manufacture a compound designed to restore normal communication patterns. This process of drug discovery has been examined in detail in Episode 5. The reader will recall that it is an arduous, decade-long research process with many methodological slips between cup and lip. The resulting treatments, though clearly progressing, are only ever partially effective and the everlasting search continues to fathom the depths of cellular communication. Here we have fragile, self-transforming cellular system made more complex by human intervention. It can never be fully controlled. But that perpetual change does not overwhelm understanding.

Fourthly, we come to social systems. They are obviously not 'closed' because there is no such system. But how and in what sense should we consider them 'open'? Here is a celebrated opinion:

> To the realist, the one factor which guarantees that social systems remain open (and even forbids thought experiments about closure) is that they are necessarily peopled. Since realism insists upon a stratified view of the social, like any other reality, then there are properties and powers particular to people which include a reflexivity towards and creativity about any social context which they confront. If, *per impossible*, we could shut the door of any social situation against the intervention of extraneous factors (thus effecting extrinsic closure) we would only have closed in those whose innovativeness enables them to design a new exit or creatively to redesign their environment (absence of intrinsic closure). There is, in short, no such thing as an enclosed order in society because it is not just the investigators but the inhabitants who can engage in thought experiments and put them into practice. (Archer, 2020)

Now there's a hard line – don't even think about closure! Before I assess it, note that it contains an import possessive that may cause puzzlement. Archer speaks 'for the realist'. Well, she certainly doesn't speak for this realist. The previous paragraph is regarded as essential reading in 'critical realism' and that is not the realism discussed in this book. Huge terminological confusions have followed from this schism, which I consign to an obituary (Box 9.1) allowing us to return to the claims in Archer's passage.

BOX 9.1   OBITUARY FOR CRITICAL REALISM

Critical realism takes as its point of departure Bhaskar's (1975) *A Realist Theory of Science*. Harré supervised Bhaskar's doctoral thesis and, unsurprisingly, his first book makes a compelling case for a model of generative causation in physical science. Then came an exploration of social science in *The Possibility of Naturalism* (1979), arguing that the same principles could be applied in social science. However, Bhaskar accepts the point made by Archer, quoted above, that social systems are perpetually open systems. For him, this means that empirical social research can never create the closed systems required to detect causal forces. Instead, he proposes a critical realist 'compensator' – intense, insightful, theoretical reasoning allows the researcher to penetrate to the underlying mechanisms that generate social order (1979). His social science is thus based on what he calls 'apodeictic' reasoning (a priori certainties). This is the exact opposite of science – indeed his book actually makes a compelling case for *The Impossibility of Naturalism*. The certainties on which Bhaskar prefers to rely are found in normative and emancipatory doctrines, initially Marxism in the 1979 book and the forms of spiritualism in later work (2002). These creeds provide for the critique in critical realism. Such a priori knowledge of how the world ought to be allows for wholesale critique of how it is. This is pure idealism, a complete reversal of scientific realism, and my reason for rejecting the Bhaskarian drama. The entire misadventure here is based on a gross exaggeration of the difference between closed and open system inquiry. The whole point of the present episode is to portray science *and* social science as the struggle to investigate *partially* closed systems.

Back to Archer on closure. The basic assertion is preposterous – if social life was indeed open in the sense of presenting no regularities, then social life would be impossible. We are creative geniuses but also creatures of habit. Everyday life is entirely premised on regularities. I get up when the alarm goes off, have a pee, go downstairs, take tea up to her majesty, have my Weetabix, tell Alexa to play Radio 4, and so on. I'm not hugely surprised if it doesn't quite work out like this – the battery runs out, I forgot cereals on the shopping list, I add toilet visitations with the passing of years, the tea is spilt, and so on (I would, however, be shocked if downstairs had moved upstairs). In most cases, when routine fails, I can get by by making amends and with a little adaptation.

All of this humdrum activity may well be dismissed as 'mundane regularities', but the important point is that on the macro level, collective actors duck and weave in exactly the same way. Rhythms pervade all institutional

activity. Take the case of the powerhouse we might describe as 'policy architects'. Their actions follow a standard set of steps known as the policy process
(Jordan and Adelle, 2012), which can be summarised briefly as follows: (i)
problem emergence and identification, (ii) consideration of policy options,
(iii) agenda setting, (iv) selection of policies and programmes, (v) garnering
political support, (vi) establishing funding and resources, (vii) creating management structures, (viii) selecting leaders and champions, (ix) appointment of
practitioner agencies, (x) implementation.

We are not surprised, once again, if it all doesn't go to plan. Failures, oversight, and unintended outcomes also have a rhythm: (i) legal wrangles, (ii)
problems of implementation, (iii) overrunning budgets, (iv) target populations
fail to fully respond, (v) benefits appropriated by the intervention savvy, (vi)
practitioner fatigue, (vii) contradictions and clashes with rival policies, (viii)
evaluation setbacks, (ix) further political change, (x) more urgent problems
emerge, and so on. Policies are then further modified only to meet with a different set of positive and negative reactions from their recipients. The flux
continues. Policy details are created spontaneously in each iteration, but the
mixed outcome pattern is entirely recognisable. Change is adaptive, episodic,
probabilistic, but realised and visible as a series of 'demi-regularities'. There
is a discernible and real rhythm to change. Instead of assuming that creative
action generates open systems, it is more realistic to understand innovation as
the permanent struggle between groups seeking to close social systems and to
open social systems (Karlson, 2011). This is the authentic realist interpretation
of the closure conundrum, never better expressed than in the following:

> Structures provide actors with different possibilities for actions, with different
> opportunity costs … Such probability relationships are *not* invariant – they vary
> across time and space in occurrence as well as in strength. Still, in a given context
> and for certain kinds or relationships, relatively strong probability relations may
> persist over a long time (yet with temporal variations in strength). Such probability
> relationships are the results of relatively stable constellations of causal mechanisms
> where some causal mechanisms are strong enough to shine through at an aggregate
> level with some regularity despite the existence of counteracting mechanisms. The
> latter mechanisms may lead to outcomes opposite of the most likely ones in several
> individual cases, but they are activated too seldom and/or are too weak to cancel out
> the aggregate patterns created by the dominant causal mechanisms. (Naess, 2019)

In summary, we can say that significant difference in modes of inquiry follow
from the type of system under investigation. This meagre truism would be even
more apparent if the above analysis had ventured beyond the four illustrations.
The point of those examples, however, has been to demonstrate that natural
science proceeds without the need for completely closed systems (because
there are none) and that social science is not stymied in the face of completely

open systems (because there are none). Partial closure is the predicament but also the opportunity for causal explanation. How is it achieved?

This brings me to my next address on closure. Instead of perceiving it as a property of the system under investigation, it is important to understand that the ability to examine relatively stable constellations of causal mechanisms depends on the actions of the researcher. The scientist, of whatever stripe, *creates* a relatively closed system by building into the inquiry the conditions hypothesised to generate the mechanisms that enable an empirical uniformity to emerge. I emphasise the creative element here, for what is involved is often a lengthy, imaginative struggle to reveal the actions of explanatory mechanisms.

Here I make note of two brief examples, showing how closure is *fought for* in laboratory experiments and in clinical controlled trials. The latter instance has been described at length in Episode 5. Years of molecular inquiry into the action, structure, presentation, and dosage of the drug and of the conditions that may best respond are built directly into the efficacy trial. The RCT begins to approximate a relatively closed system because of the incorporation of all of this prior learning. Note again that I say 'relatively closed'. Exceptions and anomalies come to light and an understanding of them is built into the next (and also relatively closed) trial.

In the case of physical science, its great empirical regularities only occur within the confines of laboratory experiments. These relatively closed systems are manufactured. Prior learning about a physical process is assembled together *within* the apparatus and instruments built to conduct the experiment. The construction of optimal measurement systems also involves years of trial and error. Without a sound theory of how measurement systems operate, empirical regularities fail to emerge (Koyré, 1968).

For brief examples, I refer the reader to historical reconstructions of some classic experiments. Taking the case of Ohm's law, nowadays every school lab has the apparatus to demonstrate the regular relationship between electrical current, voltage, and resistance. This was not the case for the pioneers who tried to construct the closed system to reveal the theoretically projected law. Shedd and Hershey (1913) demonstrate the warts-and-all historical reality, which initially involved Cavendish trying to measure current by measuring the shock he received when he completed the electrical circuit. He closed the circuit but not the system. Further down the line it was discovered that electrical circuits also produce heat, and this interferes with the straightforward measurement of resistance. The 'law' only applies in limited temperature ranges and understanding these boundary conditions consumed years of trial and error. Still later it became clear that only a limited number of conducting materials turn out to be 'ohmic' (Schagrin, 1963). Measurement systems are fragile and have to be assembled progressively. As such, they only ever produce partially closed systems. But these are treasured because of their capacity to reveal significant empirical regularities.

I reach the vital question – how can social researchers pursue this idea of sufficient closure in their empirical inquiries? I have already described, perhaps too frequently, the forbidding causal landscape – potentially multitudinous causal components, which interchange over time. Against this background, there is obviously no direct analogue of the physical manipulation involved in assembling the apparatus of laboratory experiments or the social manipulation involved in assigning subjects to experimental and controlled conditions in clinical trials. But recall that these operations only work because they are guided by assumptions, auxiliary hypotheses, prior knowledge imported from previous inquiry. The analogue we search for in social science lies in recognising and articulating the many boundary assumptions necessary to permit causal inquiry.

In social science this reasoning lies in clarity of thought about research design. Research design is normally conceived as the choice of specific data collection and analysis techniques that will lead inquiry. The specifics of the design thus involve sorting and sifting from a vast array of quantitative, qualitative, comparative, historical, and textual methods. But equally important from the perspective of causal explanations are the preceding, elemental design decisions on what will and what will not be investigated, what can and cannot be investigated. Every causal influence cannot be charted, and there is a need to clearly articulate the 'scope' or 'boundary' conditions that limit all social inquiry.

These restrictions are put in place throughout empirical research. Certain starting assumptions must go untested and are simply accepted as given and/or imported from previous investigations. Good inquiry is adaptive: in mid-course certain lines of investigation may prove ineffective and more fruitful alternatives may be uncovered. Partial closure is exemplified and should be articulated in each reconsideration. By the end of a piece of research its explanatory boundaries will gradually become clarified and should be acknowledged. On publication, the researcher is in a position to say that particular causal explanations are supported in the empirical inquiry, which depend on other assumptions which are untested but most definitely not untestable. I am going to term all the manoeuvres just described as 'stopping rules', arguing that they should be formally part of research design rather than passed over as unreported, tacit decisions. Episodes 10 to 15 present practical examples of realist empirical research and in each of them I make clear the presence and the significance of stopping rules.

Social scientists dwelling on Coleman's boat have no choice but to declare I will only investigate *particular* outcomes of *particular* contexts and of *particular mechanisms* in *particular* time periods. This inescapable limitation should place upon them the onerous requirement of providing a meticulous delineation of the said 'particulars'. This is not a matter of waving away a whole wash of potential causal influences as 'beyond the scope of my investigation'. It involves identifying the exclusions and explaining how they will be treated as 'given'. For the purpose of a particular inquiry some causal forces are assumed to remain fixed. The skeletal form of the stopping rule is that in order to permit closer inquiry into causal forces A and B, other potential forces C and D are treated as given. To repeat: what is omitted in this manoeuvre is not assumed to be 'unassailable knowledge'. Indeed, having noted the latent role of C and D in a current investigation, it is assumed that their contribution is far from fixed, and that subsequent empirical investigation will shine light on their role in explaining change. Their causal contribution is not investigated … for the time being.

In this way social inquiry proceeds as a confederation of empirical studies. In other words, learning about A and B whilst enabled by the uninspected action of C and D will eventually bring study of these latter features to the fore. Through a system of continuous inquiry, we are then in a position to understand the mutual interaction between A and B *and* C and D. Thereafter, the neglected mutual influences of E and F gain research attention. We teeter from known unknowns to known knowns, whilst leaving behind a queue of unknown unknowns. We approach closure (but never get there) as we add investigations reaching to Y and Z. The great metaphysical claim here is about the formidable utility of partial knowledge. Our understanding of order in one part of a complex system may well be modified if we take into account forces existing in other parts of a system. Understanding is modified perpetually but never completed. Modifications continue in pragmatic steps, leaving us in a proud state of inching, incremental understanding.

KEY LESSONS

Episode 9 confronts the ultimate limitation on causal inquiry in social science. Perpetual, self-generated change has endless causes, endless consequences, endless complexity. The irrefutable consequence is that social inquiry cannot proceed without stopping rules and the first task of research design is to define the boundaries of a particular investigation with great precision. The notion that each inquiry has clear stopping rules, which are then extended in the next investigation constitutes one of the most intangible and neglected rules of causal inquiry. It is unspoken but essential. There are many different ways of putting partial closure into practice, but the great methodological imperative of this episode is to celebrate partial knowledge

rather than to dismiss it – fragmental, incremental understanding is the very
nature of enlightenment.

Episode 10. Generative thinking in sociology I: Goldthorpe on social mobility

The overall template for generative causal analysis is now in place. Each inquiry must investigate how the action of particular mechanisms in particular contexts generate particular demi-regularities in particular time periods. The exact scope of each element of the investigation must be circumscribed with clear stopping rules. I now concentrate on real examples of realist research that exemplify this model. The following six examples are chosen to demonstrate the utility of realist thinking across the spectrum of research techniques and a wide range of substantive inquiries. They cover inquiries with quite different causal structures, short term and long term, local and cross-national, seeking to explain individual and institutional change.

The first exemplar collects and analyses empirical data in a contingency table. Readers will recall (Episode 4) that such tables were the butt of one of my criticisms of the successionist model of causation. Such tables reveal association but are unable to explain it. Scores of experiences, completely absent from the table, dictate the configuration of the table. This case demonstrates how to make such invisible forces visible – how to use generative theory to understand the patterns in such tables.

Table 10.1 is reproduced from the classic study of social mobility by Goldthorpe and colleagues (1980). The table provides empirical evidence on the fundamental issue of the rigidity of the class structure – are we trapped into the class of our birth or is it possible to escape these origins? Providing an empirical answer to this question is heroically complex – pushing survey research to its practical limits. I thus commence with a consideration of the many boundary conditions, the many stopping rules applied in order to interrogate the core question.

Mobility is measured via just two questionnaire items, comparing the class position of a large sample of respondents from the current generation with that of their parents. The first design decision here is about defining the class positions on which to gauge mobility. In this instance the research team settle on a hierarchy of occupational classes (in brief – (I) high-grade professionals and administrators, (II) lower professionals and high-grade technicians, (III) routine non-manual and clerical, (IV) self-employed, (V) low-grade technical, (VI) skilled manual, (VII) unskilled manual). These are derived and imported

Table 10.1   *Class distribution of sons by class of father at son's age 14*

Father's class	Son's Class						
	I	II	III	IV	V	VI	VII
I	311	130	79	46	33	37	44
II	161	128	66	33	53	59	47
III	128	109	89	51	89	108	113
IV	124	128	81	187	88	134	114
V	154	147	109	83	170	229	180
VI	201	227	216	165	319	789	660
VII	151	181	187	121	274	527	685

Source: Redrawn and simplified from Goldthorpe et al. (1980 [1987], p. 49).

from an earlier phase of the inquiry (Goldthorpe and Hope, 1974), which measured the economic and status advantages pertaining in different occupational
groups. It goes without saying that other conceptions and measures of the class
structure exist (e.g., Wright, 1985) but for the purposes of inquiry occupational
barriers are seen as the main hurdle to mobility and the Goldthorpe–Hope scale
is treated as 'given'.

What of other assumptions? Sharp-eyed readers will note that the table only
assesses father-to-son mobility – the rationale at the time of inquiry was that
in the post-war period studied there was very little penetration of women into
the workforce during the lives of the earlier generation. Assessing and assigning the occupational position of 'housewives' was highly contentious … and
simply avoided. Sharper-eyed readers will note that the historical comparison
is made with the father's occupation when the child was 14. This stopping rule
is an attempt to ensure that the parent had reached 'occupational maturity',
rather than making the comparison when he entered work as a spotty youth.
Many other practical steps are taken in the survey to ensure a like-with-like
comparison across the two generations.

The results are endlessly fascinating. For instance, look down column one
and we see that most respondents in this top managerial and professional class
originate from the same background but that there is also an unmistakable
surge up from all the other occupational origins. The table can also be scanned,
and mobility may be described in many other ways with a standard technical
toolkit (Hout, 1983). For instance, it can be ransacked for the relative totals
of 'upward' and 'downward' mobility. 'Structural' mobility, changes in the
overall numbers working in each class across generations, can be identified by
comparing the totals across the rows and columns. This can be distinguished
from 'individual' mobility (movement within the same family) and 'relative'

mobility (comparing the points in the occupational structure with more and less churn).

But these are all descriptions of the data. Where is causation and where in particular are the mechanisms of mobility? To repeat an earlier phrase, scores of forces, completely absent from the table, dictate the configuration present in the table. There are many invisible mechanisms. Under an aforementioned pretext, no women appear in the table. Yet by the 1980s they had indeed arrived in the workforce, and they do shape the table by displacing many traditional male opportunities as a consequence. They generate male mobility. The same applies to immigrant workers – absent because their fathers worked elsewhere but a hidden presence in some occupational categories. Unemployment is the most serious form of life entrapment but nowhere to be seen. Then there is the matter of new occupations and changing fortunes of old ones. Imagine for a moment locating some present-day occupations in this class structure – sales executives are not executives, cloud architects are not architects, lorry drivers are now logistic technicians, and vloggers might be different from bloggers (who knows?). The point here is that the workforce is in constant transformation under economic and technological change, and this constitutes another set of causes, another major set of mechanisms of mobility.

The above paragraph is a sobering example of a point made insistently in the previous episode. Complexity always has the potential to overwhelm causal analysis, and some potential theories must lay dormant in any particular investigation. The whole point of stopping rules is that they permit closer examination of particular causal configurations. So, what mechanisms are under scrutiny in this inquiry? Goldthorpe et al. opt to investigate the human agency of social mobility. People do not choose the choices open to them, but they choose from the choices that are available. Accordingly, the major set of mechanisms of mobility under investigation are the thousands of life histories, the tales of innocence and experience encountered as people seek to make careers, as they grapple with the world of work, as they attempt to get by, as they fight to make a living, as they fail to make a living. For each incumbent of each cell in Table 10.1 there is a tale to tell about their career pathway.

Let me extemporise:

Row VI, column I: Stanley, the father, was a miner from a family of mine-workers in Goldthorpe Colliery in Yorkshire (yes, it's real). He was a member of his local Workers' Educational Association and his life's mission was to spare his son, Graham, from life and strife underground. He encouraged every educational opening, the son gaining a place to read Civil Engineering at Leeds University, before moving rapidly up the career ladder to become a Consulting Engineer for Arup.

Row I, column VII: Rupert, the father, was a Professor of Cultural Studies at White Hart Lane University (not real). He had a firm belief in child-centred education which, alas, fostered a headstrong youth and resulted in rather poor A-level results. The young man, Digby, scraped into and then dropped out of university, being busy with 'lifestyle' experiments. He flitted in and out of work and from job to job, becoming an hourly paid bar-worker when he was interviewed by Goldthorpe's team in 1980.

Forgive the soap-opera twaddle. The point is that people are habitual choice makers. It is the totality of such real-life histories, the sum of these constrained choices that is the underlying cause of the pattern of occupational mobility presented in Table 10.1. This generates an enormous methodological problem. How can one understand and represent this sum total? How can one acknowledge but also condense the action of a thousand such narratives? Goldthorpe's team provide an answer and it is a realist answer – treat each occupational class as a context, as a collective with its own causal powers. The origin class position has causal propensities. It bestows incumbents with resources – sometimes considerable, sometimes meagre. Parents are able to provide their offspring with resources of varying degree in terms of education, resilience, skills, cultural capital, ambition, contacts, networks, and so on. The destination class also has causal powers. Occupational groups vary in terms of their desirability and penetrability. There are gateways and barriers to entry, formal and informal, high and low: educational and training requirements but also cultural and familial know-how. Movement between any two occupational classes will be enabled and constrained by the balance of these resources and restraints and their many component attributes.

There are 49 available career moves in the table, some more likely than others. Goldthorpe's team's next step is thus to assign some hypothetical probabilities to each respective pathway. To requote Stinchcombe, theorising is a practical activity. And this is theory as hard labour. The researchers mentally construct a matrix of the likelihood of movement for every single trajectory. These predictions are presented in full in Table 10.2, as a model of 'mobility densities'. Pathways that are more probable are assigned the value 1; shifts that are least likely are assigned the value 7.

Let me provide a handful of examples of the underlying reasoning behind these estimates. Remember they are all hypotheses, they are all 'predictions'. Some positions would seem easier to pass on down the generations – inheriting a small business or passing on craft skills being good examples. This reasoning predicts considerable stability within class IV/class IV positions (independents and self-employed) as can be seen in the probability assigned in Table 10.2. Downward mobility from higher class positions is most definitely undesirable and upper-class families have the resources to prevent it (the bank of mum and dad). Hence, the prediction of high levels of stability in the class I/class I cell in the table. Moreover, class I households have little experience or knowledge to assist their children into the technical and trade sectors. Downward mobility

Table 10.2   *A generative model of hypothetical mobility densities*

Father's class	Son's Class						
	I	II	III	IV	V	VI	VII
I	1	3	4	6	7	7	7
II	3	3	4	6	6	7	7
III	4	4	4	6	5	6	6
IV	5	5	5	2	6	6	6
V	5	5	5	6	4	5	3
VI	7	6	5	6	5	4	3
VII	7	6	5	6	5	5	4

Source: Redrawn from Goldthorpe et al. (1980 [1987], p. 100).

to class V, VI, VII is thus hypothesised as relatively rare but equally probable when it does happen (recall Digby).

Each cell in Table 10.2 is a conjecture, providing an estimate of the potential agility of that class position. Testing these hypotheses, testing the model, is fairly straightforward. If one plugs in the base numbers in each origin class and then applies each of the 49 forecasts it is possible to compare a simulated mobility table to the actual mobility table. Goldthorpe et al. show that there is an approximate if not perfect similarity with the contours of the real-world Table 10.1. There are a few anomalies in the model and these lead to some specific, post hoc reflections on the original density predictions. But overall, the postulated model has useful explanatory power – it is said to be a 'good fit'.

There are many, many more lines of investigation in this intricate study but I have concentrated solely on the basic understanding of generative causation. All the basic ingredients are there: (i) investigation of the essential, under-lying mechanism (the constrained career choices of incumbents of different class position), (ii) comparison across different contexts (the seven positions in the post-war British occupational structure), (iii) charting the resultant demi-regularities over time (the observed change in the 49 cells of the mobility table), and (iv) the use of generative theory to tie together the explanatory components and match them to the empirical findings.

I also stress the heroic challenge in compiling all the pertinent empirical evidence and this leads, as anticipated in the realist model, to a host of 'stopping rules' on what the investigation will and will not cover (men only, unemployment and immigration ignored, structural changes given and not explained, strict and specific historical period, etc.). Commission and omission is the lot of all empirical investigation, and it is no excuse for puerile critiques which treat such inevitable 'boundary conditions' as failures (study X is condemned because it fails to 'address' the hobbyhorses of the critic). We can only explain what we have chosen to explain. The good news is that stopping rules are an invitation to further study. All the unexplored 'givens' and 'assumptions' in this research have been put to intensive further study in subsequent years. In the second edition of the study, additional chapters are given over to the mobility of women and consideration of cross-national similarities (Goldthorpe et al., 1987).

Other scholars then take up the reins. These investigations use the same realist explanatory motif of the constrained choices associated with different occupational structures – the difference being the decision to study different incumbents in different contexts at different times. The omission of women has been refined in many studies of changes in women's occupations and occupational mobility (e.g., Dex et al., 2008; Rees, 2022). Some of these have a micro-focus on the mechanism of mobility and immobility in particular job sectors such as part-time work in the service sector (Tomlinson, 2007). Goldthorpe et al.'s study confined itself to an explanation of intergenerational mobility in a 'given' occupational structure. But, of course, people don't create the jobs that are available, and the overall workforce structure is generated in longer waves of economic and technological changes. Once again there is no shortage of complementary studies on the changing shape of the job market (Brown, 2016). Many of these note contemporary shifts to an hour-glass economy of 'lousy and lovely' jobs (Holmes and Mayhew, 2012). By 2021 approximately 14 per cent of the UK population were foreign born. Immigrants, of course, cannot be included in a study of intergenerational mobility, yet many of them take up places in the occupational structure and thus influence the job opportunities and mobility of native workers. Cantankerous political debate has ensued on the impact of immigration on the labour market, balanced thankfully by notable empirical studies on the changes that have ensued (Borjas, 2014; Edo, 2019).

Goldthorpe's study provides us with a miniature model of how causal explanations grow and confederate. The generative model described here explains some key contours of social mobility. Other features are unpicked gradually: the causal mechanisms extend and are mutually reinforcing.

KEY LESSONS

Episode 10 presents the first practical example of generative causal analysis – social mobility viewed through a realist lens. It investigates how the action of particular mechanisms in particular contexts generate complex outcome patterns. The patterns are traced through a quantitative inquiry based on survey data but the explanations for those patterns are drawn from theory. The crucial and 'hidden' causal mechanisms under investigation relate to the highly constrained choices that people make in traversing the labour market. These are investigated in a simple simulation of the resources and reasoning associated with different occupational classes. The complexity of other changes associated with and brought about by social mobility is acknowledged in the strict stopping rules imposed in the inquiry. Significant partial knowledge ensues which is enlarged in subsequent investigation.

Episode 11. Generative thinking in sociology II: Boudon on educational inequality

The key lesson of Episode 8 (the boat model) was that causal analysis in social science is better conceived as an analysis of patterns in motion. Explanation usually involves an understanding of the action of several explanatory mechanisms. These need to be expressed within a dynamic model that explains how outcomes evolve. For my second classic example, I turn to the work of Raymond Boudon, to my mind the greatest contemporary sociologist and a pioneer of generative explanation. His intellectual range was immense but here I concentrate on his most extensive empirical inquiry in the monograph *Education, Opportunity and Social Inequality* (1974).

As the title suggests, Boudon's interest is the question of whether increased educational opportunities will create a more equal and meritocratic society. This has long been regarded a truism and is the cornerstone of educational policy the world over. Boudon's massive cross-examination of this thesis begins with an overview of what he calls 'bookkeeping data', administrative records and surveys from across Europe and North America in the 1950s, 1960s, and 1970s. What realists define as demi-regs, Boudon refers to as 'trends' and the first part of the monograph is devoted to compiling a long list of broadly characteristic patterns. No assumption is made that these patterns will last forever or that they are universal.

One common trend serves as our illustration. Over time, increasing *numbers* of children from poorer or lower-class backgrounds attended in the later stages of secondary education and in college and in university. However, in the same time period, the *proportion* of lower-class children attending these upper reaches of education remains roughly constant. In other words, the expansion of higher education seemed to benefit upper- and middle-class children just as much if not more so than their lower-class counterparts. Despite the considerable expansion of educational provision, educational advantage remained in much the same hands.

To interpret this counter-balancing outcome pattern requires an under-standing of the underlying mechanism at work and Boudon proposes that we contemplate two.

i.   The first mechanism is 'cultural' or 'material' advantage. This pools together all the stock-in-trade sociological knowledge we possess about the educational advantages that middle-class households can provide and pass on to their children – resources and materials, time and space, expe-rience and know-how.
ii. The second mechanism refers to the 'utilities' or 'choices' attached to striving and staying on in the higher reaches of education. This reasoning, too, is likely to be stratified – what is considered as social failure for one family may be regarded as success for another. Middle-class households might fear that early exit from schooling would involve social demotion for their children and so do their upmost to avoid it. Poorer families, even if their children are high achievers, might be worried about how to navi-gate the system and the potential financial sacrifices involved.

In the next part of Boudon's explanatory model hypothesises that the two mechanisms have their impact in different time periods, the dynamics are distinct. The play of time is modelled as a series of branching points when students make the decision to stay or leave at various staging posts in an educational career. These 'year-groups', 'grades', 'levels', and so forth carry different labels from country to country so Boudon (1974, p. 75) settles for an abstract grid which I simplify even further as Figure 11.1. The solid line indicates that the student stays on and moves to the next level. The dashed line indicates that the student exits the educational system.

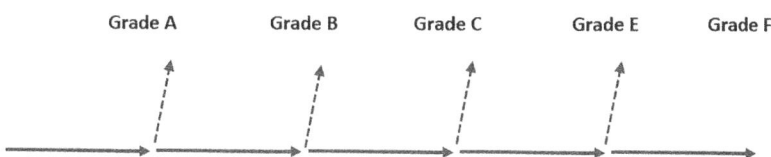

Figure 11.1   *The system of branching points in secondary and further education*

The heart of the model consists of an attempt to simulate how the two candi-date mechanisms make for different rates of progress through the branching points. How do they influence the survival rates for students from different backgrounds? To do this Boudon creates a highly simplified 'box model' with

Table 11.1   *Probability space of surviving in education at each branching point*

	School Achievement		
Social Background	A_1 (high)	A_2 (middle)	A_3 (low)
C_1 (high)	a%	b%	c%
C_2 (middle)	d%	e%	f%
C_3 (low)	g%	h%	i%

which to compare the progress of different sub-groups of students. I present the causal structure in Table 11.1. One sees, once again, that Boudon resorts to conceptual simplification by defining these sub-groups on two variables, each with three ordinal categories. Reduced to bare essentials, he is saying that the potential for progress through each educational level is shaped by the students' social background (C) and by their current classroom achievements (A), creating the nine cells in Table 11.1. In generative language, each cell, each sub-group, is predicted to have different causal powers, a different potential for survival. The probabilities are represented a%, b%, and so on.

Next comes the matter of assigning numbers to letters. How might we enumerate survival probability in each sub-group? The odds of remaining on education's high road are embroiled in the complexities of everyday life for each family. Each one of us has a story to tell about the specific influences on our choice to follow a particular educational pathway. But at the group level we can only capture this ordinary rationality in general terms, we can only say with any certainty the different sub-groups are more and less likely to make particular choices.

Boudon thus proceeds in the same manner as Goldthorpe in the previous episode, namely, by using broad estimates of what is known of the educational proclivities of different social classes. For example, one might speculate that students at A_1C_1 have a 90 per cent chance of surviving a particular branching point as compared to their equally bright but poor classmates at A_1C_3, whose chances rate at 60 per cent. Such 'informed guesses' are completed for each cell and for each branching point. This produces a massive matrix of probabilities of the likelihood of surviving through each school and university grade over time. These probabilities fill five pages of Boudon's book and are not reproduced here.

We reach the unique feature of his model. Each estimate is informed by the two mechanisms introduced at the beginning of this episode, the crucial point being that each mechanism is assumed to have different longevity. Of the cultural or material mechanism, it is supposed that its influence wanes as students pass through each hurdle. If a bright, lower-class child has manged to pass into college and university it is assumed that material disadvantage can be and has been overcome. Such achievements are hardly unknown. By contrast, the secondary effect of stratification – the choices made on the basis of the utility calculations – might well continue to assert themselves. Ambition continues to be moderated through the years – poorer families and young people play safe and choose less prestigious schools and curriculum options. A somewhat stereotypical embodiment of this idea in higher education might be the choice of a highly able but poorer student of a vocational degree at a local university rather than, say, pursuing classics at an ancient university.

Boudon then proceeds with the simulation. The model is loaded with initial conditions, namely, the numbers occupying each cell at time 1, and calculations are made of the survival percentages of each sub-group as they pass through the successive branching points. The numbers staying on or dropping out at each point provide a moving picture of educational inequality. What the simulation shows as we reach the final branching points is that the grip of social class on educational attainment remains firm. We have an explanation for the 'bookkeeping data' showing that the proportion of lower-class children attending the upper reaches of education remains relatively low and roughly constant. Although Boudon's model was built to explain trends in mid-20th-century educational inequality, note that it has some staying power. Subsequent studies of educational attainment in Italy and France reveal the same pivoting pattern of disadvantage (Manzo, 2009). The dynamics uncovered also have great policy significance; they help explain the struggles of a mass of interventions aimed at 'remedial' and 'compensatory' education (Power, 2018). Compensating for aptitudes will not necessarily shift attitudes.

Now let us ponder caveats and the issue of stopping rules in Boudon's inquiry. As ever there are many. Dozens of 'correlates' of educational attainment are simply ignored. We know, for instance, that gender, race, family size, and so on can influence school achievement. These are left for others to explore. The main restriction on Boudon's analysis, however, is the introduction of significant simplifications in the model, which are plain to see in Figure 11.1 and Table 11.1.

Boudon attempts to explain a perverse outcome that he has uncovered in records on educational achievement across Europe and North America. But, of course, the precise makeup of the school subtypes, age ranges, curricula, examination systems, and so on varies significantly from country to country. He makes no attempt to chart the causal progress through the disparate systems – the primary and secondary schools in the UK, the lycée classique and the lycée technique in France, gymnasium and gesamatschule schools in Germany, etc., etc., etc. These delivery structures are all simplified as a series of 'branching points' in the model. Yet the specifics of the 'system' can make a difference. Educational authorities sometimes have exclusive responsibility for placing children and in these particular phases assumptions about the choice mechanisms will not apply. There is a rather stark choice here. It would be impossible to simulate progress through every nuance and pathway of every national educational system. These delivery systems are questioned and reformed on a yearly basis.

So Boudon settles for abstraction. The working assumption is that the branching model has features that are common to all systems and it is the common features that are explored. We alight on a key compromise here, a methodological stopping rule that is common to all social inquiry. Causal analysis always requires a certain degree of simplification and making clear the simplifications is a basic requirement of research design. Of my six exemplars here, Boudon's research on educational inequality is the only one claiming cross-societal generality. This strategy of abstraction and simplification is also key to that mission and its precise articulation comes under scrutiny in Part III.

The other major concession lies in the way that the action of mechanisms, both material and subjective, is described. In the box model different estimates are made of the survival rates at each branching point. These estimates are expressed as probabilities – 80 per cent, 90 per cent, and so on. Placing such a numerical estimate on each transition enables us to see how the longitudinal pathways for each sub-group develop and differ over time. But remember they remain estimates whose role is to capture broad differences in the resources and reasoning of different social groups. Arithmetical precision is impossible and indeed misplaced if decimal point accuracy is claimed. All that Boudon asserts, and all that social science can even claim, is that certain actions differ according to such approximate estimates. Group A is more likely than group B to pursue a particular goal. A group's preferences at time A will differ from those at time B. This is another severe and inevitable limitation on causal analysis in social science – highly restrictive in some ways but nothing to apologise for. Boudon summarises it as follows: '[Causal analysis] takes the form of qualitative statements of the "more or less" type rather than quantitative statements' (1974).

KEY LESSONS

Episode 11 reconstructs an investigation of the action of just two generative mechanisms (material forces and rational choices) as they apply in different school cohorts through time. The mechanisms run a race; they have different force over the educational career. Boudon's model is able to explain a paradoxical outcome that can be observed in many Western nations about the stubborn retention of a hierarchy of educational advantage. One mechanism waxes as the other one wanes. The analysis makes use of available administrative data and takes the form of a simulation exercise predicting which students are likely to continue into higher education. It makes huge simplifications about the pathways through educational systems. It reduces the complexities of human choice patterns to a series of approximate probabilities. These stopping rules allow it to surface the action of otherwise invisible mechanisms. It constitutes a classic piece of realist inquiry, which still has profound implications for educational policy.

Episode 12. Generative thinking in programme evaluation: Pawson in prison

Whenever I was introduced in conference presentations, I always encouraged the chair to say something like: 'He has served a long time in prison … … … for research purposes'. Rarely were these scholarly souls able to sustain the dramatic pause long enough to convey the joke. So let me press on. We shift disciplines here to examine investigations on the effectiveness of social policies and interventions, inquiry normally referred to as 'evaluation research'. Programme evaluation is based foursquare on a causal question – did the intervention bring about the intended outcomes? In the present case the question becomes – can prisoner education reduce recidivism? The attempt to answer this particular puzzle marked the beginning of the development of 'realist evaluation' (Pawson and Tilley, 1997), which since this time has become a standard item in the repertoire of applied social research.

Details of the prison education programme discussed in this episode are described in Duguid and Pawson (1998). Here I concentrate on how the research team uncovered its causal structure. The venture was quite unique and, if I may say, profoundly Canadian. From 1973 to 1993 a university-level, liberal arts programme ran in several federal prisons (medium to maximum security) in British Columbia. Lectures, tutorials, assignments, etc. were all delivered and superintended by Simon Fraser University instructors. Insofar as it was possible, the core aim was to mimic in an off-campus environment the content and ethos of on-campus higher education. In other words, and thinking back to the previous episode, the basic aim was not 'remedial' or 'compensatory'. There are scores of correctional prison programmes of this ilk, which target offending behaviour, cognitive deficits, anger management, and so on. In contrast, the Simon Fraser programme sought to provide no more than 'education for education's sake'.

There is a twist, however, and perhaps a controversial one. Many of the instructors, some of whom had been involved for a dozen years or more, claimed that this deliberately passive intervention could be transformative. They had seen the arrivals and departures of many inmates (including return visits from some recalcitrants). Like many practitioners they saw social benefit in their work and there was considerable anecdotal evidence that many former prisoner students moved on to mainstream education, professional training, and so on. The causal spark, as hypothesised, was that sustained exposure to a liberal arts curriculum could open new horizons, trigger different ways of thinking, and develop self-reflection. Change, if it occurred, was self-generated rather than externally driven. Could this theory be put to the test?

On to method. We confront the standard question – did the programme work to reduce recidivism? The standard methodological answer at the time would be to find out using an RCT – assign prisoners randomly to the programme and to a control group and compare the ensuing rehabilitation rates. This, of course, is a non-starter in voluntary interventions. Imagine approaching Reginald 'Hacksaw' Molloy one morning and telling him, 'Reggie, like it or not you have been randomly assigned for the next two years to the Simon Fraser University course.' Since entry to prolonged education can only be voluntary, the problem then arises that any recorded benefit might be due to self-selection onto the scheme of relatively well-motivated and success-bound inmates.

The solution used in this case was to make comparisons with an historical norm. High rates of recidivism are the curse of all prison systems and it is possible to capture a predictive statistical picture of inmates who are most likely to return. All regimes make use of such tools for capacity planning. The Canadian variant was known as the Statistical Information on Recidivism Scale (or SIR scale). Common sense tells us, for example, that a more mature offender who has stronger family ties, a decent employment record, and who has served a shorter sentence for a lesser crime is less likely to become a habitual offender. A dozen or so such durable correlates are rolled to the SIR scale, which can then be applied to provide a standardised historical measure of the likely rate of return for any offender. Released prisoners are categorised into five groups ascending from those in category A with a 20 per cent historical record of recidivism in a three-year period to much more seasoned reoffenders in category E of whom 66 per cent would normally return by year three.

The SIR scale thus provides us with a relatively unbiased outcome comparator – do prisoners on the programme outperform these historical norms? The information required to enable the said comparison was gathered (laboriously) from federal prison records on the offender's background and their offence, from Simon Fraser administrative data on grades, semesters completed, etc. and from parole files on offending after release. These data provide us with a headline figure for the intervention as a whole – for the total group of prisoner students, the actual return rate to prison within three years was 25 per cent as against the SIR prediction of 42 per cent.

As described to this point, this is not yet a realist inquiry. We have a statistical, black-box picture of apparent success but no answer to the causal question, 'Why?' What are the mechanisms and contexts that generate the observed pattern? Translated into evaluation research terminology this required us to ponder what was it about the programme that worked for whom and in what circumstances. To answer the puzzle requires we begin with theory and the working hypotheses were collected in qualitative interviews with experienced instructors. We asked them to provide examples of the types of prisoners who might become involved in the programme in ways that might begin to change their lives on release. Probing like this produced a little torrent of hypotheses suggesting whom might (and might not) be so affected. Typically, these pen-pictures consisted of a combination of particular background characteristics and particular pathways through the programme that encouraged change. Here's a verbatim example:

> The men who are most likely to be changed are best described as mediocre. You shouldn't look for high-flyers. They are likely to come from a deprived background with a poor and maybe non-existent school record. They will be mediocre criminals too. They'll have gone from petty crime to street crime to drugs or armed robbery or something. Then when they come on the program, they're mediocre or worse. They just survive the first semester but gradually build up getting Cs and Bs. So by the end they have come a long way and that's what changes 'em. It is not so much a case of 'rehabilitation' as' 'habilitation'.

This was perhaps the pearl of wisdom amongst other more prosaic ideas that we gathered and collectively these hunches became the theories that guided inquiry. Verbal sketches such as the above describe different sub-groups of prisoner-students, different combinations of characteristics that are more likely to generate intervention success (and failure). Each sub-group was identified by a combination of characteristics, and the federal and Simon Fraser databases were ransacked to find sub-groups of men that shared these attributes. Several such clusters were examined, three of which are analysed in detail in the Duguid and Pawson (1998) paper, namely, the 'improvers', the 'high-flyers', and the 'hard cases'. Readers may be able to guess the group compositions from these shorthand labels.

I have already described the analytical method. For each sub-group, a comparison can be made of actual versus predicted reconviction. The results paint a stunningly diverse picture, with some groups (e.g., the improvers) easily outperforming the SIR norms on expected rates of reincarceration, and with others (e.g., the high-flyers) actually exceeding their gloomy historical predictions. Details of the sub-group composition and the spectacular differences in numerical outcomes may be found in the 1998 paper.

It is the methodological implications that are important here. The basic strategy marks a shift from successionist to generative thinking in evaluation research. Rather that asking, 'What works?' and making intervention on/intervention off comparisons in an RCT, the question becomes 'What works, for whom, in what circumstances?' and this requires study of mechanisms acting in contexts. Some students with particular background characteristics *chose* to make the intervention work for them, and some did not. And so indeed it is with all policies and programmes.

I now move to starting assumptions and stopping rules. As with all inquiry, they were numerous. I cover just two here. The first is to re-emphasise an ever-present limitation about probabilistic explanation. The explanatory mechanisms in this study are rooted in the choices that inmates make when offered a particular resource. The generative mechanism thus seeks to capture the agency involved in making complex decisions. For any individual this reasoning involves endless cogitation on the minutiae of his past and present. We cannot capture that level of detail in an inquiry about collective choices. Candidate theories can offer no more precision than to say that a particular group is 'more likely' or 'less likely' to respond in particular ways. So, when a working hypothesis says, for example, that the sub-group of young prisoners who make steady improvement in grades is less likely to be reconvicted, it is indeed corroborated when it turns out that 7 per cent of them return to prison as opposed to the SIR norm of 45 per cent. But the theory is quite incapable of predicting an exact 38 per cent difference. Testing probabilistic explanations, as Boudon has taught us, consists of capturing broad trends and clear differences in outcome data as they apply to numerous sub-groups.

The second stopping rule in this particular inquiry is perhaps more surprising. The core theories turn on the inmates' reasoning yet these are not directly interrogated in the above evidence. As with much generative explanation in social inquiry, the mechanisms are effectively 'invisible' (Cherkaoui, 2005). In this particular inquiry, our initial design had a final phase which involved contacting inmates post-release to seek their opinion on whether the broad conjectures we apportioned to their sub-group corresponded with their own experience. Was there a sense of self-recognition? As it turned out, such a far-flung tracking exercise proved impossible given privacy concerns and meagre funding.

But as with all stopping rules, there is nothing to prevent research programmes from harnessing further inquiry to support the causal explanation. The basic theory here is that education for education's sake offers the prisoner prolonged opportunity for self-reflection and that is the core trigger of change. Many qualitative studies have sought to capture this line of reasoning from the perspective of those doing the reasoning. One example is an edited volume by Wilson and Reuss (1999). Reuss's contribution is an ethnography of a UK initiative at HMP Full Sutton, which was a small-scale (and short-lived) attempt to imitate the Simon Fraser programme. The repeated message from the students was that education provided an opportunity, but it was for them to decide how to act on that opportunity. This brings me back to Pawson in prison. I did some qualitative interviews with the same men resulting in exactly the same message. One of them told me that education provision by itself didn't change anything but was a 'mere catalyst' and he certainly knew the exact derivation of that term. I might also add that he was a previously educated 'high-flyer', so there might be some doubt about whether he went on to beat the relevant odds.

KEY LESSONS

Episode 12 examines the causal mechanisms involved when those in authority attempt to engineer social change. The causal structure of policy effectiveness is profoundly realist. Interventions always decompose into many different pathways according to the resources and reasoning of their recipients. The basic causal question in policy evaluation becomes highly conditional, changing from 'What works' to 'What works for whom, in what circumstances, in what respects, and over what duration?' As with most realist inquiry, this question brings forms of sub-group analysis to the fore. In this instance, sub-groups of prisoners undergoing a prolonged period of education were found to respond in quite different ways. The sub-groups were first identified via qualitative hunches, which were transformed into formal hypotheses, which were then tested using record-keeping data that compared actual outcomes with historical norms. This mix of methods is typical of realist inquiry.

Episode 13. Generative thinking in comparative historical research: whether protest movements?

We swap disciplines once more and move to a research domain that you are more likely to discover in the 'Politics' section of your library. I refer to comparative historical research and the aforementioned study of big structures, large processes, and huge comparisons – democratisation, dictatorship, (de)industrialisation, welfarism, revolution, war, secessionism, protest movements, and the like. Here the term 'realism' makes less of an appearance, but as Gerring (2010) puts it, 'In recent years, the importance of mechanism-centered explanation has become an article of faith.'

The literature is a dense forest. There are countless accounts of first principles (Falleti and Lynch, 2009; Gerring, 2008; Hedström and Swedberg, 1998; McAdam et al., 2001; Tilly, 2001). As its name suggests, the core research design is based on a comparison of social change across nations. Why democracy here and dictatorship there, why war then but not now, why centralised welfare provision here and not there? It must be stressed that there are different ways of organising such comparisons, different ways of digging out the explanatory mechanisms. Some researchers prefer comparisons between two countries, others prefer 20 or so (formally, small-n and large-N). Some researchers choose comparisons between outwardly similar countries, others start with stark differences (formally, 'most-similar' and 'most-different' designs). To add complexity there are widely used technical variants such as 'process tracing' and 'agent-based modelling' (Beach and Pederson, 2013; Bennet, 2010; Collier, 2011: Mahoney, 2012). Finally, note that the raw data used to build the comparisons can be quantitative or qualitative, preferably both (Goertz, 2017). Perhaps the clearest guidance through this forest is provided by Little (2005, 2015).

I will return to a fuller discussion of this range of research designs in Part III. I focus this episode on just one strategy – the method of 'paired comparison' (Tarrow, 2010). I do so because it adopts closely the basic causal formula identified throughout Part I, namely, that understanding outcomes patterns requires attention to both pre-existing structural forces and the mechanisms residing in people's choices and opportunities. Tarrow's paper takes the reader through a number of alternative paired comparison designs as utilised in a number of celebrated inquiries. Here, I concentrate on a particular sub-strategy he terms 'dual-process tracing' and use as my case study a recent comparative study of protest movements.

The method of dual process tracing begins with the idea of comparing systems with close similarities. These 'most-similar designs' are often and quite erroneously understood as a weak subset of controlled experiment designs. If two countries or regions have many similarities on many measures, then any difference in their development can be attributed to the smaller subset of variables that differentiate them. We have already witnessed the demise of this variable-based approach to causality. It does not work because at a national level there are always endless potential differences and endless potential similarities (Goldthorpe, 1997). We are not about to return to that same garden path. Similarities and difference do not provide the causal explanation; they are the topic for causal explanation.

What is traced in dual process tracing is change over time. The forces and movements that come under examination in comparative macrosociology have a different tempo in different countries. They work their way through many agents and agencies over time. They pass through different stages. They operate in fits and starts. They may fire and they may misfire. The core task is to explain these differences in tempo. The basic causal sequence is depicted in Figure 13.1. Change is broken down into a series of shorter stages or phases. For example, in the diagram we have two nations following a similar trajectory at input but then deviating at output. The causal explanation asks 'Why?' What accounts for the similarities and the differences? What is the sequence of actions and reactions responsible for *both* the convergence and the divergence of the causal pathways?

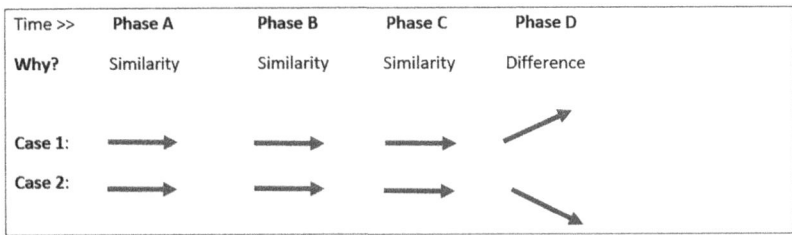

Figure 13.1   Dual process tracing

For a substantive example I turn to Lee's (2021) study comparing anti-austerity protest in South Korea in 1997–98 and in Greece in 2009–10. Protest movements gather pace rapidly, they are fired by powerful ideas and narratives, common grievances have to be identified, and success depends on alliance building from group to group. Accordingly, protest movements have a different trajectory from instance to instance, country to country. They pass or fail to pass through different phases at a different tempo. And it is the trajectories that are the subject of causal analysis. The empirical backbone of Lee's study can be depicted reusing Figure 13.1. The respective historical changes follow the sequence: (A) mounting debt and economic crisis; (B) enforcement of austerity policies; (C) intensifying grievance and gathering protest; (D) contrasting protest outcomes in the longer term.

The causal puzzle is to explain why, despite remarkable uniformity in the process through stages A, B, and C, does divergence occur at D? Why, given closely matching input histories, does protest fizzle out in Korea and intensify in Greece? Lee's empirical task is to collect and construct evidence on each of these phases. He uses a vast array of sources, including macroeconomic indicators, governmental records, administrative sources, policy proposals, media reportage, and existing academic commentary. Here, I provide a very brief summary, omitting the hard graft of research and all references to the primary sources.

- *Phase A*: The economic indicators building to crises are remarkably similar in the two countries. There were highly prosperous earlier years in which welfare provision was stepped up. Then arrived the financial crisis in which foreign debt mushroomed and borrowing levels shot up – to the same degree in both nations. Economic crash begins and Lee goes on to provide graphical data on the huge percentage declines in employment levels and wages and household disposable income in the first year of each crisis. If anything, the deterioration in living standards was slightly worse in the Korean case. Crisis deepens with both countries on the verge of defaulting on major international loans. These baseline data are important to the overall thesis. A simpler explanation for the difference in protest levels is an 'economic pain' theory – the bigger the debt crisis, the bigger the protest. No such correlation holds here. The similar system assumption holds good in phase A.
- *Phase B*: In both countries austerity policies were proposed as the solution – immediate sharp reductions in earnings and benefits and steep rises in taxation. These were implemented in highly analogous political environments – initially recommended and executed by the governing party and supported by the opposition in predominantly two-party systems. Crucially, there were also major similarities in external control. International bodies (International Monetary Fund, European Commission, and European Central Bank) mandated stringent tax and benefit changes in order to guarantee huge financial bailouts. These manoeuvres gave those

on the receiving end in both countries a convenient and legitimate focal target – expressed via growing narratives about 'foreign occupation' and 'conceding sovereignty'. The similar system assumptions hold good in phase B.

- *Phase C*: Protest flared up immediately in both cases under a common grievance. As they saw it, the public through no fault of their own were being required to repair losses due to governmental economic incompetence by enduring a further round of economic pain. In Korea, mass rallies broke out spearheaded by the Korean Confederation of Trade Unions. The KCTU seceded from all negotiations with the government. The Hyundai Motor Workers Union called an all-out strike against plans to dismiss 4830 workers. In Greece, the anti-austerity movement was spearheaded by the two largest unions, the Civil Servant's Confederation and the General Confederation of Greek Workers. Collaboration between the two led to two general strikes in March and then in May 2010 supported by mass rallies with tens of thousands of followers. The similar system assumptions hold good in phase C.

- *Phase D*: Lee now follows dissent beyond the immediate uprisings and explains protest curtailment in Korea and its amplification in Greece. He does so by examining the respective opportunities, alliances, strategies, and tactics of the protesters. In Korea, protest soon hit a plateau. It had a population four times larger than Greece and rallies were confined to the capital city, Seoul. The movement was unable to develop sufficient political allies. Minority parliamentary parties kept at arms length with one (United Liberal Democrats) being sympathetic with austerity policy. There was further support for austerity at the civic level, most notably the people's Gold Collection Drive, donating $2.2 billion to government coffers. Splinters in labour opposition to austerity emerged. The aforementioned joint union leadership fell out, one pursuing more strikes and one joining government negotiations in an effort to mitigate austerity's worse effects. Another union (KIA Motors) joined in efforts to save the company. In Greece, strikes spread across all employment sectors – private and public, industrial and administrative, professional and manual. Seven general strikes were called, with sustained support. Several minority parliamentary parties supported the protesters, with three left-wing groups joining its leadership. The focus of protest was enlarged with corruption and lack of governmental accountability being added into the grievances. Survey research suggested that 'novice' protesters with no experience of collective action joined in anti-austerity opposition. Rather than fragmentation, Lee provides evidence showing that the Greek response was closer to a mass movement.

The methodological argument here is realist. Only in certain contexts will mechanisms of action flow to their intended consequences. Pre-existing conditions in South Korea were such that protest flared but faltered. Pre-existing conditions in Greece allowed for the building of a wider range of alliances so that the protest movement bit deeper. So, Lee is realist but is he right? I cannot claim any expertise on the details of each national case study. Instead, let us ponder the crucial lesson of Episode 9, namely, that empirical inquiry cannot proceed without stopping rules and can only undertake investigation of a limited range of hypotheses. In advocating the strategy of paired comparison, Tarrow (2010) also insists that the boundary conditions of any historical causal claims must be made clear.

Lee's (2021) study was unfunded and, I suppose, an extension of a doctoral thesis. Accordingly, it has limited scope and leaves behind many untested theories. As noted above, he provides compelling evidence to dismiss one key rival hypothesis – the economic decline in both nations was closely comparable, killing off the 'economic pain theory'. But there are always unconsidered causal forces. Might not his account of the pre-existing conditions to protest in Greece have failed to take sufficient account of a greater historical predisposition for public outrage and indeed political violence? And what of the years following the height of the protest? The Greek protest did indeed gather in further waves, culminating in January 2015 with electoral success for the radical SYRIZA party (Karyotis and Rüdig, 2018). Thereafter, protest became subdued, and a punishing long-term international rescue deal was agreed. The methodological point again is that tracing causal pathways can only reconstruct change within well-defined boundaries. Rival antecedents and alternative consequences can always be conjectured and subjected to further inquiry. But this does not deny the worth of causal claims in partially closed systems.

KEY LESSONS

Episode 13 finds generative causal inquiry burgeoning in another domain, namely, comparative historical research. The same basic formula pertains – pre-existing contextual forces are interpreted and reinterpreted, offering different opportunities for different agents and agencies, generating different outcomes patterns. Those outcomes, moreover, will themselves change over time. Comparative research provides a range of different designs to follow and tease out the emerging causal pathways, each of them dependent on clear stopping rules. Tracing empirically the evolving interconnections between contending parties calls upon the full repertoire of quantitative and qualitative data collection methods.

Episode 14. Generative thinking in qualitative longitudinal inquiry: following young fathers

We hurtle from the macro to the micro in this episode and enter the domain of qualitative inquiry. Customarily, qualitative research has had little interest in causality, let alone an aptitude for generative causal explanation. The guiding impulse has always been to gain close access to individuals in their social settings in order to gather rich, evocative descriptions of their lifeworlds. Qualitative longitudinal inquiry (Neale, 2021) stays true to and indeed celebrates the importance of understanding how people think. The difference is that it follows these ruminations through major life course transitions. Tracing how people think and think again and then going on to understand the consequences of these considerations and reconsiderations demands attention to causal forces. This episode gives a glimpse of the methodological requirements.

The case study here is drawn from a three-year 'Following Young Fathers' project, itself part of a larger UK, ERSC-funded 'Timescapes' programme. The scene is set as follows: 'The entry into fatherhood is a major life course transition involving the fashioning of a new identity and the take up of new responsibilities' (Neale and Davies, 2015). Very young fathers face exceptional challenges in this respect and this study explores their aspirations to provide financially and materially for their children.

Design details can be summarised as follows, the first being to note that tracing, contacting, and maintaining the interest of unsettled research subjects over a number of years is a tough challenge and requires considerable resources. Thirty-one young fathers were followed for periods extending between two and four years, some using five waves of interviews, some two. Eighteen of the young men were school-age fathers (15 and 16), the remainder being spread evenly between 17 and 24. Only two had planned to enter parenthood. Insofar as these small numbers allow, the respondents were selected from a variety of social backgrounds and, importantly, went on to follow different education, training, and work pathways. As with all of the case studies in Part I, the research was based on the idea that identifiable sub-groups at input (the birth) go on to follow complex, non-linear trajectories at output (moving into fatherhood). The experience of the same momentous event leads to quite different consequences, which require careful explanation.

Copious interview material is analysed and presented in a way which shows how the young men came to terms with their own life choices and chances. Verbatim sections of interview transcripts are published in order to capture differences in how they tried and tried again to figure out how to regain control of their disrupted lives. Here I can only produce miniaturised versions of already much condensed journal paper transcripts to convey the emerging patterns. The findings are organised into three sub-groups identifying 'skilled', 'semi-skilled', and 'low-skilled' trajectories.

'Dominic' is representative of the former category. He entered into parenthood at 16 and tried to combine studying and working and childcare, with considerable help from parents. His trajectory is depicted via interview waves 2 and 4 reproduced below, which I might describe in the local vernacular as moving from 'knackered and despondent' to 'knackered but coping'. The frequent references to exhaustion, however, reveal a pay-off, namely, that for young men like him it was just about possible to 'keep on track' and maintain their original careers ambitions:

> Wave 2. I'm not best pleased with this job ... 'cause it's really mind numbing ... I'm purely there just to take money out 'cause of financial constraints ... before this happened, you know, I had aspirations of what I wanted to do ... what's the point ... everything is a struggle.
> Wave 4. [After a change to part-time work and study]. Going down to part-time from full-time's a massive shift in your lifestyle ... in some ways it's lucky how it turned out ... I knew I wasn't going to Uni just for the sake of going ... as I say it's very tiring 'cause I'm up at eight and working till ten. It's all building towards, hopefully ... a career path in the future.

Turning to the semi-skilled trajectory, I reproduce a smidgen of the developing testimony of 'Kevin' and 'Senwe', both of which indicate a different kind of resilience. They accepted the blow that fatherhood delivered to youthful ambitions and settled for the lower-skilled sector and so began the humbling, protracted process of securing slightly better pay, better hours, better conditions.

> To come out of college, no real grades from school. Not even completed a year of college, I was worried ... who would employ me? ... I had four cleaning jobs and I just worked and worked and provided. It was hard ... looking back maybe I could have stayed at college and got a few years under me.
> It's just that the challenge of growing up, manning up, knowing that you've got a kid coming ... I was really upset and down, 'cause most of my friends had gone to Uni or college ... I didn't want to let my mum down ... and just stay at home and do nothing ... I applied for three apprenticeships ... Yeah I got it, so after two years I'll get the job ... it's made me a better person to provide for my daughter and just knowing I'm working for her.

Fourteen young men fell into the 'low-skilled' trajectory. They had accrued negligible qualifications, skill, and experience before the birth of the child. Their financial circumstances were precarious, and they remained stuck on unemployment benefits. Relations with their partners and babies also tended to deteriorate. Both 'Marcel' and 'Andrew' understood the obligations of fatherhood but the gap between aspirations and actuality were pronounced.

> So I've worked a couple of times but it's just because it's always been temporary … they always lay me off … so I'm always looking again and again … and I start right over again … it's just really hard to find something permanent because I didn't finish my studies and didn't do no apprenticeship course.
> I had to go to school on us own … and that's how I came to end up acting like an idiot … I'll just do as I please … and I look where I've ended now … but obviously I could change it … it's just like hard isn't it, really.

What of the caveats, assumptions, and stopping rules in Neale and Davies's inquiry? There are many as we shall see. But interestingly, because this 'employment sub-study' was part of the larger 'Timescapes' project and because the Following Young Fathers project is dissected as an exemplar throughout Neale's (2021) huge manifesto for qualitative longitudinal research, the boundary conditions are made perfectly clear.

First is the issue of sample size. The core idea is to track subjects intensively, to capture those many moments where the young men are figuring out 'what the bloody hell to do next'. Accordingly, there is no interest in and no possibility of following a large representative sample. Neale and Davies thus opt for a small opportunistic sample, gathered and then boosted through contacts with support agencies working in this field. This allows the researchers to follow what they set out to follow, namely, the rapid emergence of subtly different pathways in response to unplanned fatherhood. These pathways can be identified but cannot, of course, be quantified. The purpose of such a sample is not to count how many individuals flit hither and thither. The goal is to unearth formative rather than summative outcome patterns.

It is useful to compare this stopping rule to that applied in Goldthorpe's quantitative study of social mobility (Episode 10). Both understand the operative generative mechanisms in the same way, namely, residing in the choices and resources that people utilise in trying to forge a career. Goldthorpe and colleagues, because they are aiming to explain the totality of intergenerational mobility in Britain, opt for formulating abstract, broad-brush choice mechanisms, which are used to simulate the decisions of 49 different sub-groups. Neale and Davies, by contrast, concentrate on concrete choices, the intricate details of the short-term decisions made in just three nascent sub-groups. Different boundary assumptions, different payoffs.

Another set of boundary conditions are given (and thus unavoidable) in the pre-exisisting social, political, economic, geographical, and cultural contexts surrounding the research subjects. Although it was 'longitudinal', Neale and Davies's study took place in a restricted locality; under the same political and policy regimes; against a bleak background of a weak labour market, the growing casualisation of work, and reducing welfare entitlements. Context matters and these and other background features are bound to play some part in the young fathers' reasoning. The precise impact of these causal forces can only be gauged in comparative inquiry but it is important that they are recognised in a local inquiry.

Neale and Davies supply a useful example. The brief excerpts above give expression to the sense of frustration experienced by these young men in trying and often failing to gain a foothold in gainful employment. It may well be that these sentiments are exacerbated (i.e., caused) by wider public expectations about support for children and in particular the prevailing norms about the 'male breadwinner'. In the given time and place of the Following Young Father's project, the authors point to the overriding assumption about gendered responsibilities – material support is the domain of fatherhood, caring responsibilities reside with the mothers. Dominic, Kevin, Senwe, Marcel, and Andrew may well have felt its force. Arguably, this convention is a disappearing stereotype and there are certainly different cultural expectations elsewhere. But that matters not one jot – as long as the boundary condition is made clear.

There is another interesting scope condition associated with the raw materials of qualitative longitudinal research. The very idea is to encourage the respondent to tell stories, to engage in spontaneous descriptions of why they reckoned this and why they reckoned that. The goal is to prompt the respondent's own narrative on the myriad influences in their life course. People's inclination to do this varies. Some, like Tristram Shandy, rattle on, so that their narratives burst the covers of thickest tomes. Some, like the Lonesome Cowboy, are reluctant to respond to questions with anything other than a 'yup' or 'nope'. There are various interview tactics available to restrain or encourage each type of respondent (Neale, 2021, chapter 6).

But the problem with the raw data remains. Life histories are infinite. There is nothing to exclude recall of the significance of what stepfather Sid said about his sons on a sun-drenched Sunday in Scarborough in the sixties. Here's the rub. People recollect without stopping rules. Social research is impossible without stopping rules. The social scientist's task is to locate, distinguish, and find evidence on the generative causal process within these oral histories. And no doubt to the horror of phenomenologists and oral archivists, the researcher has to impose order onto discourse. So, as with the excerpts above, the researcher selects out and codes the bits of the young men's testimony that

provide direct reference to education, training, and employment. In doing so
they inevitably omit other reflections on other aspects of a chaotic life.

Such omissions are inevitable, and the first response is always to make clear
how the practical boundaries of data collection are drawn. After that, and in
a well-resourced inquiry, it may be possible to investigate other causal pathways propelling the young persons' lives. In this manner, Neale and Patrick
(2016) go on to investigate the evolving relationships between young fathers
and their co-parents, Neale and Lau Clayton (2014) follow trajectories into
the wider family of the young men, and Tarrant and Neale (2017) look more
closely at influences of public policy on the life chances of young parents.
Beyond this there are studies of other 'crisis events' such as redundancy and
illness (discussed in Part III) that generate understanding of kindred coping
strategies. Reading across such accounts builds up a picture of the intersecting
causal forces. Suites of studies reach into the causal complex without exhaust-
ing it.

KEY LESSONS

Episode 14 examines yet another variation in causal forces, reaching down
into the micro level – as when a single crisis event produces immediate
changes in an individual's way of life. In this case study, qualitative longitudinal research provides a vehicle to follow the varied consequences of
young, unplanned fatherhood. The same causal process is uncovered – identifiable sub-groups interpret the birth in different ways according to social
background. Future opportunities are interpreted and reinterpreted generating different career pathways. The research method provides the wherewithal to follow these trajectories by placing clear boundaries on their reach
and generalisability.

Episode 15. Generative thinking in legislative analysis: Megan's Law

Laws of the legislative rather than of the scientific kind constitute one of the great causal forces in modern society. There is a lot of it about – family law, commercial law, criminal law, penal law, contract law, land law, civil law, and so on. Then there is the regulatory apparatus that goes with it – courts low and high, tribunals, ombudsman services, policing, prisons, probation, and so on. A whole arena of inquiry, namely, 'empirical legal research' has grown up in an attempt to understand the causal power of laws as they apply 'on the ground', rather than 'on the books' (Leeuw and Schmeets, 2016).

Put simply, laws seek to manufacture compliance and/or act as deterrence. That is the intended mechanism. They work, if they work, in long causal chains passing through many hands over prolonged periods of time. The passage of a law through its various stakeholders provides a neat example of the boat model of social change. Governmental bodies set the conditions and the enforcement infrastructure to constrain the actions of the public. The public responds in different ways – some sub-groups comply, others ignore, others actively resist. The effectiveness of the law on the ground rather than on the books is thus generally mixed. Laws and regulations are then debated, tweaked, and reshaped in a continuous effort to make them more effective.

An obvious way to assess the force of law and to understand its revisions is to follow this causal sequence through its many carriers and through time. This was the basic design I employed in a study of Megan's Law (Pawson, 2002), employing a method known as realist synthesis (Pawson, 2006). I will not recount the technical details here, other than to mention that it exemplifies the incremental, confederational system of inquiry noted in Episode 9. As its name suggests, realist synthesis is a form of secondary analysis trading on the findings and the labours of many previous researchers. Unlike meta-analysis no attempt is made to provide a statistical summary of the findings; rather the goal is to extract, develop, and refine causal explanations of the reach of the law.

Seven-year-old Megan Kanka was raped and killed in 1994 by a recently released sex offender who, unbeknown to her parents, lived in their neighbourhood. Public outcry followed and within one month the State of New Jersey passed a law for mandatory public notification of the whereabouts of released sex offenders. All other states followed within the year. A mighty surveillance mechanism was unleashed – with what effect? The underlying logic (or programme theory) was clear and simple – providing an opportunity for intense public surveillance of the offender would prevent reoffence. Putting theory into practice, however, is never simple and the intended implementation pathway was sketched out as the first step in the research process. Box 15.1 presents a simplified version of the one used in the actual research.

BOX 15.1 CAUSAL PROCESSES IN MEGAN'S LAW

- **Problem Identification**. Released sex offenders may live anonymously in a community, denying residents the opportunity to protect their families against reoffence.
- **Proposed Solution**. Create valid and reliable registers of released offenders carrying public and constitutional endorsement.
- **Proposed Implementation**. Issue bulletins to the local community identifying high-risk released offenders and explaining the citizens' rights and duties in response.
- **Community Sanction**. Informed citizens take precautionary measures and together with police and probation officers they provide the surveillance capacity to monitor suspicious behaviour.
- **Offender Response**. Recidivism reduces with the offender recognising reduced opportunities, higher risks of arrest, and being exposed to public shaming and stigmatisation.

All of these hypotheses were reviewed in the research. Existing primary evidence, in copious quantities, was available about the reasoning of actual lawmakers, citizens, law enforcement officials, and former offenders in the face of these proposals. I will only cover a tiny fraction of this material here, omitting information on search procedures, evidence quality appraisal, data extraction, and so forth. Technical details are all covered in the aforementioned manuscript. My mission here is methodological – to discover how causal processes flow through different stakeholders and through time. Laws on the ground look very different from their depiction on paper. I sketch just a few major bumps on the road, simplifying the extracted data and omitting all primary sources. Whilst the example of Megan's Law is, of course, highly specific not to mention highly charged, its uneven and unforeseen discharge has great similarities with the unfolding of many other laws.

The first challenge is the identification of risk of reoffence. Discharged sex offenders have served their time, have committed offences of varying seriousness, with different frequencies and different victims. They are likely to have undergone therapeutic interventions and some are often significantly older and have more physical limitations on release. Both the relatively unchanged and the relatively reformed will be discharged. As with many labels, 'sex offender' masks untold differences. So, who should appear on the registers? There is no exact formula for predicting reoffence at the individual level and the consequence is that from state to state there were considerable and inevitable discrepancies in responsible personnel, in the volume of information, and in the type of profiling used to register risk. At the farcical extreme one state official acknowledged over-aggression – a paraplegic person and a man in a coma had made it onto the register.

The next practicality concerns the method of public disclosure. The community had the right to know but how was knowledge disseminated? Practice varied markedly across different jurisdictions, varying from *passive* (records 'made available' rather than circulated), *restricted* (access only to families deemed vulnerable) to *active* (itself a range including the internet, mailed flyers, door-to-door notification, and neighbourhood meetings). The law's intentions twist further when it comes to community reactions to disclosure, which ranged widely from: (i) overt harassment of the named individual to (ii) some sympathy for time-served prisoners considered unfairly picked upon.

Next consider the preventative power of local community notification. What proportion of offences might the law preclude? An analysis of 136 current sex offences and the respective offenders in the Boston district revealed the following: 100 had no previous criminal record, a further 24 were already know to the victim's family, and six offenders were from out of state. In total, only six cases had any potential to be stopped by local community notification. It was fear of 'stranger predatory' attacks that ushered in Megan's Law, but it is poorly equipped to prevent them.

Finally, consider the ultimate purpose of the law. Information on offender response on being subject to community notification was harder to locate. The few interview studies that had been undertaken again revealed discrepant testimony. I quote just two that show that public disclosure might not always carry the intended effect: (i) 'If you are going to reoffend there is nothing that can stop you … The only person that can stop it is the offender himself'; (ii) 'If these people know you're a sex offender and keep pointing at you … everything breaks under pressure. If you taunt a dog long enough it's going to bite.' Surveillance can subdue or miscarry or provoke.

The purpose of this brief reconstruction is not to demonstrate that Megan's Law failed in its worthy mission. Let us settle for a verdict 'uneven implementation' and 'varying effectiveness'. Despite widespread acknowledgement of its limitations, the law remains on the statute books in all states, with regular practical revisions trying to better identify risk, to improve notification, to reduce the hounding of named individuals, and where possible to balance surveillance with the rehabilitation of former offenders.

The topic here is causation and the episode has important lessons in that respect. The first is about the dissipation of causal forces in society. Megan's Law, for all its uniqueness, follows a routine path trodden by much legislation and law enforcement. During implementation, the potential force of the law flows literally through many agencies and many hands. Its causal powers are fragmented and undermined. Impact is not only of academic interest. There are many different agencies involved and as the limited reach of the law becomes clearer, policy makers and managers go back to the drawing board and tweak implementation. Other stakeholders respond to each adaptation and the cycle continues.

Hopefully, even within this brief reconstruction, it is possible to recognise that social research can chart and explain the intricate nature of social change. The case study reveals a leaky policy pipeline or what might be regarded as a classic open system, yet it is quite possible to understand how it morphs. In this respect several details of the research method employed are important. The first is that it is a secondary synthesis of many different primary sources. Getting a clear purchase on social change within a single study is always difficult. Causal mechanisms fire in iterative, overlapping sequences and the combination of many existing research sources enables a better grasp of the dissipating system. The second feature is that these primary sources utilise a deep toolbox of data and methods – qualitative, quantitative, textual, longitudinal, administrative, etc. All manner of contexts, mechanisms, and outcome patterns can thus be pinpointed and assessed. The third feature is that the research goal is synthesis, realist synthesis, so what is pursued and refined is a theory of social change. There is no summative claim that Megan's Law is perfect, imperfect, or otherwise. The emerging theory unearths its underlying, often invisible workings and that is the basis of causal explanation.

As ever there are limitations and associated stopping rules. Public reaction to community bulletins formed part of the research but not public reaction to the very existence of the law. One suspects that it proved popular and is still proving popular. This could easily be verified in supplementary research, and it may help to explain the longevity of an inefficient law. This line of inquiry might take us to further evidence on the importance of 'moral laws'. Other major pieces of legislation have equivalent weakness in terms of enforcement but remain solidly on the statute books (see Episode 24). Note further that the empirical materials in the study were confined to the United States. Many other nations have dillied and dallied with versions of Megan's Law. Much of this procrastination follows from policy debate about how many of its loopholes and unintended consequences would apply in a different context. What have usually followed are more limited and tightly controlled versions of public disclosure. Further research could review these modified interventions, providing a more comprehensive understanding of the limitations in the social control of this class of offence. In short, there are many more unanswered questions but of the present answers it is no conceit to claim – so far, so good.

KEY LESSONS

Episode 15 completes the case studies of research using generative explanation. Although the substantive topic is highly specific it speaks to the whole domain of law-making, in which causal forces pass rapidly and recursively through many agents and agencies. The causal structure is dissipative, progressively losing focus. In order to capture the moving picture, the chosen method (realist synthesis) is a secondary analysis, combining evidence from a plurality of primary studies, deploying a plurality of research methods. Calling on hundreds of studies to confederate evidence on an emerging repertoire of causal mechanisms represents the fulfilment and the ceiling of realist thinking.

Episode 16. Interlude

Part I has assembled a set of ingredients that together make up a model of generative causal explanation. That model entails a bold claim about the unification of science, namely, that all scientific disciplines employ this generative approach. Needless to say, I have failed miserably to cover all of science in this first part, but as an initial step I have attempted to draw a solid connection between causal analysis in physical science, in clinical science, and in social science. All of them explain by discovering underlying mechanisms that act in particular contexts to generate identifiable outcome patterns. To be sure, social science has some particularities in this respect. We are all able to recognise and navigate a social world that is undoubtedly patterned. We are not surprised, however, when the patterns change. Social science thus needs to tackle causal outcomes that are relatively fleeting and are better understood as demi-regularities. The durability of patterns thus becomes a core issue in causal explanation in social science. It requires a time dimension. Societal patterns form and reform and research needs to explain the transformation from one state to another.

Social science faces another predicament not entirely shared by the sibling sciences – boundless complexity. The transformations that we choose to explain are potentially limitless as are the mechanisms and contexts that could be used to explain any particular adaptation. Accordingly, any individual inquiry must make clear the explanatory configurations that come under investigations. It should contain an explicit map of those processes which are investigated and those which are not. Partial knowledge ensues, which may be expected to modify and will modify with the incorporation of evidence from previous and subsequent investigations. Partial knowledge remains useful knowledge.

If I may make so bold, I would claim that the main contribution in Part I is to forge a clear connection between principles and practice, between the methodological explication of generative causation and the empirical work that bears its stamp. As noted, the research exemplars have been chosen in an attempt to cross the wide substantive concerns of social science and to sample the vast repertoire of techniques used in digging for evidence. I have showcased a mere six. To win my case might require a few (thousand) more. Of course, I'm confident that they exist, though it is important to point out that they do not always come packaged and certified as 'realist'. This applies even to the six studies

I have covered. My contributions are indeed labelled 'realist evaluation' and 'realist synthesis'. Goldthorpe and Boudon have favoured the term 'generative explanation' to signal their epistemological preferences. Lee might well join other comparative historians in preferring the term, 'mechanism-based' to convey his causal claims. Neale has fought to pursue qualitative researchers into the fold under the term 'complex causality'. I am also happy to acknowledge allegiance to a range of siblings and cousins that have developed similar basic notions under somewhat different terminology such as process tracing, relational sociology, rigorous sociology, complex realism, relational realism, and so on.

A similar point can be made about the philosophical origins of the realism described here. It is a family and like all families it has closer and more distant relatives. I commenced with Harré, who always preferred to describe his philosophy of science as 'realist'. But there are many, many others. I might have started with Popper or Campbell, and we will certainly hear more from them in due course. I've always smiled at Campbell's description of his own perspective: 'I am some kind of realist, some kind of critical, hypothetical, corrigible, scientific realist. But I am against direct realism, naïve realism, and epistemological complacency.' I too am some kind of realist. For instance, my version involves being wholeheartedly behind what Campbell means by 'critical' and flatly opposed to Bhaskar's usage of that term (Pawson, 2013, p. xviii). But to repeat, the realist guidelines developed to this point are intended to directly inform the conduct of research and make no claim to perfect the philosophical understanding of causation.

What comes next? Remember, realism is corrigible. The formula for causal explanation developed here is not foolproof, studies making use of generative explanation are always prone to modification and further development. To repeat, the changing patterns that we choose to explain are potentially limitless as are the mechanisms and contexts that could be used to explain any particular transformation. There is always an overabundance of causal pathways that could be put to inspection. But does this mean that one partial explanation is as good as any other partial explanation? Of course it doesn't – otherwise we would be stuck in the never-never land of relativism. This begs the question of how we adjudicate between contending hypotheses. On what basis is it possible to claim objectivity for a particular generative theory? This a formidable question requiring a long answer, which I tackle in Part II.

There is another unanswered puzzle left behind at this point. I have argued for the importance of stopping rules; causal explanations only apply within carefully constructed boundaries. Does this mean that the findings of empirical investigations are not transferable? Are we limited to investigations that apply in one particular pigeonhole and not to a thousand others? Of course not – otherwise we would be stuck in the never-never land of solipsism. On what basis is it possible to generalise, to use and re-use explanations from one study to the next? This is a formidable question requiring a long answer, which I tackle in Part III.

PART II

How to think about objectivity

Introduction to Part II

Part II tackles the ultimate problem in social science methodology – is it indeed a science? Is it capable of generating objective truths by following a systematic methodology based on evidence? Our topic and our challenge here is the status of evidence in all of its forms – observation, statistical data, administrative records, attitude measurement, personal testimony, historical documentation, psychological tests, opinion polls, etc. Can these routine features of social inquiry be considered objective? Do they constitute valid and reliable tests of our theories and hypotheses? Perhaps more than any other issue in social research, opinions differ on these questions. Opposing paradigms have gathered and glowered across a wide methodological chasm.

I can foreshadow the debate by considering some founding contributions. Most famously, Durkheim (1895 [1982]) argued for 'social facts as things'. These are the basic ingredients of empirical sociology, things considered by Durkheim as external to and coercive of the actor. They exist in their own right and are independent of individual manifestations. His usage of social facts covered social institutions such as kinship and marriage; laws and constitutions; cultural norms and customs; political and governmental institutions; economic and financial regulation; religion and belief systems, etc. These social facts give shape to our everyday interactions with other members of our communities and societies. They also provide the possibility of objective measurement. Data can be rooted in these institutional realities, in these external forces. Durkheim's most famous exemplar is, of course, his study of suicide (1897 [1951]). He maintains that this seemingly most intimate and personal of acts is in fact ordered by wider cultural and religious norms. Accordingly, by measuring and comparing the 'suicide rate' in different communities it is possible to go beyond the countless subjective motivations of its victims and to provide objective evidence on these external, shaping forces.

Running in parallel with this stream of thought are numerous declarations that social *science*, political *science*, psychological *science*, and so on are imposters! There are dozens of schools of thought that lie on this side of the methodological fence to which, to begin with, I apply the collective label 'constructivist'. These start from the premise that social research deals with human experience. Accordingly, perception, thought, memory, imagination, emotion, desire, volition, and language are the requisite topics of inquiry. These intensely personal and resolutely subjective acts should be studied for their own sakes rather than being seen as the products of external forces. Thus, Sacks (1963) opines that 'in terms of the history of sociology, nothing is more tragic that Durkheim's *Suicide* should be conceived as a model of inquiry'. The appropriate means of inquiry under this constructivist lens might be characterised by Douglas's (1967) qualitative inquiry into the social meanings of suicide. He seeks explanations for suicide in individual motivation (revenge, escape, sympathy, despair, etc.) and as for 'social facts' or 'suicide rates' these too are deemed to be composed of nothing more than the perceptual understandings, nay the guesses, of the coroners responsible for compiling them.

Prepare yourself, dear reader, for a slugfest. These fisticuffs go back, I don't doubt, to the Greeks. In the modern era, Comte's first pronouncements on sociology as 'social physics' and as the 'queen of sciences' were roundly ridiculed in the early 19th century (Scott and Marshall, 2005). Many readers will remember their introductory research methods courses, often structured around the 'paradigm wars' – 'positivism versus phenomenology', 'quantitative versus qualitative', and so on. Mutual incomprehension is perhaps most famously captured in Snow's famous Reith Lecture (1959) on the 'two cultures', in which he introduces the 'have you read?' test. The arts aficionado teases the scientist with the challenge, 'Have you read a word of Shakespeare?' to which the scientist responds, 'Could you describe the second law of thermodynamics?'

All of these academic disputes on objectivity might be regarded as gentle (and perhaps even gentlemanly) jousts in comparison to their modern incarnation in public discourse. It came without warning. At the turn of the century most policy makers and indeed many politicians were inclined to speak up for evidence. Programme evaluation, policy analysis, implementation science, cost–benefit analysis, forward planning, risk estimation, and engineering design were in their heyday. Some even spoke of 'evidence-based everything' (Fowler, 2003; Oakley, 2002). Then in the blink of time's eye we found ourselves in the thick of a new 'post-truth' epoch. President Bombast and Prime Minister Bluster were elected to populist acclaim. Experts are hounded. Technocrats are berated. Feelings have taken over and a new emotional politics has become normalised. The emerging orthodoxy was captured, with a characteristic hint of satire, in the words of the journalist Marina Hyde (2019), who instructs us: 'Remember: ideas ought not to be considered on their merits but fawned over or spat upon because of who is suggesting them.'

Part II, it transpires, has a fearsome fracas on its hands and I begin with an outline of the argument, which once again is told in 'episodes', each one concluding with a summary of its key lessons. The ten instalments are as follows:

Episode 17: The empiricist myth of direct, sensory observation
Episode 18: The constructivist myth of omnipresent, omnipotent opinion
Episode 19: The empiricist myth of balanced, impartial observation
Episode 20: The constructivist myth of partisan science
Episode 21: Objectivity reclaimed: introducing post-empiricist science
Episode 22: Theory-informed evidence: excavating data in social science
Episode 23: Theory adjudication in social science
Episode 24: Building evidence networks in social science
Episode 25: Organised scepticism or mutual incomprehension?
Episode 26: Postscript: post-empiricism versus post-truth

Here is an initial summary of proceedings. I set off in the relatively quiet waters of academic debate and begin with some fundamentals. What is the nature of objectivity? How is the factual status of evidence established? What is the difference between evidence construction in natural and social science? On these matters the paradigms splinter, and two venerable schools of thought are examined: (i) empiricism, which assumes that the scientific method is rooted in direct, sensory observation providing objective, impartial, and reproducible facts that leave no room for doubt or opposition; (ii) constructivism, which assumes that there is no such thing as direct, unmediated access to the truth, requiring that researchers must always speak subjectively from a particular standpoint.

Both of these perspectives have burrowed their way deeply into mainstream empirical social research. Both have profound implications for the debate on post-truth. The key point, however, is that both are fundamentally flawed. Key objections to empiricism are described in Episodes 17 and 19. Key contradictions in constructivism are detailed in Episodes 18 and 20. These critiques clear the stage for the entry of the realist perspective in pivotal Episode 21. I outline its origins in 'post-empiricist' philosophy of science and introduce a radically different approach to objectivity. The key principle is clear – do not seek objectivity in data. Post-empiricist science assumes that there will always be alternative explanations for any event or phenomenon and understands objectivity as the process of cross-examining the relative strength and plausibility of the rival theories on offer. We can never attain absolute certainty, but we approach truth in a continuous process of theory building, theory testing, and theory adjudication. Episode 21 then searches for applications of this key principle in the workaday practices of physical and clinical inquiry. Objectivity is approached through four key strategies: (i) by excavating data to ensure the independence between theory and evidence, (ii) by seeking out the relative strengths of rival theories, (iii) by building interconnecting networks of theories, and (iv) through a culture of organised scepticism. These four notions are the cornerstones of Part II, not widely understood methinks, but basic to my realist manifesto.

The core test of this framework is mounted in Episodes 22 to 25. Each of the four pillars is examined for its potential application in *social science*. Episode 22 shows how evidence can be excavated to reveal its underlying presuppositions. Episode 23 shows how it is possible to come to a preference for one explanation over another. Episode 24 shows how objectivity gathers across networks of theories. Episode 25 is more circumspect. Is there a collegiate system for careful, mutual inspection of the claims made in each empirical inquiry or has social research fragmented into scores of perspectives with no regard for each other? Social science emerges here, forever fighting a rearguard action against its doubters but also carrying much of the key institutional apparatus for approaching objectivity.

The final episode, 26, makes a return to the monster. I do not suppose for the moment that realist social research, or any other social science perspective, can provide the material antidote to the epidemic of post-truth politics. But can it provide the counterintelligence? It is confirmed, despite the aspirations of so-called 'fact-checking' agencies, that empiricism provides no answer. Constructivism, to its embarrassment, has only encouraged the brute. But what of realism? Is there a place for data excavation, theory adjudication, network explanation, and organised scepticism in public discourse?

Episode 17. The empiricist myth of direct, sensory observation

Empiricism is often dated back to the 17th century 'British School' and particularly the work of Locke, Berkeley, and Hume (Priest, 2007). They, along with many other philosophers of the time, were impressed with the advances that science had made over the previous centuries, and they sought to establish the source of the inherent superiority of science over all other systems of thought. The founding principle, as they saw it, was that valid and reliable knowledge must be based on sensory experience. If all people witness an event in a certain way, then they should agree on what has taken place and 'factual' status is achieved. In 1660 the Royal Society set out to formalise and institutionalise the rules of scientific inquiry and this principle becomes paramount: 'In all reports of experiments brought into the Society the matter of fact shall be barely stated without any preface, apologies and rhetorical flourishes' (Shapiro, 2000).

Over the years, this axiom is enlarged. The reliability of observations becomes crucial. Objectivity is guaranteed only by systematic and repeated observation, with evidence having to withstand rigorous tests for *replicability*. Observation *precision* becomes another requirement. Science's observational language must deliver decimal-point accuracy, contrasting with the vagueness and ambiguity that pervade other thought systems. Empiricism also involves a clear claim about existence. Empiricists are 'strong realists' believing that what we experience as reality is *really* out there in the world. In ontological terms, these real objects and events are entirely independent of the observer's volitions, perceptions, beliefs, linguistic practices, etc. The properties scrutinised by science are thus *intrinsic*, properties that an object or a thing has of itself, independently of other things, including its context. Empirical research, in short, is tasked with providing hard data about 'the world as it is'. In this way, it is able to deliver the unassailable evidence that is able to settle the veracity or falsehood of any idea, hypothesis or theory.

These goals were historically important in separating the concerns of the aforementioned 'two cultures' – the sciences and the humanities. Social science, I should add, has always sat uncomfortably between them. Though relabelled thanks to Comte as 'positivism' (Pickering, 1993–2009), there remains to this day a resilient empiricist faction based on similar principles, namely: (i) sociology should strive to be scientific in that it trades only in 'social facts' external to the observer, (ii) sociological inquiry should strive to be value-neutral and entirely free from moral, religious, and political influence, (iii) sociological methods should be precise, reliable, verifiable, and replicable and should thus adopt forms of quantitative inquiry.

Compelling as the above principles may seem, none of them has stood the test of time. Each and every one of the core assumptions (about the immediacy, objectivity, precision, replicability, intrinsicality, etc.) of data derived from sensory experience has come under severe censure in the philosophical literature. The first casualty is the idea that evidence is born out of direct, sensory observation. Popper (1963 [1989]) puts his finger on an elementary error as follows: 'Observation is always selective ... It needs a chosen object, a definite task, an interest, a point of view, a problem.' Something needs to precede sensory observation otherwise it will fire off in multitudinous, unrelated directions. I can adapt Popper's method of demonstrating this inevitability to a lecture audience by asking you, esteemed reader, to record observations of the room in which you are now sitting. As you soon appreciate, the task never ever ends; for example, you've probably forgotten to list potential observation #7548, namely, the thick dust layering those redundant, recordable CDs (#7549) sitting at the very back of your desk drawer (#7550). Direct observation does not close in on inviolable facts but leads to the realisation that the world is infinitely describable.

If we move to the laboratory, it becomes evident in a much more practical way that science does not rest on direct, sensory observation. Scientists measure using voltmeters, chronometers, thermometers, manometers, accelerometers, magnetometers, spectrometers, and so on. Evidence is gleaned in investigations using instruments, which are themselves based on engineering principles constructed from the findings of previous investigations. If we take perhaps the simplest physical property, namely, length, it can be measured approximately by eye – that is, by sensory observation. But such a methodology has yet to gain much traction in the *Annals of Physics* and instead data on distance are manufactured using: a ruler for accuracy against a standard; a hodometer for irregular lines; triangulation for longer distances; travel times of sonar signals if underwater; the brightness of stars in astronomy; barometric pressure in an aeroplane altimeter; X-ray diffraction for atomic spacing; the GPS function on your phone and dozens more. We come to understand the nature of properties via the explanatory systems in which they are embedded.

If we shift to social science a parallel conclusion holds. Typically, data are constructed using a complex administrative apparatus. If we take a significant concern of public policy like crime rates, measurement depends on an intricate sequence of events and interactions – the offence occurs, it is noticed, it is reported to the police, the police assess and verify the claim, it is then logged and enters central records, where it is classified and counted by type of crime, and the aggregate numbers enter the public domain as 'crime rates', which themselves are often used as performance measures, subject to all forms of political and media scrutiny (Lohr, 2019). There are many pressures on under- and sometimes over-reporting all along this pipeline, provoking familiar claims about the overlooked 'dark figure of crime' (Coleman and Moynihan, 1996). These uncertainties lead to proposals for alternative measurement systems such as crime surveys of the general public. But in the same manner, this rival measurement system involves dozens of tricky methodological decisions on sampling, question design, and respondent sensitivities (Lynn and Elliot, 2000). Whatever method is employed, we are light years away from direct sensory observation of crime.

There is another, quite different, approach to measurement widely used in social research. It is known as attitude scaling, the most familiar version being the Likert scale. A statement is posed, such as 'The People's Political Party has the best policies on crime' to which the respondent chooses between tick-boxes labelled 'strongly agree', 'agree', 'don't know', 'disagree', 'strongly disagree' (sometimes enumerated +2, +1, 0, −1, −2). The answer is then understood as a measure of the individual respondent's attitude and the aggregate score is considered as an indicator of 'public opinion'. But, once again, consider the lengthy interrogative sequence involved. Political party A makes policy proclamations B, and voter C may or may not register these pronouncements and may or may not approve of them. Some Cs are then confronted by researcher D with a questionnaire E, containing the Likert scale F on their reactions to A and B. Public opinion is manufactured in the process of statistical aggregation H. This whole framework of inquiry and the particular numerical values for measuring attitudes are imposed entirely and arbitrarily by the researchers (Cicourel, 1964). Regardless of whether they are interested in the issue, regardless of how they might view the issues, each respondent is left to interpret the scale and complete the task as best they can. Once again, we are light years from direct, sensory observation.

One concludes that the idea of the sensory apprehension of facts is a myth. Empiricism is dead. Facts do not speak for themselves. Data are not simply collected; they are always constructed. Evidence, as we see in these embryonic examples, is always manufactured using a complex apparatus, requiring both material equipment and human manipulation. 'Facts' are therefore slippery, and evidence is always fallible.

Note well, though this should not really require saying, that this is not an argument against the usage of data, against the usage of empirical evidence. Science without data and evidence is impossible. What is rejected is the idea that objectivity depends on the production of hard data that is 'factual', 'given', and 'beyond dispute'. As we shall see in later episodes, evidence survives and indeed gains in credibility because of our cumulative, progressive knowledge of these underlying processes that go into its making.

But before we swap 'empiricism' for 'post-empiricism' a couple of caveats are relevant. The first is to acknowledge that Locke, Hume, et al.'s efforts remain historically significant in their critique of the then prevailing wisdom that truth resided in innate ideas and traditional beliefs. In short, empiricism can be said to have provided great service in resisting creed, superstition, idolatry, blind faith, and doctrinal influence. It was, to coin a phrase, against 'pre-truth'.

Secondly, and more significantly for present purposes, note that this unwavering vision of scrupulous sensory observation still underpins what might be thought of as the lay or popular understanding of science. Scientists are those fastidious, white-coated citizens who spend their time in endless, meticulous observation, peering down microscopes, plotting readings, and devouring computer printouts in order to unearth the given 'facts' that constitute reality. It is thus unfortunate but perhaps unsurprising that the dominant opposition to present-day post-truth politics still remains faithful to the battle-cry of 'fact-checking'.

Hundreds of such fact-checking or reality-checking organisations have emerged in response to partisan claims about what is 'news' and what is 'fake news'. The clarion call is epitomised in piece by a prominent UK journalist, 'Remember that facts are sacred' (Harding, 2017). Clear-sighted observation is seen as the antidote to the bullshit and to the lies. The Reuters editor-in-chief recommends old-fashioned 'boots on the ground' inquiry: 'reporting fairly and honestly', by 'doggedly gathering hard to get information'. Similar sentiments are echoed in the United States, the American Press Institute insisting that 'fact checkers investigate verifiable facts, and their work is free of partisanship, advocacy and rhetoric' (Elizabeth, 2014). These are all admirable sentiments, but I note that they fall into the trap of assuming that it is possible to provide unmediated access to the facts. They are not a world or an epoch away from the 17th century Royal Society proclamations about recording 'the facts of natural history avoiding all kinds of rhetorical flourishes, oratorical garnishes and all sorts of paraphrases and circumlocutions' (Shapiro, 2000). Some myths are hard to shift.

KEY LESSONS

Episode 17 provides an uncompromising lesson. The traditional and the common-sensical view of objectivity understands it as a property of factual data. We arrive at truth by getting to the facts of the matter. The flaw here is

How to think like a realist

the assumption that we can 'get there' unequivocally by direct, immediate, consensual observation. It turns out that all observation is theory-laden; it is always guided by particular assumptions. This inconvenient truth provides the conundrum for the remainder of Part II – how can we test theories with data when all data carry and embody theoretical assumptions?

Episode 18. The constructivist myth of omnipresent, omnipotent opinion

Contemporary post-truth thinking rests on the ancient truism that everyone is entitled to an opinion. Hundreds of utterances, popular and poetical, have gathered to acknowledge the significance of 'viewpoint'. Who doesn't know that 'beauty lies in the eye of the beholder', though less well known might be Benjamin Franklin's couplet: 'Beauty like supreme dominion / Is but supported by opinion.' The same idea travels through politics, as in the conundrum, 'One man's terrorist is another man's freedom fighter', into criminology under Howard Becker's slogan, 'deviant behaviour is behaviour people so label', and into historical writing, as in Hilary Mantel's barb, 'History is a process, not a locked box with a collection of facts inside.'

These aphorisms are uplifted to matters of first principles via a range of philosophies concerned with human interpretation – 'phenomenology', 'hermeneutics', 'symbolic interactionism', 'standpoint theory', 'ethnomethodology', and so on as well as the umbrella term I use here, namely, social 'constructivism'. It is impossible to trace the full family tree in the space available, but a couple of examples may suffice to signal the utter denial of the notion of 'objective facts'. Husserl (1952) was contemptuous of the attempts in psychology and sociology to apply the methods of natural science (as he understood them) to human behaviour. Living subjects, he argued, do not react automatically and in a law-like manner to external stimuli but respond according to their own perception of what these stimuli mean. A similar sentiment denying that there are objectively correct interpretations of real-life situations is promoted in Thomas's famous dictum: 'If men define situations as real, they are real in their consequences' (Thomas and Thomas, 1928). Another of his propositions presages the mentality of self-absorbed, post-truth politicians: 'subjective impressions can be projected on to life and thereby become real to projectors' (Thomas, 1951)

A vital question jumps off the page at this point – how far should we take this philosophical notion that all beliefs are local constructions? The idea of a singular, unimpeachable truth is abandoned. But what is the alternative? Are there partial truths, shared truths, many truths, or no truths? As we shall see, the constructivist perspective begins to fracture on this issue. Constructivism does not confine itself to philosophy but also informs empirical research via strategies, known variously as participant observation, ethnography, qualitative research, field research, etc. As the first label suggests, perhaps surprisingly, the core data collection activity within these methods has affinity to the empiricist notion of direct observation – though in this case of social life rather than the natural world. 'Fieldwork' is the method of choice with the researcher participating in the location under study, observing, interacting, gathering ideas, learning, taking notes, and writing a journal. When such fieldwork observations are analysed and published, what is their status – are they truths or are they opinions?

The answer to this question turns out to be deeply contested. I illustrate the dissent as it occurs over time across what may be summarised as the 'three phases of ethnography'. Traditional ethnography (phase 1), whilst never subscribing directly to objectivity, always made strong claims for rigour, authenticity, and indeed truth-telling. Thus, whether the subject matter was street gangs (Whyte, 1943), or mental hospital wards (Goffman, 1961), or jazz musicians (Becker, 1951), or local communities (Dennis et al., 1956), the overriding aim was to capture the 'shared experience', the 'life world', the 'ways of acting', the 'culture', the 'normative structures' of the people studied. The overriding objective of phase 1 ethnography, and incidentally its claims to methodological superiority over quantitative methods, is made manifest in its ability to 'get closer to' or to 'dig deeper' in order to represent 'faithfully' the true nature of social interaction (Blumer, 1986). The assumption was that 'in-depth participation' into and 'thick description' of the everyday activities and relationships in these situations provided a consensual and, in that sense, a true-to-reality account of the people chosen for study.

This claim is then undermined in phase 2, which I will call 'partisan ethnography'. Becker's writings (1967, 1973) exemplify this tradition. He argued that all social situations, localities, organisations, and interactions are characterised by hierarchies and power differentials. Dig deeper into the social world and it will reveal difference and discord. The venerable objective of getting closer-to-the-people only succeeds in getting closer-to-some-of-the-people. And this leads to his famous dictum – 'there is no position from which sociological research can be done that is not biased one way or another ... the question is not whether we should take sides, since we inevitably will, but whose side we are on' (1967). The researcher has no choice but to adopt a perspective and *then* to dig deeper for evidence to exemplify it. Accordingly, in his empirical work of the period he refuses to accept the validity of such questions as 'Why is it that group X engage in higher rates of criminal offences?' Instead, empirical observations should be politically guided: why do certain behaviours come to be labelled as deviant by those in authority and how are such designations resisted by the 'underdogs' castigated as group X?

All changes yet again within phase 3 ethnography, often termed 'autoethnography', under the proposition that fieldwork accounts are necessarily and inescapably authored. The focus of attention within this variant changes from the political to the personal. It is argued that the individual experiences and values of authors cannot be removed from their fieldwork observations and from the research narratives they concoct. And since different kinds of people have 'a multitude of different ways of speaking, writing, valuing, and believing', this means that researchers cannot help but remember selectively and write one-sidedly about their fieldwork experience (Ellis et al., 2011). Accordingly, in making use of these experiences autoethnographers opt for implicating themselves directly within their reports, writing in the first person, telling of their encounters, expressing their feelings, and so on. Viewpoint is thus celebrated under autoethnography. Ethnographic narratives are no longer valued as truth-telling but cherished because of their textual qualities – emotional appeal, aesthetic qualities, storylines, personal epiphanies, character portrayal, and so on (Ellis, 1999).

Within one empirical strategy and in the passing of a few decades, constructivist inquiry has shifted from neo-empiricism to relativism. It began with what modern-day journalism might praise as 'boots on the ground' reporting. Truth is what passes for truth in a given community and the researcher attempts to grasp that 'particular truth'. It moves to a notion of 'divided truths' with the idea that there will always be differences of opinion, understanding, beliefs, and ideology within a particular social setting and the researcher's task is to favour a predetermined normative truth. It terminates in the idea that the truth is what individuals decide for themselves – and that fieldwork generates no more than a 'version of the truth'.

Little was at issue, and perhaps these differences were not so pronounced when these 'tales from the field' landed thickly and harmlessly on the shelves of the university library. But when observational studies turned from tribal societies to urban tribes and then to political tribes the stakes multiplied. Latter-day claims that truth comes only in 'versions' provide the academic licence, the epistemological alibi, for post-truth politics. If it is inevitable that unhurried field researchers pick and choose data to support predetermined perspectives – then this is exactly what we should expect the scurrying political classes to do (with brass neck and at volume).

I now want to argue against the proposition that social research is forever locked into different versions of truth. It is another monstrous myth. The basic problem is simple to utter – it is a self-defeating claim. If researchers go to the bother of compiling detailed evidence to demonstrate that 'there is no one truth', then they are essentially claiming that 'it is true that there is no one truth'. On what basis can those denying the possibility of value-neutral knowledge still claim validity for their own knowledge claims? Do they not cut off the branch on which they sit (van den Berg and Jeong, 2022)? Research inspired by relativism always involves this self-contradiction and in the last analysis most constructivist analysis will shy away from it. After prolonged and detailed fieldwork on the thinking of a particular group or community, after months of hard slog in making fieldwork notes and turning them into publishable academic prose, few researchers will discard their own efforts as a throwaway commodity, as will-o'-the-wisp opinion. Constructivist researchers write assuming that their prose carries some weight and eventually within that prose it is usually possible to detect a covert, whispered claim amidst the clamour of opinion that 'my version is correct'.

This is a combative accusation and it, too, requires evidence. Here follows a brief case study chosen precisely and deliciously because it is constructivist analysis written in the midst of the post-truth controversy (Uscinski and Butler, 2013). How does constructivism compile evidence about post-truth politics … and does this testimony then constitute the truth? Uscinski and Butler's paper seeks to provide an 'epistemology of fact checking' no less and features a critique of the major US fact-checking agencies. My objective here is not to defend these agencies; I have already hinted at a crude empiricism in some of this work.

Uscinski and Butler begin with a similar assertion: 'Fact checkers share the tacit presupposition that that cannot be a genuine political debate about facts, because facts are unambiguous and not subject to interpretation.' They go on to champion the polar opposite perspective:

> the subject matter of politics is often complex, ambiguous and open to a variety of conflicting interpretations, even when empirical claims are being made. Therefore, people genuinely disagree about the truth. The fact that a politician disagrees with a fact checker about the facts does not make the politician a liar any more than it makes the fact checker a liar.

The main body of the paper seeks to demonstrate the inevitability of viewpoint, the inescapability of opinion in the work of journalists. Uscinski and Butler's empirical work aims to reveal the ubiquity of 'selection effects' in everyday reporting. One of their examples concerns the selective reporting in US press coverage of the *Kay Report*, congressional testimony on whether prior to the Iraq war Saddam Hussein's regime did pose a threat in the form of weapons of mass destruction (WMD). Uscinski and Butler extract four items of media coverage at some length. The first pair show that the two news outlets sympathetic to the war chose to lay stress on Kay's reportage: (i) of Iraq's research and development 'potential'; (ii) of military equipment and activities 'undeclared' to the UN inspectorate; and (iii) of Saddam's abiding 'interest' in nuclear and chemical weapons. By contrast, two examples of anti-war journalism are extracted, which dismiss these pro-war claims as: (i) a 'sandstorm of suggestiveness' and concentrate on Kay's other findings that: (ii) Iraq's WMD programme 'barely existed' and (iii) it 'posed no immediate threat to the international community'. The same 'story' in the hands of different agencies ends, inevitably we are told, with two selective and contrasting 'storylines'.

But what is the status of this evidence? Is it aspiring to the truth or is it itself an opinion? Does it demonstrate the inevitability of selection bias in the work of journalists or is it itself the product of the selection effect? As we are about to see, our authors slide very quietly between these poles. Take, for instance, Uscinski and Butler's long and considered conclusion about the inescapability of selection effects:

> In each story it is not the number of accurately reported facts but their juxtaposition with other facts, to the author's analysis, and to the writers' and readers' prior assumptions that drive the conclusions ... The very possibility of these various interpretations is created by the ambiguity of the objective situation as it is subjectively perceived ... There is a huge universe of facts from which human reporters must select a handful as *the* (representative, significant, telling) facts. This entails that there will usually be plausible arguments for a different selection of them, a different contextualisation of them, a different grouping of them or a different definition of some of them ... Therefore, most journalism may be subject to the problems we have identified in its fact checking branch. So, too, may most political science – and social science.

Here then is the basis of the argument that journalism is politics incarnate, that fact-checking is futility incarnate, *and* that social science is subjectivity incarnate. It is starkly constructivist – *no one* it seems can escape their convictions. But it is an argument that bites its own tail. Constructivism denies the Archimedean vantage point. It *requires* that we pick and choose. Following the logic of the passage above, political discourse is inherently ambiguous, so journalists have no choice but to select and impose their own meaning. It also follows that journalist discourse is inherently ambiguous so that media researchers have no choice but to select and impose their own meanings. By their own admission, there is nothing to prevent Uscinski and Butler hand-picking fragments of text that reflect their hypothesis about journalism's entrapment in incommensurable political truths and failing to register those episodes that do not.

Unsurprisingly, there is a retreat from self-annihilation. Note some subsequent text, which suddenly makes a claim for truth, albeit modest and fallible, in the authors' own empirical labours.

> Wise social scientists ... lay out their analytic and case selection criteria as explicitly as they can; they stipulate definitions of ambiguous terms; they do not claim that the authority of an expert or non-partisan source establishes the truth and, most

import of all, they do not ever declare that the case is closed because the facts are self-evident. (Uscinski and Butler, 2013)

If, as wise social scientists, our authors are aware of a potential approach to non-partisan truth, then where is the problem? The culprits, it transpires, are journalists:

> the openness of the social scientists to new evidence is incompatible with the needs of citizens, politicians and therefore journalists for clear cut binary answers. The journalist who saw the world as ambiguous would never get a story written and the fact-checker who saw it that way would never be able to do his job. (Uscinski and Butler, 2013)

Journalists are thus written off, either as inveterate relativists or as naïve fact-checkers. However, social scientists, wise ones at least, may after all be dispassionate truth seekers. We go in seek of this tribe in subsequent episodes.

KEY LESSONS

Episode 18 leaves us far, far away from nailing down the methodological strategies that will lead us to objectivity. Once again, and from a completely different perspective, the idea of directly ascertained social facts is roundly and quite properly dismissed. But this episode also raises the spectre of relativism. Constructivists celebrate other people's subjectivity but are subdued on the subjectivity of their own labours. Constructivism is a deeply divided tribe that dallies with relativism and then dithers on its consequences. Social science requires an approach to objectivity that denies both the certainty of facts and the inevitability of opinions.

Episode 19. The empiricist myth of balanced, impartial observation

Shapiro's (2000) book traces the origins of British empiricism and notes two vital foundations. Alongside the Royal Society's insistence on sensory observation, already discussed, she maintains that the 'culture of fact' also resides in certain principles of justice and legal doctrine that came into prominence in the 16th century. 'Legal fact-finding' gradually gained the status to challenge spiritual certainty by advocating the principles of impartiality, balance, even-handedness, and fair-mindedness. Justice requires truth and, accordingly, the law should be based on objective criteria, applied without bias and without regard to the power or status of complainants or defendants.

Centuries later the proposition that objectivity resides in impartiality still exerts a powerful force – a careful examination and exposition of all viewpoints is thought to remove the bias inherent in any one of them. This is a precept that has considerable common-sense appeal. It is celebrated in bronze or stone with public statues of Lady Justice (or Justitia) wearing a blindfold and carrying a set of scales as well as the broadsword of truth. It is perhaps *the* guiding principle in public broadcasting, a domain to which I will return presently, given the presumed role of impartiality in combating post-truth propaganda.

Firstly, let us consider the application of the balance principle in social research. There are dozens of practical recommendations across the methodological spectrum about how it might be put into practice. In questionnaire construction, a balanced question is one that presents the respondent with all reasonably plausible sides of an issue (Sue and Ritter, 2007). Balance is the very basis of survey methodology: we assess public opinion by obtaining a representative sample of all opinion. National sampling is nothing but a constant battle to retain representativeness (NatCen, 2012, appendix). Balance is the starting point of much content analysis. Rather than cherry picking excerpts from a text to assess its ideas and convictions, one should scrutinise the whole text (Krippendorff, 2018). Balance is also central to the core logic of meta-analysis. Rather than relying on one study to gain an estimate of the effectiveness of an intervention, we pool results of all such inquiries (Borenstein et al., 2021). The size and number of available data sets have grown rapidly in recent years leading to claims that their combination within 'big data analytics' can yield greater explanatory power (Breur, 2016). The call for balance even turns up in some qualitative research. Rather than rely upon the observations of the single (and possibly biased) researcher, calls have gone out for team-based and multi-site ethnography (Bikker et al., 2017). I curtail the list with the most celebrated proposal for widening and balancing the empirical materials used in social research, which lies of course in the many calls for 'mixed method' approaches (Johnson et al., 2007).

Alas, I have no space to pick the bones out of these massively varied prospectuses. All of these aims have surface plausibility, and it can seem churlish to question the aim of seeking balance in research. But I want to do so, and I do so on the basis of a simple counter claim, namely, that the source of objectivity does not lie in data. Adding ever more of it to a study or mixing in different sources is more likely to result in data agglomeration rather than sound explanation. In and of themselves, mountains of evidence are no more objective than molehills.

The basic problem is that the logic of balanced inquiry only applies to topics in which the unit of analysis is finite, and the research question is one-dimensional. It breaks down when the focus of investigation is complex. For example, the population of the UK is large but most certainly finite at approximately 67 million. If one wants to build a broad picture of, say, voting intentions, then indeed it is best to consult all of them (or at least a good representative sample). But how does the idea of balance apply when the research topic has many different, overlapping, and changing components? Is it possible to produce impartial, comprehensive analyses of complex, evolving, adaptive, self-transformative systems? I maintain that the answer is 'no' – what tends to ensue in the pursuit of balance is massive detail on one aspect of the substantive issue and silence on the rest. I am going to make this case here with an extended example from content analysis, but before we get lost in detail note that it applies to all other research methods which seek balance by extending the observational platform. For instance, claims for the objectivity of statistical meta-analysis are based on the idea that it combines outcome data from a large pool of intervention studies. Examined closely, it becomes apparent that the aggregate intervention effect size is obtained by obscuring all information about process and context in those interventions (Pawson, 2006, chapter 3).

For the sake of continuity, let us return to the topic of media bias, chosen again because it presents a simultaneous examination of impartiality in the mass media and impartiality of social research on the mass media. The classic critique of media study from the perspective of balance is that researchers are often highly and deliberately selective in their empirical inquiries. For instance, as just described, Uscinski and Butler (2013) presented evidence showing that US journalists ransacked the *Kay Report* in two completely different ways that reflected the prevailing two-party political power play on the legality of the war. It is a theory known as 'indexing' (Bennett, 2010) – basically, journalists report the news as proxies to the dominant political parties. The underlying problem, put somewhat differently, is that the researchers are also indexers. Uscinski and Butler can be said to have self-selected the particular themes and the particular sources of evidence to support their selectivity hypotheses.

How might the picture change if one attempts an 'impartial' overview of all sources? Answers are to be found in a further paper that returns to the same issue – 'Whose views made the news? Media coverage of the march to war in Iraq' (Hayes and Guardino, 2010). Lest I am accused of picking upon a straw man here I should point out that it is an exemplary piece of empirical work. It exudes balance, consisting of a systematic content analysis of the entire body of 1434 pre-war US TV broadcasts (i.e., a media source prone to speed and simplification). Comprehensive content analysis uncovers the reportage of not two but 24 different political viewpoints as well as depiction of not two but 30 different 'primary story foci'. I list them in highly abbreviated form as follows:

- *Source categories*: Republican Party, UN official, Conservative group, Ordinary citizen, Pro-war group, Veteran, Not aligned/Independent, Expert, IAEA official, Anti-war group, Bureaucratic source, Liberal group, Celebrity/Prominent citizen, Democratic Party, NATO source, Foreign official/Leader, Foreign citizen, Iraqi source, Religious leader, Military source, Local official, Bush administration, Retired military, Other interest group.
- *Story focus*: Debate over invasion, UN resolution, Weapons inspections, Military action, Protests/Rallies, Government formation, Casualties, Political developments, Reconstruction, Speech by official, Military strategy, Insurgent activity, Cost/Economics, Impact on allies, Violence in Iraq, Iraq election, International support, Legal debate, Iraqi dissidents, Military planning, Domestic politics, War prospects, Impact on soldiers, Impact on Iraqis, Civil liberties, Domestic security, Terrorism/Al-Qaeda, Saddam war, Aftermath, Other.

We have an example, par excellence, of a massively comprehensive research project. It goes out of its way to seek balance, but can it be said to be objective? The authors certainly think so:

> From a normative perspective, one might view pre-war Iraq coverage as a case of the media playing its watchdog role more effectively than the indexing argument suggests. Even in the absence of domestic elite dissent, the broadcast networks sought out sources with divergent views, giving the public access to a broader debate than was occurring inside the Beltway. (Hayes and Guardino, 2010)

I take a rather less charitable view – not remotely with the colossal effort and hard-won data on the disparity of broadcast perspectives, not remotely with the critique of contrived selectivity in work in the indexing tradition, and not remotely with the discovery of a presence of minority views in the media. The problem lies with the notion that a comprehensive overview is an objective overview. Hayes and Guardino's study was published some eight years after the broadcasts under scrutiny (for very good reasons – such a massive exercise takes time to win funding, to execute, and to find publication). The chosen method is content analysis. It involves a comprehensive search for all relevant news items in a two-year period, then line-by-line scrutiny, and then classifying and then aggregating the varied themes and storylines – which are indeed shown to proliferate.

The problem lies with the gap between the impressive mass of data and the conclusion that it is an objective demonstration that the media play an effective watchdog role, providing the public access to a broader range of opinions than in the political bubble. So, what exactly is the problem? Remember the closer one looks, the more issues become apparent (recall Popper's lecture on sensory observation). The world is infinitely describable, and one can never exhaust the potential viewpoints from which to portray it. If one examines hundreds of hours of broadcast material, it follows that it too can be described and redescribed ad nauseum.

If one examines the large number of 'source categories' and 'story focuses' listed above, what is to say that they are correct? The classification system is the authors' and is not inherent in a broadcast or intrinsic to a broadcaster. It might be that a still finer classification could be achieved – rather than saying, for instance, that the 'Republican Party' was one key source, might it not be important to see if different wings of the party are represented? On the other hand, might not some of these categories be usefully collapsed since they might seem to exaggerate the range of responses to the war; for example, are reports on 'domestic security' and 'domestic politics' fundamentally different? Then, of course, there is the ubiquitous 'other' category, which crops up in most content analysis. Who and what falls under this classification and might unpacking this content reveal other important influences? What about double counting – is it the news item itself or utterances within that item that should be tallied? Content analysis always has to wrestle with many such practical problems and one can summarise by saying that different analysts might come up with different solutions – no classification system can claim to be 'objective'.

Problems deepen when one considers the crucial matter of what content analysis does not cover. A major omission in the present case is that matter of the broadcaster sentiment (i.e., Uscinski and Butler's passion). A particular theme may be present in a broadcast but is the portrayal itself negative, positive, inflamed, or impassive? Counting themes does not reveal their intent. Furthermore, in the present case there are media sources other than TV broadcasts, many more potential pundits, many more potential points of view, and many more phases of the conflict, all of which might be added to describe 'whose views made the news'.

Another imponderable, perhaps the classic problem with content analysis, is that it necessarily omits the audience, the huge number of potential responses to material uncovered. A practical problem ensues – absolutely no one reports, encounters, or digests the news in the comprehensive, unhurried, and persevering fashion applied by Hayes and Guardino. The authors are thus poorly placed to make claims about 'public access' because their method does not permit a study of public access. Jo Public processes only a fraction of the broadcast output. She cannot be aware of and indeed rarely seeks awareness of its many viewpoints and sources. Meanwhile, other influences and other influencers proliferate in her world.

Media bias finds its way to the public through myriad channels. Hayes and Guardino's gigantic overview thus remains a partial view. It is a vast 'agglomeration' of data on one aspect of media production that omits several others. Like its predecessor it is selective – but in a different fashion. I should add and indeed insist that there is no way of avoiding the truncation of any research project and to make clear that the above analysis is most definitely not a charge that Hayes and Guardino have omitted to cover this, that, and the other. The critique is not about the authors' formidable labours, but rather a general point about the inability to gain ground on complexity by adding more and more data. However hard it is bashed and filleted, the inspection of more and more data does not provide for objectivity. Rather than peering ever more deeply and broadly, much more needs to be said about the role of theory development and theory competition in seeking objective research. We need a constant reminder of Popper's (1976) dictum that 'it is a mistake to assume that the objectivity of science depends on the objectivity of the scientist'. This alternative way to the light is described in Episodes 21 onwards. Here I stick with the negative conclusion that the notion of impartiality is crushed by complexity.

Before we leave the topic, it's well worth examining the efforts to maintain impartiality in broadcasting circles. This quest has redoubled in importance in the post-truth era and will receive a final comment in Episode 26. I begin by noting that the Royal Charter of the BBC promises 'accurate and impartial news … so that all audiences can engage fully with major local, regional, national, United Kingdom and global issues' (BBC, Royal Charter Archive, 1927–2017). The major global news agencies follow a similar mission (Fenby, 1986):

> To achieve such wide acceptability, the agencies avoid overt partiality. Demonstrably correct information is their stock in trade. They avoid making judgments and steer clear of doubt and ambiguity. Though their founders did not use the word, objectivity is the philosophical basis for their enterprises – or failing that, widely acceptable neutrality.

One appreciates the proud intentions but as we are about to see once more impartiality is not the route to objectivity.

Broadcast news, unlike social research, is made in a day, by the day. And it is at the level of the single bulletin that the balance hypothesis comes really unstuck. It is impossible to include the totality of relevant voices in a couple of minutes. Interviews and participants always have to be 'stage-managed'. Cushion and Lewis's (2017) research on the UK's 2016 EU referendum (Brexit) shows that working solutions come in the form of 'tit-for-tat' reporting. This tactic was used unerringly in news items in which statistical claims came under discussion. Unintentionally but unerringly, there was a tendency for the 'quest for balance' to retreat into and reinforce existing political bunkers. Statistical claims were rarely interrogated but instead were simply batted back and forth.

Harding (2017), a senior BBC editor, explains the situation like this, commenting on the notorious Brexit Battle Bus's claim about the soaring weekly cost of EU membership. Where the £350 million Leave campaign figure was queried, it was often merely referred to as being 'disputed' or 'uncertain' or 'controversial' … It was of course the BBC's job to present both sides of the argument … But it was also part of the BBC's job to scrutinise the claims of both sides. This did happen, but too often coverage lapsed into passive reporting of claim and counterclaim. Expert views were reported but countered by a dissenting voice seemingly inserted for the sake of appearing balanced.

The same preference for impartiality-as-balance reporting is demonstrated in analysis of other news items. Wahl-Jorgenson et al. (2017) cover broadcasting between the years 2007 and 2012 on immigration and religion as well as the EU and reveal a 'focus on party-political infighting rather than the substance or context of these issues … the tendency toward an elite and relatively narrow range of debate only intensified'. A similar picture can be seen in the coverage of climate change. Corry and Jorgensen (2015) bemoan the standard-issue presentation of the clash between 'deniers versus believers'; thus, largely omitting the real debate rests on 'problem-definition' and 'solution-framing'.

Another example of the woes of impartiality occurs in regulating televised 'leadership debates' during election periods. Which parties should be represented, by whom, and on what basis, to be interrogated by whom, under what format? How might these issues be decided impartially? A study by Anstead (2015) of the broadcasting of election debates in the UK, Australia, Canada, and Germany discovered little by way of a common rulebook on eligibility and much disagreement on the way forward. To quote but one oddity, in Canada, in addition to numerical entry rules about a party's share of the vote, another understandable but hopelessly chimerical requirement was that the party leader 'must also be recognized as a national political figure'.

Similar confusions occurred during the 2019 UK general election in which much disgruntlement and several legal challenges followed in the wake of decisions to exclude the Scottish National Party and the Liberal Democratic Party from certain televised debates. The current state of play remains at stalemate. Each party is able to argue for its unique entitlement to a podium position, but the selection rules remain at the discretion of individual broadcasters. If there is a trend the goal, almost literally, is to redouble efforts at balance and inclusivity and this is achieved by increasing the numbers of politicians and by using different interrogators. Both tactics have unintended consequences.

The latter turn, using lay inquisitors, is particularly worthy of comment because it affects the nature of the debate. Increasingly, questions to the panel are put by members of the public selected, yet again, to achieve balance across the political spectrum. But in order that the same query can be put to an increasingly diverse set of respondents, the questions become anodyne, clumsy and, above all, predictable. The consequence is that the politician can respond by rote. Rather than tackle specific content they can rely on a preconceived 'frame' or 'schemata' or 'script' (Chilton, 2004). Advisers and spin doctors gather in the first act of any political campaign and decide on its main set of symbols and slogans. Take your pick – 'La République En Marche!', 'Mut zur Wahrheit', 'Avanti, insieme', 'Make America Great Again', 'Take Back Control', and 'Get Brexit Done'.

Beneath these are another set of metaphors, aphorisms, and maxims that differentiate the righteous objectives of the chosen party from the despicable opposition. The good guys use 'virtue signalling' and so deem their policies 'progressive', 'eco-friendly', 'ambitious', 'world class', which will be unleashed on behalf of 'one nation' or 'hard-working people' or 'for the many not the few' or 'those who cannot help themselves'. Opposition parties are dealt with using bad-guy symbolism and are dismissed as 'self-interested', 'ideologues', 'short-termists' and even 'enemies of the people' who 'cannot be trusted' and whose ignorance will generate financial 'crisis' and 'emergency', which can only be undone by getting 'back to basics' and even a 'draining of the swamp'. Insofar as any data are used to support these generalities, they take the form of endlessly repeated 'killer statistics', selected to show off a particular policy in the most favourable light. In the trade these are known as 'lines to take' to the press, which civil servants pre-prepare by the dozen for their minister (Jary and Bryant-Smith, 2015). In the hurly-burly of news broadcasts these data fragments pass like ships in the night and receive no serious scrutiny.

In summary, it has to be said that the quest for balanced news rarely delivers on well-meaning charter promises on objectivity. In practice, it involves selectivity, simplification, and the fear of stepping on toes. There is a significant semantic clue here – neutrality has the tendency to neutralise evidence.

KEY LESSONS

Episode 19 notes that the quest for impartiality has a proud history. It is not, however, a source of objectivity. In social science impartiality is often associated with seeking a balanced perspective by collecting copious evidence from multiple sources using multiple methods. But faced with investigating complex and constantly adapting systems there is no end to the causal forces that could be inspected. Accordingly, attempts at comprehensiveness always give way to selectivity. In broadcast news timelines are compressed, rendering even more superficial any attempt to achieve balance of viewpoints. The statues of Lady Justice need a rethink. The message to future sculptors is clear. Forget the scales – they become overloaded with information and misinformation. Forget the blindfold – evidence depends on painstaking, well-informed scrutiny. Concentrate on the broadsword – we cut to the truth by dissecting claims and counter claims.

Episode 20. The constructivist myth of partisan science

I shift back to constructivism and identify another branch line that has given succour to post-truth thinking. The notion that professionals, technical experts and, above all, scientists are trustworthy has always been integral to modern democracies. We live in an information age and, traditionally, these citizens are deemed responsible for producing valid and reliable information. Ordinary members of the public cannot be expected to know about rates of economic growth, the melting of the polar icecaps, the dangers posed by epidemics, levels of military threat, and so on – so they come to rely on and believe in scientific expertise. That was then. All this has changed in the post-truth era, one of the main characteristics of which is the complete breakdown of trust in knowledge elites, since it is they who have created the turmoil in which these ordinary members of the public have to struggle ... so the story goes.

Such scepticism about science is actually nothing new and has a considerable academic pedigree. There are several variants of the thesis, some more philosophical going by such tags as the 'Duhem–Quine thesis' (Harding, 1976) and 'epistemological anarchism' (Feyerabend, 1975), some more sociological, namely, the 'strong programme in the sociology of science' (Barnes et al., 1974). Here, I trace out the latter perspective and begin by sewing it to the constructivist research methods identified in Episode 18. The core approach is the same; data collection takes the form of fieldwork observations, boots-on-the ground reporting. The perhaps surprising difference is the subject matter. The substantive focus shifts from the village, the street corner, the hospital ward, and marches to the laboratory for a close-up examination of the working practices of scientists.

The strong programme produced a bevy of empirical studies (Collins, 1985; Knorr-Cetina, 1981; Latour and Woolgar, 1979) attempting to show that, contrary to its public image, the daily routine of scientific activity was not organised around the objectivity of experimentation and the precision of measurement. By getting closer to everyday practice, routine choices on evidence collection and research strategy were shown to be considerably more affected by their social context than had previously been believed. This resulted in an ambitious polemic against technocracy 'by showing how expert advice rested on a sea of social assumptions' (Collins and Evans, 2017).

As noted, the method of choice was ethnography and the studies just cited chart in vivid detail how everyday life in the laboratory was fuelled continually and conspicuously by social issues and interpersonal relationships. Laboratory life revolved around: gaining acclamation, the drive for publication in high-ranking journals, antagonism against other research teams, selective and vested interest in particular lines of inquiry, abrupt floods of attention to the latest breakthroughs, the presentation of findings to maximise impact and to minimise opposition 'noise', the protection of individual status and even local jealousies like the struggle to maintain grade and pay differentials. Laboratory findings are always partial and precarious and are always open to rival interpretations. So, for the strong programmers privileged, 'scientific' findings are always infiltrated by social forces.

All of this, of course, has significant implications for our examination of the role of evidence in the post-truth era. The undermining of experts, the intelligentsia, and the cognoscenti are central to the development of the new politics. The average citizen, of course, doesn't give a hoot for the 'strong programme' but the public's increasingly headstrong proclivities are most certainly exonerated in its core epistemological assumption, namely: 'there is no sense attached to the idea that some standards or beliefs are really rational as distinct from merely locally accepted as such' (Barnes and Bloor, 1982).

Supporters of science have not fallen silent under the strong programme/ constructivist onslaught (Collin, 2011; Sokal and Bricmont, 2004). The first rebuttal comprises a pertinent reminder of the nature of the evidence gleaned in the laboratory visitations. What is the status of these fieldwork observations of the everyday jealousies, power plays, short-cuts, and presentational ploys? Are they to be considered objective accounts or are they partisan opinions? We are talking ethnography here, so we already know the answer – constructivism has made no attempt to disguise the reality that empirical observations are selective and partial. In narrative style the laboratory reportage ranges from thick description (Collins, 2004) to deeply metaphorical (Latour and Woolgar, 1979) but they remain unavoidably selective and partial. The resulting critique is rendered self-contradictory. The inside stories read and are intended to be read as detailed indictments of scientific objectivity. But what really happens is the authors pass off evidence that they know to be selective and partial in attempting to convince the reader that laboratory science is a power game. In the words of one of their fellow-travellers: 'they play the game of Reason in order to undercut the authority of Reason' (Feyerabend, 1975).

Another factor in the strong programme's downfall concerns the scope and timeframe of its empirical work. The raw material is based on workplace ethnography, typically studying the daily encounters in one lab over the short period funded for fieldwork. And indeed, as in most workplaces, one doesn't have to look too far to find authority figures, jealousies, single-mindedness, careerism, and so on. But is that the end of the story? What is omitted is the big picture, the long durée. When findings emerge from fractious labour in the laboratory, they have to face absorption, replication, refereeing, and critical scrutiny from an entire community of fellow scientists. They also have to confront the history of inquiry. All laboratory investigation is preceded, prompted, and enabled by decades of previous inquiries. Thus, what is missing in the ethnographer's snapshot is science's basic dynamic which lays down some secure advances but also leaves behind other puzzles to be solved by the next laboratory cohort, and so on. Scientific objectivity and progress depend on a slowly unfolding process called organised scepticism and I beg the reader's patience in waiting for this denouement in the next episode. The laboratory studies showed that *scientists* were variously fickle, fearsome, and frail but as a method of understanding of *science*, they are akin to trying to understand the economy on the basis of a short sabbatical in Pawson's Porkpie Factory.

Finally, we come to the strong programme's response to the argument that it unwittingly fostered a climate of post-truth. The laboratory studies described how scientists cherry-pick and present data to support preferred theories. They uncovered open rivalries and the blocking of dissenting views. They argued that knowledge is local and socially constructed rather than rational and universal. And in so doing, the strong programme opened the door to pseudo-science. If there are no scientific facts, if there is no one scientific method, if social influences permeate, if anything goes, then who is to deny the deniers. If evidence is always selective and power-primed, then on what basis can we decry the assertions of climate-change sceptics, anti-vaxxers, tobacco-lobbyists, flat-earthers, creationists, snake-oil salesmen, and so on?

With friends like these, who needs enemies? And having spent decades resisting the uncritical acceptance of scientific authority, the strong programme, in its latest incarnations, has found the need to respect it. Having pulled the rug, it finds a need for the red carpet. Collins, formerly a strongman of the strong programme, now wants to defend science as a 'moral choice' and goes on to co-author a book named *Why Democracies Need Science* (Collins and Evans, 2017). Fuller (2018) reckons that the post-truth condition is a sign of greater 'epistemic democracy', which will eventually encourage 'ProtScience' and widen access to 'instruments of knowledge'. Latour (2004) admits that 'dangerous extremists are using the very same argument of social construction to destroy hard won evidence that could save our lives … why does it burn on my tongue to say that global warming is a fact whether you like it or not'. And Feyerabend who once taught that 'science is essentially an anarchic enterprise' (Feyerabend, 1975) ends up musing, 'I often wished I had never written that fucking book' (Feyerabend, 1994). Strong programme constructivists embraced relativism with gusto – until it was stolen by the real fanatics.

KEY LESSONS

Episode 20 takes us to the end of the line of constructivism, in the absurdly self-defeating, strong programme critique of scientific practice. If power play and intrigue are said to be the daily currency of the physical sciences, then the same must apply to the sociological study of science. The one positive lesson of the programme is to recognise that the scientific method and its most cherished goal, namely, objectivity, rests on a social process. That social process is not, however, the daily dose of rivalry and jealousy that pervades life in the lab. The cultural backbone of science is provided by the long-term, never-ending, study-by-study process of mutual inspection and cross-examination.

Episode 21. Objectivity reclaimed: introducing post-empiricist science

Here endeth the bad news. Empiricism fails as a defence of objectivity. Constructivism is mired in self-contradiction. The problem with both camps is that all of their essential claims are expressed in terms of 'data'. Data derived from sensory observation or balanced observation end with a proliferation of information rather than narrowing on the truth. The data used to proclaim bias and selectivity are themselves partial and selective. There is nothing as vacuous as data. Without a purpose, data are meaningless. Without a purpose, data just squat in ever-growing lumps. If, however, we start with the notion of 'evidence', then a different tale is to be told. Evidence is purposive, it is always for (or against) something. Its overriding purpose, I will argue, is to test and refine theories. This goal, simple as it is to utter, is in practice difficult, fallible, and never-ending. But, as we are about to see, it is the bearer of some good news.

The purpose of the remaining episodes is to refute epistemic relativism and post-truth agnosticism by reinvigorating the aim of striving for objective truth. In natural science, of course, this is a goal that hardly needs revivification; the pursuit of objectivity remains the unchallenged first principle. The precise manner in which evidence is marshalled will, of course, vary from discipline to discipline, subject matter to subject matter. But there are some fundamental and shared strategies, which are well understood. This consensual understanding of the scientific method, and by this I refer to a hundred-year literature, has come to be known as 'post-empiricism'. Realist inquiry stretches across the physical and social sciences and realism can be said to have inherited many post-empiricist principles. This episode explores and explains these core tenets as they apply in physical and clinical science. These lessons are then applied to social science in the remaining instalments.

Note that I use the blanket term 'post-empiricism', whilst acknowledging an array of contributory ideas from the philosophy of science with labels such as 'conjectures and refutations' (Popper, 1963 [1989]), 'evolutionary epistemology' (Campbell, 1974; Popper, 1972), 'competitive cross-validation' (Campbell, 1988), 'fallibilism' (Peirce, 1955), 'scientific research programmes' (Lakatos, 1970), and indeed 'realism' (Harré, 1986). There are also many contributions from social science methodology such as 'organized scepticism' (Merton, 1968b), 'ordinary rationality' (Boudon, 2013), and 'theory adjudication' (Pawson, 2013). A gigantic literature has accumulated, and I insert a humble plea that this episode only seeks to introduce four, kernel ideas about how evidence is understood.

Post-empiricism proclaims 'theory-building' as the core scientific method and the ultimate source of objectivity. Evidence enters the picture as the means of testing, refining, and adjudicating between theories. Throughout, I use the shorthand 'competitive cross-validation' to refer to the overall mode of evidence construction. Within this umbrella term there are four different ingredients that make up post-empiricist inquiry, expressed in shorthand as follows: (i) 'data excavation', (ii) 'theory adjudication', (iii) 'building evidence networks', and (iv) 'organised scepticism'. Brief illustrations follow on how these elements are built into natural science inquiry.

TESTING THEORIES WITH THEORIES: EXCAVATING THE ASSUMPTIONS BUILT INTO DATA

The first post-empiricist revision of empiricism is the correction to the idea that evidence is borne out of direct observation. I have already quoted Popper on the requirement that sensory observation is infinite and thus needs something to guide it. So, what is that 'something'? Back to Popper – 'the belief that we can start with pure observation, without anything in the nature of theory is absurd' (1963). Post-empiricism thus asserts the crucial role of *theory* in creating explanations. Evidence does not lay around waiting to be discovered but is created in a remarkably active and imaginative process: 'Bold ideas, unjustified anticipations, and speculative thought, are our only means for interpreting nature: our only organon, our only instrument, for grasping her' (Popper, 1992). In short, making observations of puzzling events, happenings, relationships in the world is carried out in the service of testing guesses and conjectures on why these regularities arise.

How is asserting the primacy of theory in post-empiricism different from upholding the inevitability of viewpoint in the constructivist paradigm? If we use theory to guide observations how can these self-same observations become construed as a test of that theory? This would seem akin to making the case that we test theories with theories. This conundrum is widely recognised, so much so that it bears a couple of names – the 'theory-ladeness of observation' (Hanson, 1958) and the 'circularity objection' (Hesse, 1974). Scientists lose little sleep on the issue, however, solutions being self-evident and omnipresent in the everyday conduct of research.

They do indeed test theories with theories. The fact that evidence is 'theory-informed' is seen as benefit rather than blight. Consider a simple example. Your family doctor suspects you have a fever (based on theory 1 –

your immune system has increased your body temperature to fight infection) and once upon a time she checked that theory using a glass thermometer (based on theory 2, the linear expansion of mercury under increased temperature) or nowadays using a digital thermometer (based on theory 3, a thermopile to detect change in infrared energy under increased temperature). The theories at work are essentially independent. The theory that in response to an infection, illness, or some other cause, the hypothalamus may reset the body to a higher temperature is unrelated to the theory of how thermal energy converts to electrical energy. This initial parcel of theories, moreover, provides the platform for further inquiry as when our medic begins to sort through many potential hypotheses on which illness or infection has produced your fever.

All physical properties are connected to dozens of other physical properties and knowledge of these relationships provides dozens of separate ways of measuring them. The reader will recall this point being made in another cause, namely, dismissing the empiricist idea that facts are gleaned by direct sensory observation. The many different and decidedly indirect ways of measuring length were noted. To stress the same point, any primer in thermometry will embark on a substantial list of measurement instruments: liquid thermometers, gas thermometers, infrared thermometers, thermocouples, thermistors, pyrometers, resistant temperature detector, Longmire probes, and so on. Each instrument is based on a theory. Indeed, the respective theories are deliberately engineered into the construction of the device (Pawson, 1989, chapter 4). Circularity is avoided when science tests impending and tentative hypotheses using a measurement apparatus embodying mature and much scrutinised theories. The humble apparatus of laboratory measurement (voltmeters, chronometers, thermometers, manometers, accelerometers, magnetometers, spectrometers, etc.) acquires authority because it is the bearer of evidence from a previous history of inquiry.

To think ahead for a moment, it would be fanciful to suppose that measurement in social and political science could ever employ instrumentation (imagine the 'understanderscope' or the 'feelingmometer'!). But that, of course, is not the lesson we seek to extract here. Lakatos (1970) supplies the key message as follows: '[Empirical testing] is not "between theories and facts" but between two high level theories: between an interpretative theory to provide the facts and an explanatory theory to explain them; and the interpretative theory may be on quite as high a level as the explanatory theory.' There's the lesson – evidence has its own level of complexity and is constructed on the basis of many assumptions founded in previous inquires. In social research, measurement systems (or interpretative theories – to use the Lakatosianism) are indeed high level. They involve all kinds of complexities. They are buried in administrative procedures. They involve subtle interchanges between researchers and subjects. Accordingly, what needs to be checked in testing the adequacy of such evidence is whether the data so generated are compromised by or independent of the explanatory theory under test. We need to excavate the data to clarify its presuppositions. Examples await in the next episode.

ADJUDICATING BETWEEN RIVAL THEORIES

There is another routine way that natural science avoids the circularity problem that also may be adapted for social explanation. The core idea is explained by Harré in his history of *Great Scientific Experiments* (2002). The popular understanding of experimental inquiry is that the researcher begins with a pro-visional theory and then builds a particular experimental apparatus that will affirm or falsify that particular hypothesis. But this view is a simplification, Harré explains, because the theories in any branch of science (optics, mechanics, thermodynamics, electromagnetism, organic and inorganic chemistry, botany, zoology, microbiology, and so on) are internally complex and interre-lated. A good theory will have many empirical consequences and any empir-ical relationship will be explicable by more than one theory. Accordingly, Harré overturns the standard model, explaining: 'In real science hypotheses are usually conducted in pairs, the one conceived as a rival to the other.' The experimentalist's task is thus to construct some empirical evidence that rival theories will accept as legitimate but will then have the power to adjudicate in favour of one of the contending explanations. Theories A and B provide rival explanations of some real-world phenomenon. The circularity problem is confronted and avoided if proponents of the rival hypotheses agree on an observation that would adjudicate between the contending conjectures.

Amongst Harré's examples is Gilbert's pioneering 1581 experiment on the nature of the Earth's magnetic forces. At that point in history, naturally occurring magnets in the form of lodestones had long been discovered. Simple magnets made of iron, magnesium, and cobalt could be constructed and the attraction and repulsion of their north and south poles was routinely observed. The basic nature of magnetic force, however, was not understood. Then came the compelling but unexplained observation that a magnetised compass needle would always point to the geographic north. Enter theory. Was there a 'point attractant' at some northerly point in the Earth or in the heavens, which liter-ally pulled the compass needle in that direction (theory A)? Or was the Earth itself a 'field' in which magnetic attraction is carried along 'lines of force' (theory B)? To adjudicate between the theories, Gilbert devised the famous 'wineglass' experiment (Figure 21.1). Instead of using the standard fixed compass pivot, which would automatically scupper theory A, he floated a mag-netised needle in a cork. The cork tilts northwards but is otherwise stationary. There is no pulling or drawing of the whole needle as would be anticipated by theory A. Theory B wins the day. (Nowadays theory B is confirmed in the schoolroom experiment in which a few iron filings are shaken onto a sheet of paper under which sits a magnet. The filings obediently arrange themselves along the now-visible lines of force).

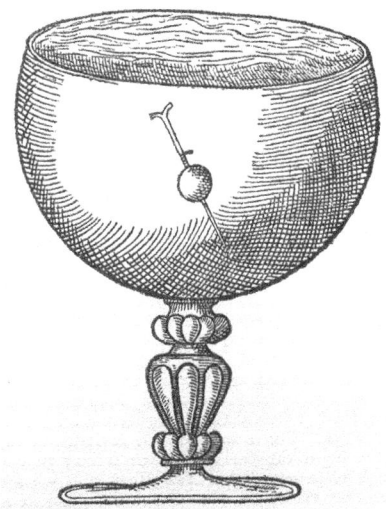

Source: https://www.gutenberg.org/files/33810/33810-h/images/illo194.jpg.

Figure 21.1   Gilbert's wineglass experiment (circa 1581)

Once again and obviously, there can be no exact replication of this strategy in social research. We cannot wish for such experimental manipulations to sort and sift contending theories. But one basic ingredient is most certainly there in social and political discourse – rival theories exist in superabundance. And this can lead us to a broader strategic lesson of Harré's model. It is the process of building upon commonly held assumptions of rival theories and not by any withdrawal to neutral or objective observations that provides for crucial empirical tests. Illustrations will be pursued in Episode 23.

BUILDING EVIDENCE NETWORKS

Particular scientific theories may be tested in ones or twos (as above) but science as a whole grows as a network of theories and sub-theories. Lakatos (1970) refers to these as research programmes – any theory will carry within it many different suppositions; any test of that theory will involve many different assumptions. Accordingly, progress in science is the business of articulating and drawing in evidence on the many, many suppositions that underpin explanations about how the world functions (Musgrave and Pigden, 2021). Objectivity arrives when whole sequences of theories are tested by consolidated blocks of evidence.

There are any number of such research programmes as one ventures across the sciences – thermodynamics, general relativity, quantum theory, cell theory, natural selection, and so on. Each has this concatenated structure of theories within theories. For an example that might be rather more approachable I return to the clinical research process we examined previously known as the 'drug development pipeline' (Figure 5.1). The interdependence of theories and the cumulation of evidence built into an inquiry is clear to behold. I refer the reader back to Episode 5 for a fuller account, but it is perhaps worth offering a handy summary (Box 21.1).

BOX 21.1   EVIDENCE ACCUMULATION IN DRUG DEVELOPMENT

1. *Therapeutic discovery.* The requisite biological process underlying a therapy has been identified. Researchers then provide evidence on specific chemical compounds to deliver that process in an effective fashion.
2. *Preclinical development.* Drug compounds need to be transported into the anatomy with great precision. Evidence is gleaned on whether the drug is effectively absorbed, properly distributed, and remains at its site of action long enough to produce an effect.
3. *Animal testing.* Drugs need to be tested for safety as well as efficacy. The primary purpose of animal testing is to contribute evidence on the former. Is the drug, in prolonged doses, carcinogenic, mutagenic, or teratogenic?
4. *Dose finding.* Safety studies continue in the next phase, which uses healthy human volunteers. The purpose is to find a drug dosage that maximises the requisite biologic activity but minimises the toxic risk.
5. *Feasibility studies.* These are methodological 'dress rehearsals'. They provide evidence that large-scale clinical trials are feasible. They check out some practical assumptions on which that inquiry will be based. Will patients be willing to be randomised, will they follow protocols, etc.?
6. *Randomised controlled trial.* The candidate drug is tested in large patient populations with the specific disease. Patient volunteers are divided randomly into two identical groups. The experimental group

receives the treatment as developed to this point. The controls receive an inert placebo. The difference in clinical outcomes between the groups provides summative evidence on drug efficacy.

7. *Regulatory approval.* Pharmaceutical drugs may not be supplied and sold without formal governmental approval. Experts in a particular field are drawn together to consider evidence provided by the drug companies and their researchers on all aspects of safety and efficacy as above.

We have followed this journey previously in studying causality. Recall that causation is established in the entire sequence of inquiry rather than, as is sometimes supposed, in the formal RCT. Exactly the same applies in thinking about objectivity. Confidence in the objectivity of the claim that 'drug X is effective in treating condition Y' rests on a sea of evidence gathered over a dozen years or so, in vitro, in animals, in healthy volunteers, and in real patients, using a huge medley of research methods. We know moreover that 'approved' drugs only ever work for a portion of treated patients. Evidence on heterogeneous effects gathers, which feeds into potential improvements in any of these contributory theories, which are then put to empirical test.

What does this all portend for objectivity? Empirical inquiry turns out to be agile and never-ending – interweaving evidence, ruling in and ruling out particular claims, adding supplementary evidence where it can to specific hypotheses, crafting novel designs to test out the implications of previously hidden assumptions. All of this whilst being aware that its conclusions are provisional and will be improved upon. We are now a healthy distance away from the sensory observations of empiricism (not to mention a country mile from the conceptual kaleidoscope of constructivism). This shift from decisive, inviolable, hard data to partial, accumulative, interwoven evidence is articulated vividly in this famous 'swamp' metaphor from Popper (1992).

> The empirical basis of objective science has thus nothing 'absolute' about it. Science does not rest upon solid bedrock. The bold structure of its theories rises, as it were, above a swamp. It is like a building erected on piles. The piles are driven down from above into the swamp, but not down to any natural or 'given' base; and if we stop driving the piles deeper, it is not because we have reached firm ground. We simply stop when we are satisfied that the piles are firm enough to carry the structure, at least for the time being.

This is not the orthodox, common-sense view of objectivity. Objectivity in science rests on a judgement, a provisional verdict that we have a body of evidence from a variety of sources, using a variety of methods, testing a portfolio of the theories, that encourages the conviction that we are approaching certainty. Social and political discourse, of course, is a swamp of swamps. We investigated the feasibility of pile-driving in this mire in Episode 24.

ORGANISED SCEPTICISM

The above 'ingredients' of post-empiricism are best regarded as 'modes of inquiry' or 'research strategies' or even 'research designs'. They are practical ways of conducting and organising inquiry. Our fourth component of objectivity is of a different order and is variously referred to as 'organised scepticism' or as 'organised distrust' or, once again, as 'competitive cross-validation'. These latter concepts refer to the scientific culture or social system required to sustain the requisite practical modes of inquiry.

Science is much more than a collection of single inquiries that follow set procedural rules. Any individual inquiry is led by an explanatory theory and tested using evidence derived from interpretative theory (as Lakatos has decreed). But the process never ends there. As we have seen, an individual inquiry may end in confirmation or adjudication in favour of the theory, but it may equally turn to failure, mistaken conjecture and most certainly to the production of further unanswered questions. The question here is – who should make these judgements? Who decides on progress, failure, and the way ahead? The crucial premise of 'organised scepticism' is that this verdict is not the responsibility of the individual experimenter but of the wider scientific community.

Campbell puts it like this:

> The objectivity of physical science does not come from turning over the running of experiments to people who could not care less about the outcome, nor from having a separate staff to read the meters. It comes from a social process that can be called competitive cross-validation and from the fact that there are many independent decision makers capable of rerunning an experiment, at least in a theoretically essential form. The resulting dependability of reports (such as it is, and I judge it usually to be high in the physical sciences) comes from a social process rather than from the dependability of any single experimenter. Somehow in the social system of science a systematic norm of distrust, combined with ambitiousness, leads people to monitor each other for improved validity. Organized distrust produces trustworthy reports. (Campbell, 1988)

This upping of the defence of objectivity to the collective level changes its dynamic. The expectation remains that any individual inquiry is led by the researcher's hunches, best guesses, and tentative hypotheses. The expectation remains that the investigator will test these provisional theories with evidence elicited on the basis of the best practices described above. The difference comes at the next stage, which supposes that the investigator's emerging explanations should always be regarded as provisional and tentative. No investigation is inviolable. We cannot be certain because errors can be made, further alternative explanations may be left unexplored, and fresh, unanswered questions will have been created. The whole process is thus managed by external scrutiny, by peer review, by trial and error, and by attempted replication. And then, before the dust has settled, there is a subsequent testing of rival explanations as proposed by independent teams. Post-empiricist inquiry, in short, is deemed to be led by guesswork but then controlled by criticism.

We can illustrate this collective, corrective impulse using two of our previous case studies. A basic function of organised scepticism is to scrutinise research for oversights or unanswered questions. Pray the reader return to 1581 for another look at Figure 21.1. The magnetised needle in the cork is stationary and not attracted to the pole or some heavenly body as once predicted. Magnetism must be carried in some other way – along some yet-to-be-explained lines of force. But witness also the dip angle or the 'magnetic inclination' of the needle. This phenomenon was well known to compass builders who rectified the problem by counter-balancing the pivoted needles so that they were able to move freely in the correct plane. Gilbert was, of course, thoroughly acquainted with the dip but for many years was unable to explain it or calculate it. The 1581 wineglass experiment answers one question but leaves behind another. And it was left to 1600 when Gilbert explained the variation in the dip by modelling the 'orbis virtuous' of the Earth's entire magnetic field (the full story unfolds in Harré, 2002).

Another function of organised scepticism, and this is one of Popper's (1963 [1989]) favourite motifs, is that critical scrutiny permits science to 'learn from its mistakes'. To illustrate, allow me to retrace a particularly tragic mistake that occurred in one journey through the drug development pipeline (Figure 5.1). Thalidomide was developed in the 1950s on the basis of stage 1 and 2 investigations that hypothesised that its mechanism of action was psycho-active (sedative) and antiemetic (anti-nausea). Studies proceeded along the pipeline demonstrating significant effectiveness in these two respects. After widespread application to prevent morning sickness in pregnant women came the unfolding disaster of 10,000 cases of foetuses with limb malformation, of whom only 50 per cent survived. This drove investigation back to stage 1 and 2 and closer examination of the basic biology of the treatment. More adequate investigation of its mechanism of action led to the discovery that thalidomide was in fact a potent inhibitor of new blood vessel growth (angiogenesis) and thus potentially lethal to the unborn (Somers, 1963). It is now known that 'sustained angiogenesis' is also one of the 'hallmarks of cancer'. Paradoxically, thalidomide's ability to suppress the supply of nutrients to growing tumours has since led to its development as a form of cancer treatment (D'Amato et al., 1994).

Organised scepticism is thus seen as a constructive impulse rather than a destructive force. It is acknowledged that there will always be alternative explanations for any set of observations and science is a process of working through and sifting out the more from the least successful. Even theory failure is instructive – surfacing our mistakes provides a better understanding of the nuances of the problems which we try to solve. But to do any of this requires a positive willingness to face mutual, critical scrutiny. On first hearing, that does not sound too much like a common cry of paradigm-ridden sociology. It is hardly a credo of politicians and policy makers. We will seek more positive signs in Episodes 25 and 26.

KEY LESSONS

Episode 21 is not so much a lesson, more of an agenda. Close inspection of how inquiry is organised in physical science and clinical science reveals a different agenda for truth-seeking, which rejects the empiricist quest for immutable facts and impeccable balance. Objectivity in post-empiricist science is founded on a research framework that utilises: (i) 'excavating evidence', (ii) 'theory adjudication', (iii) 'weaving evidence networks', and (iv) 'organised scepticism'. Realist social science shares the quest for objectivity. Can it utilise the same foundations?

Episode 22. Theory-informed evidence: excavating data in social science

This episode wrestles with the problem of the independence of evidence in social science research. Remember that the point has been conceded that there is no such thing as an independent observation language. All observations carry assumptions. All data are theory-laden. The upshot, the corresponding conundrum, is the aforementioned circularity objection. If evidence is underpinned by theory – does this not imply that science tests theories with theories?

Well, yes, indeed it does but rescue is at hand via Lakatos's (1970) notion that evidence is delivered in the form of 'interpretative theory'. Laboratory instruments do not provide direct observation but are themselves the carriers of theories, which may be every bit as elaborate as the explanation under test. In the natural sciences there is a clear separation of the two theory modes: the explanatory theories are tentative, provisional, and fallible whilst the interpretative theories are independent, settled, and embodied in the construction of measurement apparatus. The reader will recall examples above of how the humble apparatus of laboratory measurement acquires authority because it is the bearer of autonomous evidence from a previous history of inquiry.

The measures used to assess social theories, political claims, and policy predictions can never, of course, involve physical instrumentation. The point holds, however, that these measures and the evidence they provide are in no sense direct but are based in some pre-existing assumptions. An important task for the evidence-checker is to scrutinise, to dig deeply into these interpretative theories, for they provide important clues on the durability and utility of the evidence so generated. The strategy might be usefully termed 'data excavation'. The idea, at its most basic, is to examine the rationale, the conventions, the assumptions that underpin data construction and then to consider whether the ensuing evidence consists of a reasonable test of the substantive theory under test. We excavate the data to ensure that the interpretive theory is independent of the explanatory theory.

I now turn to working examples of data excavation – one detailed, two brief. For an in-depth example I call on a classic controversy on the measurement of waiting times for hospital care. The management of waiting lists is one of the most pressing issues in healthcare given the need to secure evidence both on patient satisfaction and on hospital performance. Reducing waiting times has the potential to fulfil endless policies and promises on the importance of early intervention and on the efficient management of services. There is a pressing need for objective evidence but the whole exercise is politically charged and institutionally challenging given the unstoppable rise in demand for services.

Taken at face value, gauging waiting times for elective care would seem to be a relatively simple task for enumeration – a measure of the time elapsed between the clock starting (referral for treatment) and the clock stopping (commencement of treatment). Assembling (and thus excavating) the actual data turns out to be massively complex. The basic calculation requires a host of subsidiary rules on: (i) the type of referral and its clarity and accuracy; (ii) who is eligible to make the referral; (iii) whether intermediary agencies and stages are involved; (iv) how to accommodate failures to attend; (v) how often and on what basis the clock can be paused; (vi) whether the patient actually wants a particular treatment and is fit enough for treatment; (vii) whether initial treatment constitutes the definitive treatment; and so on. This maze of decisions is made tangible in Figure 22.1 taken from a National Audit Office (NAO, 2014) investigation of how different hospital trusts record waiting times. Note that this diagram is itself a simplification of the Department of Health (2012) 'Rules Suite', a highly complex, 32-page exposition, featuring explanatory 'case studies', of the National Clock Rules.

The NAO investigation included a detailed review of 650 orthopaedic patient waiting times across seven trusts, reported as follows: (i) in 281 cases, waiting times had been correctly recorded and were supported by documented evidence; (ii) in 202 cases, waiting times were not supported by enough evidence to say whether they had been correctly recorded; and (iii) in 167 cases, there was evidence of at least one error, leading to under- and over-recording of waiting time. Alarming stuff, perhaps most of all the second finding; the audit trails of many trusts were simply incomplete leaving no evidence of whether the Clock Rules had been followed.

What are the implications? The NAO's conclusion is a typical masterpiece of bureaucratic understatement. Waiting time data

> is not as reliable as it should be and masks a great deal of variability in actual waiting times … Value for money is being undermined by the problems with the completeness, consistency and accuracy of patient waiting time data; and by differences in the way that patient referrals to hospitals are managed. (2014)

Such handwringing is doubtless appropriate but what should we actually make of this wayward data? Is it perfectible? Is it somewhat flawed or simply useless? Might it be used for some purposes and not others?

These are difficult questions but the first thing to establish is that the NAO inquiry is decidedly *not* a form of fact-checking in that it reveals the 'true'

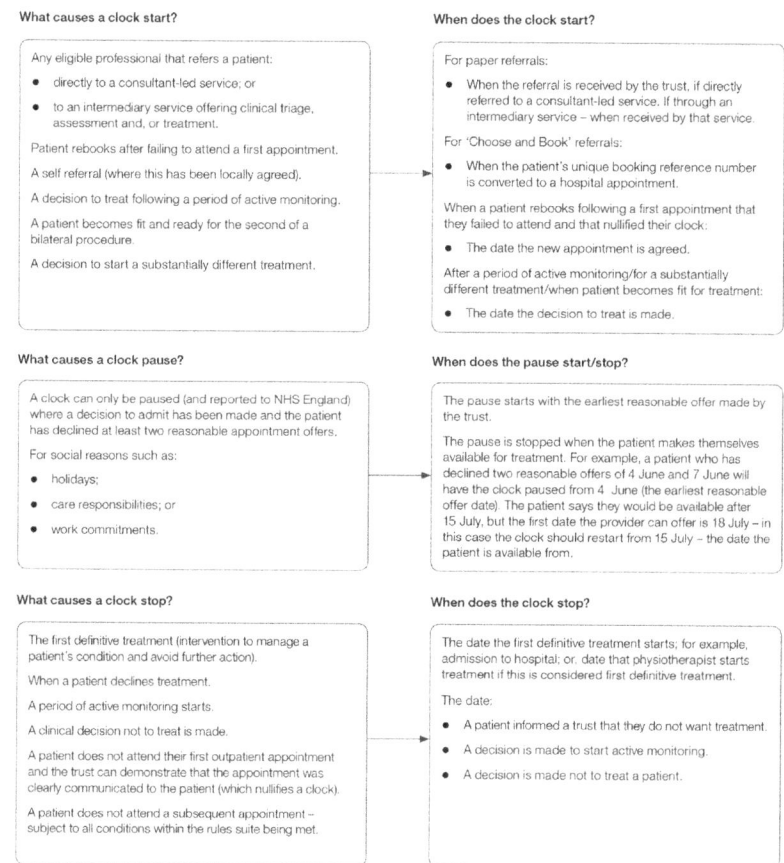

Figure 22.1   Measuring treatment waiting times

figure for waiting times as opposed to the 'inaccurate' times as reported locally. To take but one example, there is no 'correct' way to stipulate or administer or perfect a rule on the legitimacy of a patient-initiated pause (e.g., 'a previous work commitment') and whether it constitutes a proper reason for halting the referral clock. This particular rule will have different ramifications for different patients with different medical conditions being referred to different consultants in different centres. Practical experience tells us that it will be applied flexibly, sometimes leniently, sometimes stringently and sometimes fraudulently, according to the urgency of treatment need and the capacity of the unit to provide and reorganise treatment (Curtis et al., 2009). This same interpretative tractability will apply to many of the other items in the suite of national rules. It follows that the more ambitious the measure, the more that it attempts to capture 'macro' shifts in waiting times, the more it is likely to be inundated by discrepant local reasoning and practice. National estimates of waiting list trends can only ever produce untrustworthy, ball-park figures.

We should not, however, jump to the (constructivist) conclusions that such data are contrived or meaningless. We need to revert to the post-empiricist rule to assess the assembled findings. The objectivity of evidence does not depend on the impregnability of data construction. What needs to be checked in great detail is the independence of that data from the substantive theory or the policy claim which it purports to assess.

Let us start with a prime example of the inauspicious usage of waiting time data. Unreliability is likely to increase as waiting list times become policy instruments in themselves, through public disclosure instruments, or by being built into hospital star rating schemes, or being subject to rewards and fines. Under such pressure, what is presented in the NAO report as error and perhaps ineptitude can easily turn to gaming and perhaps subterfuge. Countless academic studies and journalistic reports have pointed to the dangers of managing public services by performance indicators – showing that institutional effort and capacity is often displaced from overall performance to its specific indicator (Van Dooren and Hoffman, 2018). Interrogation of this general proposition is beyond the scope of the present episode. The purpose of the example is to demonstrate the unintended manufacture of *interdependence* between the policy expectation and the chosen measures. Lakatos's axiom for sound measurement, remember, requires *independence* between the explanatory theory and the interpretative theory.

Here then is the post-empiricist challenge. If we change its purpose, if we change the explanatory role, can waiting list data become more useful? There are several ways of approaching this objective. The first is to descend from the macro to the micro. The NAO inquiry was, so to speak, at the meso level. It examined only orthopaedic waits, but this subsumes many different procedures and patient pathways and, crucially, it does so across seven different hospital trusts. And it is at this level that measurement noise begins to exceed waiting time signal. With this realisation, the Department of Health changes tack. The national Rules Suite turns out to be not so national. It is now conceded that consistent measurement can only be achieved locally:

> There are very few national waiting time rules. Models of service provision vary across the country, and each patient will be different. It is for the NHS locally to decide how these rules are applied to individual patients, pathways and specialties, based on clinical judgement and in consultation with other NHS staff, commissioners and, of course, patients. (Department of Health, 2022)

It is deemed possible, therefore, for specific units to apply and monitor specific waiting list measures in respect of specific procedures. Changes in *local* waiting times can be measured with more confidence – but for what purpose? This brings us to a second potential modification to the underlying 'theory' of waiting list measurement. Rather than being used within a system of accountability (performance measurement) the data might be used to prompt learning and dialogue (quality improvement). Data can and have been used to identify specific blockages in specific referral chains (NHS Improving Quality, 2017). These have gone on to prompt local initiatives such as 'one stop shops' (which may add speed by consolidating tests, diagnostics, and simple treatments in one location), 'patient decision aids' (which may prevent indecision, reduce clock-stops and even increase self-care), and 'referral gateways' (which may bring primary and secondary care providers together to provide feedback on the accuracy of referrals).

None of these interventions are panaceas, of course, and require specific evidence to prove their effectiveness. Accordingly, we never completely escape the dreaded circularity problem – evaluation of these improvement initiatives can potentially inflate their worth by self-selecting particular measures at particular time periods. And what is then required is a fresh round of data excavation. What the example demonstrates, however, is that it is perfectly possible to gauge the interdependence/independence of hypotheses and evidence, and much is to be gained by doing so. But it is also clear that such a project is ongoing. It is no technical fix and it depends on sustained vigilance of the community of researchers rather than being left as a matter of individual judgement. Much more will follow on 'organised scepticism'.

I close the episode with two further brief illustrations. What I refer to as 'data excavation' is the simplest of the strategies for approaching objectivity in social research. As such, it is widely applicable and already widely used as the following examples demonstrate. The objective measurement of crime rates and crime patterns has proved a long-standing methodological challenge. Accordingly, there are many masterful examples of data excavation, one of which is the chapter by Maguire and McVie in the *Oxford Handbook of Criminology* (2017). I have space to recount a few baby steps in their methodological deconstruction of crime data.

We learn from the outset that there is no such thing as a 'factual' measure of the most basic of statistics, namely, the crime rate – the number of offences committed per year. The official measure, using police records (PR), are the most comprehensive in that they track a huge range of 'notifiable offences' (only omitting minor motoring and public order offences). Such records have, of course, the major drawback in omitting the many, many crimes which are never reported to or recorded by the police. The main alternative, the Crime Survey for England and Wales (CSEW), uses a random population survey asking people of their experience of crime victimisation. The survey thus includes non-reported crime but is limited to personal and household crime and does not include crimes against organisations, fraud, sexual crimes, and so on. Respondents, of course, are free to choose whether or not to respond to CSEW and this probably biases responses to thus who wish to 'make a point'. Neither method provides a meaningful measure of 'total crime'. Any substantive hypothesis or political claim that due to policy X overall crime rates Y are rising or falling needs to be assessed against the crude 'interpretative theory' assumed in these measures.

Changes in the crime rate are of abiding interest, an example being the much-publicised claim that there has been a widespread 'crime drop' in recent years in most Western countries. Attempts to measure crime trends present good and bad methodological news. There is no removing the ingrained selectivity in measures like PR or CSEW. But there is an argument to say that their inbuilt filters and biases remain constant from year to year, so that trend data are a respectable indicator of real change. Inevitably, this claim is also contested: 'However, law change and new kinds of criminal behaviour (and new sources of information about them) emerge, so that if one sticks rigidly to the same approach, the statistical series will lose both comprehensiveness and relevance to current crime problems' (Maguire and McVie, 2017). The upshot, as ever, is that there needs to be constant vigilance in ensuring that substantive hypotheses and measurement assumptions remain independent. In terms of the so-called crime drop, there is an interesting similarity with the thinking on waiting times, namely, that comparisons of macro rates, pulling in all types of crimes, time periods and reportage systems, are much less meaningful than plotting and explaining meso/micro changes in specific trends such as vehicle crime, violent crime, or gun crime. Farrell et al. (2014) provide an exemplary example delving into which of these reported reductions is robust.

Another age-old controversy in measurement in social science concerns the accuracy of 'self-report' in the face of the 'social desirability' effect. A contemporary example concerns the reliability and validity of people's reports on their own compliance with governmental directives on hygiene and social distancing during the Covid-19 pandemic. Many self-report surveys on frequency of hand-washing and avoidance of close contact report admirable levels of compliance (Wright et al., 2022). But to what extent are the results influenced by the powerful need to report support for the fight against the pandemic? There is little incentive to own up to infractions. What does data excavation reveal? For many years studies that 'question the questioning' reveal how self-reports are strongly influenced by question wording and format, by poor recall, and above all by the perceived desirability of the answer. The latter syndrome carries a name – 'faking good' (Winfred et al., 2021)

Research by Hansen et al. (2022) tested the accuracy of self-report on Covid rule compliance in a study which asked people to report on hand-washing – but which posed the question in different ways. They compared the unstructured, open-ended, 'How many times?' format used in official Danish government surveys with other formats that were 'anchored' for the respondent using specific scales with numbered intervals. Self-reported behaviour changed markedly according to how it was elicited. Note, importantly, that the authors do not claim to have discovered a superior way of conducting self-report inquiries. Trying to recall fleeting, routine behaviours like how many times per day one has washed hands may always be loosely connected with reality. Answers simply tend to 'pop up' in the respondents' heads. On this basis Hansen et al. make two forthright recommendations. The first is to condemn Danish government Covid policy which simply accepted and directly acted upon the validity of the original self-report statistics. The second is that in the final analysis the only way to avoid a respondent 'faking good' is to have others report on the behaviour. There are studies, for instance, using observers to measure longitudinal usage of sanitisers on entry to public locations. This measure, of course, contains a different set of methodological challenges and behavioural assumptions but they might improve the all-important independence of evidence.

KEY LESSONS

The basic lesson of Episode 22 is that data are always 'constructed' and never simply 'collected'. It follows that the best means of interrogating the validity of evidence is not to cling to the idea of locating the hard facts but rather to inspect, to excavate the assumptions which underpin the assembled data. Those assumptions must be relatively independent of the theories under test, rather than being self-confirmatory. Measurement conventions in social research are often deeply hidden. They sometimes go unreported, and this can lead to confirmatory bias. Nevertheless, data excavation is a relatively simple undertaking and should be much more widely used in the appraisal of empirical work. As we shall see in Episode 26, the same procedures occasionally find a place in investigative journalism. Fact-checking turns out to be data excavation.

Episode 23. Theory adjudication in social science

We turn to the second realist revision to the empiricist understanding of objectivity discussed in Episode 21. It called upon Harré's thesis that natural science experiments often have the function of adjudicating between rival theories. Experiments are indecisive if they raise specific hypotheses and test them selectively with specific observations – for such a procedure is always open to the charge that the experimental observations are chosen to favour the favoured theory. If, however, and as usually happens, there are several potential theories to account for a physical phenomenon, then it is possible to devise a test based on evidence that both theories would agree upon but would turn out to favour one of the rivals. I have already acknowledged that such experimental manipulation is impossible in testing social theories and political claims. However, the overall 'adjudicationist' logic is applicable and not as convoluted as it first appears, so let us proceed directly to detailed illustrations. As previously, I offer one substantial example and two briefer ones.

Example one begins in the dark arts of politics and with the esoteric practices involved in the way that civil servants are required to deliver evidence to ministers. In the trade this is referred to as providing 'lines to take' to ministers. They take the form of 'killer statistics' that politicians in power will broadcast endlessly in a way that gives credit to their actions, that can be quoted succinctly, that sound impressive … and are factually accurate. Andrews (n.d.) provides a forensic examination of one such statistic from recent UK educational policy. Again, our interest is in his method which, to repeat for emphasis, does not challenge the accuracy of the proclaimed datum but instead proposes and tests a series of rival hypotheses on how it came to be.

The sound bite in question, about educational performance, was used about 40 times by UK politicians in office in 2018 and goes as follows: 'There are now 1.9 million more children in good or outstanding schools than there were in 2010.' The School Inspection Service in England provides performance data on all state-funded schools including the classification used in the political claim, namely, an overall quality rating of: (i) 'Outstanding', (ii) 'Good', (iii) 'Requires Improvement', or (iv) 'Inadequate'. Does the quoted figure bear out what it is designed to proclaim, namely, (theory 1) that attainment standards have risen under governmental patronage and, as a consequence, that more schools are now performing at these top two levels.

Evidence never speaks for itself, and Andrews investigates a number of rival explanations that might also account for the observed shift. One plausible alternative (theory 2) concerns the potential influence of the growing pupil population. It turns out, thanks to an earlier baby boom, that there was a 7.5 per cent rise (560,000) in the state school population between 2010 and 2017. Half a million additional children entered the system, and this alone should boost the numbers in the higher rated schools. Does this simple change in demography (theory 2) rather than school-specific activity (theory 1) account for the rise in numbers encountering the higher standards?

This revised question needs careful empirical adjudication, which Andrews provides by examining the change in headcount at the schools classified under the four quality ratings. It turns out that schools rated as good or outstanding expanded much more quickly than the overall school population. Between 2010 and 2017, schools rated outstanding gained 212,000 additional pupils, those rated good increased by 367,000, whilst those rated requires improvement lost 10,000 pupils and the headcount at the inadequate schools declined by 20,000. As well as the demographic explanation (theory 2), this suggests that parental choice in sending children to the higher rated schools (theory 3) was also a significant factor in driving the statistical headline.

There are also further questions about the rating system itself that need interrogating before we can decide on the merits of *any* claim about school improvement based upon it. Can we assume that the inspection regime remains both even-handed across the four school categories and constant over time? Is there any support for a counterhypothesis (theory 4) that good and outstanding schools benefit from a softer inspection system that preserves their status? This is a significant but devilishly difficult theory to test, and I report on just a couple of Andrews's efforts.

During the period in question there were significant changes to the inspection framework. Once 'Outstanding' status is achieved, schools are no longer required to face further formal inspection (unless external monitoring uncovers serious safeguarding problems or an exceptional drop in examination results). 'Good' schools wait three years for the next inspection. Schools that 'Require Improvement' have compulsory re-inspections the following year. An 'Inadequate' rating means that the school goes directly into special measures and an enforced change of management. In the period in question Andrews discovers that these different trajectories meant that '579,000 pupils attended schools that were rated as good or outstanding but had not been inspected since 2010'. Theory 4 thus bears some fruit in that the changes to the re-inspection regime mean the ranking of the topmost schools is to a certain extent self-fulfilling.

Another potentially telling feature of the rating system in the period in question is a revision to the nomenclature of the performance categories; a previously used rating of 'Satisfactory' was updated to 'Requires Improvement' as noted above. This was undertaken with the idea (theory 5) of using inspection to increase focus on schools perceived as 'coasting' – that is, a way of adding pressure on those deemed not-bad-but-should-have-been-doing-better. Andrews offers a rival conjecture on the renamed categories (theory 6) that might also be boosting the number of higher ranked schools. He warns of 'the risk that the "requires improvement" outcome is seen as more punitive than "satisfactory" making inspectors less likely to give it'. Inspecting the inspectorial mind presents a really difficult terrain on which to gather evidence. Andrews tries to test whether the inspectors are reluctant to award the new label by comparing the number of schools awarded this third-tier grading immediately before and after its introduction. The thesis holds good – but only for some reason for primary schools (pupils 5–11 years).

The partial success (and partial failure) of this particular hypothesis marks an auspicious point on which to close this example. The school inspection regime discussed here is in constant flux and the data it generates are always open to interpretation – but the methodological implication of the entire episode is quite clear *and perfectively generalisable*. Providing good evidence is not a matter of its factual accuracy. There is no point in searching for decisive (killer) facts to settle political claims. Political ambitions are transmitted through policy changes, which are embodied in complex programmes, mounted in different circumstances, which generate multiple consequences, intended and unintended. Accordingly, there are always multiple, often contending, interpretations for any outcome consequent on ungainly policy processes. Striving for objectivity in empirical inquiry *is* the business of trying to decide between these explanations – even if those attempts only succeed incompletely and temporarily.

For further, and alas brief, examples of objectivity-as-theory-adjudication I turn to two examples explaining very different forms of social change. The first returns us to the 'crime drop' and the major study by Farrell and colleagues (2014). In the previous section I examined their data excavation affirming the decline – 'Crime has declined in many advanced countries, though sometimes with considerable variation in the timing and trajectory.' This takes us to explanations and the authors' literature review of an extraordinary list of candidate theories that *might* explain the fall in rates. For the purpose of illustration (Box 23.1), I abridge to the round dozen the huge list of potential explanations uncovered by the authors, noting that their common causal structures all hypothesise different contexts and mechanisms that might account for the crime decline.

BOX 23.1 RIVAL THEORIES FOR THE CRIME DROP

1. Demographic change reducing number of offenders and targets.
2. Prison population increase reducing the number of potential offenders.
3. Increased policing and better strategies to apprehend more criminals and increasing risk.
4. Strong economy increases wellbeing and reduces need to commit crime.
5. Capital punishment increases deterrence.
6. Gun control and weapons restrictions reduce homicide and injury.
7. Changing demographics generates proportionately fewer young offenders.
8. Institutional and cultural control over public behaviour increases.
9. Improved household and commercial security reduces opportunities.
10. Changing lifestyles, work patterns, and home ownership increases surveillance.
11. Decline in specific drug markets association with crime.
12. Lead pollution damaged children's brains in the 1950s with subsequent cleaner air causing the crime drop.

This brings us to the core analysis, which is an exemplary exercise in theory adjudication. For each conjecture existing evidence was reviewed in order to see if it could explain the observed changes. Is the theory consistent with crime patterns across nations and across time and across a variety of offences? I have no space here to review that review, so let me summarise. Of some of the explanations (e.g., theory 12) the authors are too kind to say that they are bonkers. Many others fail in terms of cross-national comparisons. For example, the United States did increase the prison population (theory 2) signif-icantly at the time of the drop, but imprisonment levels in other countries were stationary or falling as crime declined. The exercise continues, winnowing out inconsistent explanations leaving us with the most promising: 'The evi-dence examined here identifies the security hypothesis as the most promising explanation of why crime has declined.' The increased usage and increasing sophistication of security devices (theory 9) is common across all walks of life, every type of institution and most countries. Thousands of evaluative studies have shown the utility of such opportunity reduction measures in shoplifting, theft, robbery, vehicle, electronic, fraud, commercial and cooperate crime. Every theory has its limitation, of course, and Farrell and colleagues concede, for instance, that the observed reductions in homicide require a different expla-nation. Whilst they cannot explain the overall crime drop, some of the other candidate hypotheses apply closely in respect of smaller perturbations.

Another brief illustration takes us to Cornwall, the so-called 'English Riviera', and to Williams' (2021) study of counterurbanisation into that area. Population movement within a country is normally associated with urbanisation and the pull of jobs and wealth. By the 1990s Cornwall was one of the poorest areas in the country and remains so – yet for decades it has experienced high levels of inward migration. How can the paradox be explained? In an investigation using multiple methods and lasting over many years, Williams (2021) strove for an answer and that answer required theory adjudication, Box 23.2 providing a highly simplified list of potential mechanisms and contexts.

BOX 23.2   RIVAL THEORIES FOR CORNISH COUNTERURBANISATION

1. Economic decline was based on the almost total loss of mining and engineering.
2. Environmental attraction arising from perceptions of 'tourist Cornwall'.
3. Life course appraisal by migrants.
4. Perceptions of economic opportunity by migrants.
5. Lower house prices in Cornwall compared to migrant home areas.
6. Medium-term central government investment for poorer regions.
7. Local government policy of Cornish population led growth.

A vast amount of empirical work was undertaken in relation to each proposition. Here I summarise only the basic findings. In this instance theory adjudication was not so much about seeking outright 'winners' and 'losers' but about refining and blending the candidate theories. That said, two theories were regarded as extremely unlikely. Governmental incentives (theory 6, 7) launched to bring about economic regeneration were evaluated as too sporadic and too modest to have had significant impact on migration to Cornwall. Evidence indicated that theory 2 did identify a significant, initial draw – the far southwest of England having a benign climate and outstanding land and seascapes. Yet tourism is traditionally seasonal, producing little permanent migration and limited economic opportunities. It is a mere curtain raiser. Investigation of theory 3 showed that most migrants were well into their housing and economic careers. They arrived with little perception of breaking into local job markets but with resources of their own, which were invested in commercial opportunities in seaside towns (theory 4a). These towns became leisure industry 'honeypots', which in turn attracted younger, less skilled, less wealthy immigrants (theory 4b). Theory 5 is supported by strong evidence on lower house prices in southwest England as compared to other regions (this is eventually reversed but only in the seaside towns). Meanwhile, most of the rest of northern and central Cornwall, having lost its traditional industries (theory 1), continues to decline and is untouched by these processes. The conundrum is explained – counterurbanisation will not necessarily counter economic decline.

KEY LESSONS

Episode 23 articulates one of the most important and yet little heralded strategies of approaching objectivity in social research. Theories are not tested using unassailable facts but in competition with each other. It is frequently the case that empirical regularities are explicable under more than one theory. Further evidence should then be sought with the specific purpose of adjudicating between one and another. Theories will make common claims but will differ in some respects and these points of difference are the crucial location for inquiry. This strategy is especially important in sociology, where theories proliferate in effortless abundance (recall Stinchcombe in Episode 3). Theory adjudication itself does not end in unassailable truth but winnows down the set of theories that lead us nearer to the truth.

Episode 24. Building evidence networks in social science

The examples in the previous episode presented a method to decide objectively between one theory and another. Here I turn to my third strategy for pursuing objectivity based on the idea of constructing networks of evidence. Recall that in complex systems, scientific explanations grow as networks of theories and sub-theories. It is the linkage and interdependence between the component theories that make for sound causal inferences. I illustrated this idea with the example of the 'evidence pipeline' in the development of therapeutic drugs (Episodes 5 and 21). A drug is shown to 'work', to be causally efficacious, only if it fulfils a complex sequence of specific hypotheses on its biological mechanism of action, its chemical structure, its presentational properties, its safety record, its dosage parameters, and its efficacy in clinical trial. The same logic provides a different and superior way to think about objectivity. The assembled network of evidence interconnects and brings reliability and validity to the explanatory whole. Causality is captured in networks of theories. Objectivity is exemplified in the corresponding networks of evidence.

Social policies and programmes are resolutely complex and always have to confront a series of challenges if they are to initiate change. Essentially, the same network strategy needs to be adopted to evaluate their causal efficacy *and* to lay claim to the objectivity of that explanation. For an example, I reconstruct some research I conducted over a decade ago, which was published most fully in Pawson et al. (2011). The study reviewed the evidence on the likely effectiveness of banning smoking in cars carrying children. It was carried out prior to and as a prelude to the enactment of such legislation in many different jurisdictions. Details of the research strategy (namely, 'realist synthesis') can be omitted here other than to say that it was a theory-driven inquiry led by a range of hypotheses about the many conditions the proposed legislation should satisfy if it was to reach the statute books and, more significantly, if it was going to be effective in reducing harm from secondary smoking. I mimic the pipeline motif by presenting the sequence of challenges confronting the proposed ban in Figure 24.1 and Box 24.1. A rapid sketch of the network of evidence follows. For brevity, the citations to all of the primary sources utilised here are omitted here as is the data excavation work in assessing their rigour. All details can be consulted in the aforementioned paper.

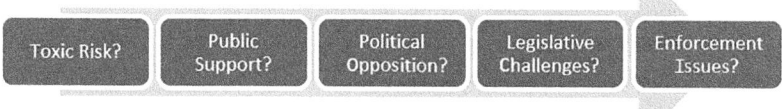

Figure 24.1   Barriers confronting legislative change on smoking

BOX 24.1 THE CHALLENGES SPECIFIED

1. *Toxic risk?* What is the prevalence of smoking in cars with children? What levels of toxicity are experienced? How do the risks compare with other smoking environments? Are children's metabolisms at particular risk? Does ventilation make a difference?
2. *Public support?* Will there be public support for the ban? Will smokers support the ban? Will parents who smoke in cars support the ban? Will support be stronger if other smoking bans are already in place?
3. *Political opposition?* How fiercely will the tobacco lobby oppose the bill? How strongly will the health lobby support the bill? How will other interest groups align?
4. *Legislative challenges?* Will lawmakers be willing to legislate on behaviour on private spaces? How will they define 'children'? What penalties (if any) are proposed?
5. *Enforcement issues?* Will law-enforcement support the bill? Will the police take action? Is public health within their remit? How easy is it to recognise, stop, and caution offenders?

The synthesis sought to review existing evidence on all five questions and their sub-conjectures. Some of these issues were thickly populated with previous investigations, on others the evidence was sparse. The first point to make is none of the hypotheses, even the ones turning on physical properties such as toxicity levels, is settled with a 'fact'. The toxic risk associated with 'second-hand smoking' comes from the emission of very small particulates known as $PM_{2.5}$. It is relatively easy to measure these levels in a car – simply replace the child with a portable air quality monitor. Such findings then entered the public domain and were widely reported as demonstrating that air quality in the rear seat of a car was 23 times worse than at a home in which parents smoked, and 10 times more toxic even than in a smoky bar (a location in which bar-workers had recently been protected by a smoking ban). We arrive at the customary question. Are these claims objective?

I respond with the customary answer – yes and no. The evidence does not provide an absolute risk estimate because a range of further environmental, biological, and social factors also contribute to the risk equation. $PM_{2.5}$ levels in the car and the comparators all vary. Ventilation in the car reduces toxicity by a rather small but statistically significant amount. Conversely, the dilution of toxins is much different in the wide surrounds of the home and in the confined car cabin. The length of exposure is a further crucial difference – in short, intermittent journeys provide less risk than an eight-hour bar shift. Another element in this causal chain is sensitivity. Although an increasing body of research exists indicating that children's bodies are more susceptible to toxic threats, the extent of this in relation to second-hand smoke is still largely unknown. The weight of evidence for the first sub-theory in our sequence of theories proves *conditionally* correct and initiates a provisional case for legislation.

What about its potential effectiveness? Effective law-making requires societal accord. Evidence on pre-existing public support for a ban approached consensus, perhaps surprising consensus. Smoking cessation is a favourite topic of survey research and surveys conducted worldwide indicated substantial support for a potential ban, especially in countries in which other restrictions were firmly in place. A crucial, somewhat counterintuitive, nugget of evidence is that the majority of smokers consulted in such surveys also supported a potential ban. Asked why they did so, powerful evidence emerged not about their own habit but on their protective instinct for their children.

The next requirement for the successful enactment of any law is for it to circumvent excessive counterpressure from powerful lobby groups. The tobacco lobby has a long history of skulduggery in opposing an unending series of restrictions on cigarette sales using the 'free choice' argument – it is for individuals to balance risk and pleasure. But in this specific instance, there was silence – indeed we did discover some tobacco company press releases which offered muted agreement with the proposed ban. Again, the key factor is the protection of children. Since minors rarely have free choice in being able to avoid second-hand smoke, the tobacco lobby feels able to concede in this exceptional instance and to concentrate on business elsewhere.

Legislative changes have to find their way onto the statute books. The drafting of such a ban had to confront many objections and legal niceties. Free choice campaigners argued that the law should not protrude on the 'private space' of the car, an argument that failed miserably given many precedents. The age of responsibility (for perpetrators and victims) provided a legislative headache, handled as it transpired rather variably across different jurisdictions.

Effective bans need to be clear on enforcement and penalties. On this score the impending legislation lacked consensus, proposals ranging from heavy fines to formal cautions to verbal warnings.

Is such a ban enforceable? This was the final imponderable under review. Recall that the investigation took place before the widespread introduction of the law and at that stage it was met with widespread disinclination by police authorities. They pointed out that public health matters were not part of their remit, and that such a fleeting, surreptitious offence would be exceedingly difficult to detect, which would require an inordinate amount of police time. Later evidence showed that apart from occasional and well-publicised enforcement 'blitzes' the ban was left to police itself.

The policy outcome of this evidence trail is well enough known. Across the world legislation banning smoking in cars carrying children arrived on the statute books with relatively little opposition. Enforcement and penalties have been applied with progressively lighter touches. Yet compliance seems to have held firm and is indeed improving, without being flawless. This latter eventuality requires explanation under a yet further theory, known under the concept of 'moral law' (Zaborowski, 2010). In this manifestation, the passing of legislation and the associated publicity seems to act as an initial trigger to compliance, which is hardened in resolute public confirmation that it should be followed out of personal conscience because of its intrinsic value.

At issue here is the methodological outcome of this particular tale. What does it tell us about objectivity in social research? I want to spell out the consequences carefully, beginning by articulating what is *not* implied in the above illustration. Although there were deeply conflicting views on the ban, the resolution explained here is *not* a balanced or impartial overview. Quite the contrary, it seeks to explain why certain viewpoints prevailed. Moreover, it is *not* a case of what I referred to, rather uncharitably, as 'data agglomeration' in Episode 19. Recall the example of Hayes and Guardino's painstaking dissection of the mountain of broadcast opinions on the legitimacy of the Iraq conflict. By contrast, the copious evidence used in the smoking ban review moves from issue to issue, source to source, method to method, and thus *theory to theory*. It begins to grasp the many-sided complexity of legislative change.

Although, as just acknowledged, the study calls on primary evidence that utilised all manner of different methods (toxicity analysis, surveys, document analysis, time series, etc.) the payoff is *not* simply a matter of what is often referred to as 'data triangulation' or 'mixed method research'. The danger here is that multi-method research can be reduced to a technical imperative, namely, that studies should be designed to have qualitative and quantitative components, with their findings being combined to produce a more objective overall picture. The problem with that scenario is that the findings produced by two methods may be complementary, but they may contradictory, or they may simply sail past each other (Pawson, 2008). Studies that combine RCTs and process evaluations are often oil and water, the former providing a statistical estimate of overall efficacy of an intervention, the latter providing a folk tale of the tribulations in its implementation (Blackwood et al., 2010). Derived separately, qualitative and quantitative findings may still carry the signatures of their fundamentally discrepant origins in positivism and phenomenology. Accordingly, mixed methods research may even preserve the distinctions that it seeks to bridge (Hammersley, 2008).

For the realist, data (without theory) simply accumulate in haphazard heaps. The approach to objectivity pursued in this episode speaks directly to the power of 'evidential networks'. To pin the idea down further I suggest the reader returns to Popper's swamp metaphor, quoted in Episode 21. To paraphrase, he suggests that we build explanation, we construct theories, over a 'swamp' of evidence. Each empirical study drives a pile down into that swamp. Any one pile can never reach solid ground (i.e., objectivity) but can provide a tentative contribution to an emerging explanation. That tyro explanation, if it is to be fruitful, will have many different components and consequences. Empirical research seeks to support an emerging explanation with an emerging body of evidence. A first study assesses a preliminary hypothesis. It leaves behind many untested hypotheses. Other studies set off into the swamp piecing together partial support for an emerging theory. The exercise repeats itself until the accumulated body of evidence seems firm enough to carry the theoretical superstructure. At least for the time being.

To my pleasure and perhaps surprise, this metaphor had profound resonance when I undertook the above review and in many others that contributed to the development of realist syntheses (Pawson, 2006). Social policies and programmes have complex causal structures, which need to be evaluated supposition by supposition in order to assess their overall effectiveness. But the same applies to all social explanation. To repeat the formula. Causality is captured in networks of theories. Objectivity is exemplified in the corresponding networks of evidence.

It is surprising that the notion of expanding explanatory networks has received relatively little formal exposition in social science. There are exceptions of course. Another venerable and closely related contribution comes from Kaplan (1964) with his notion of 'pattern explanation'. Here is his masterful and masterfully brief quotation on objectivity: 'For the pattern mode, objectivity consists essentially in this, that the pattern can be indefinitely filled in and extended: as we obtain more and more knowledge it continues to fall into place in this pattern and the pattern itself has a place in a larger whole.' Another closely related idea, namely, the construction of a 'repertoire of causal mechanisms' can be found in Miller (1987). Fielding (2008) captures a similar formula for seeking objectivity in mixed method inquiry under the term 'analytic density'.

KEY LESSONS

Episode 24 articulates another frequently used but little heralded approach to objectivity. As ever, there is a rejection of the idea that objectivity resides in empirical data – since data tend to disgorge in an undifferentiated swill. According to the network model, something is explained when it is related to a set of other elements that together create a unified system. The function of empirical research is to provide plausible evidence to demonstrate the coherence of the interconnections in that system. Objectivity resides in the process of filling and extending the explanatory network. Evidence on previously unknown and uncertain elements of a system gains traction by gradual incorporation into the known network.

Episode 25. Organised scepticism or mutual incomprehension?

The previous three episodes covered practical research strategies – modes of inquiry used to generate objectivity in natural science research, which are shown to be readily adapted for social science. These strategies are not spontaneous; they are not an automatic product of the conduct of research. Rather, they are sustained because of a particular culture or social system that pertains in science, variously described as 'organised scepticism', 'mutual distrust', and 'competitive cross-validation'.

For an immediate grasp of these ideas, I refer the reader back to the stirring quotation from Campbell (1988) in Episode 21, which ends in the pithy phrase: 'Organized distrust produces trustworthy reports.' The classic exposition belongs, of course, to Merton (1968b), which begins with a prophetic warning about creeping anti-intellectualism.

His historical studies of the development of science reveal a range of characteristics that embody its distinctive culture. I paraphrase four key principles in Box 25.1.

BOX 25.1 MERTON'S CORNERSTONES OF SCIENTIFIC CULTURE

1. The substantive findings of science are the product of social collaboration and are assigned to the whole community. Boyle's Law is not his but ours.
2. The acceptance or rejection of claims entering the canons of science are not dependent on the personal or social attributes of their protagonist. There is no such thing as Aryan Science or Soviet Science or Feminist Science.
3. There is keen competition in science, an emphasis on being first to a discovery. But such accolades are determined over the course of time and by others. Ultimate accountability is in the hands of compeers.
4. There is a stock of accumulated knowledge and a corresponding willingness to acknowledge and build up on the work of predecessors. As

Newton put it, 'If I have seen further, it is by standing on the shoulders of giants.'

There are many sciences, of course, stretching from astrology to zoology, and across the board these characteristics doubtless apply in different measure. This brings us directly to a consideration of the social system that surrounds social research. The academic infrastructure is much the same as all other disciplines, being made up of international associations, academic departments and divisions, research institutes, disciplinary specialisms, and sub-specialisms. Knowledge is disseminated through conferences, teaching, libraries, journals, editorials, reports, books, essays, and reviews. The question for this episode is whether the spirit of organised scepticism pervades this edifice.

The social sciences, especially sociology, are full of self-doubt and procrastination. For instance, over the years there have been numerous books proclaiming the 'crisis in sociology' (e.g., Boudon, 1980; Gouldner, 1971; Lopreato and Crippen, 1999). There is even a recent paper comparing sociology to phrenology, thus announcing the 'coming end of sociology' (Vandenberghe and Fuchs, 2019). What has worried these commentators is the increasing fragmentation of the discipline. The number of journals, the number of authors, the number of citations, the number of 'mentions' on social media have all increased dramatically in recent years (Filippo and Sanz-Casado, 2018). And with this comes a fragmentation of research programmes, substantive issues, conceptual preferences, research techniques, theories, and meta-theories (Scott, 2005).

An appropriate yardstick against which to measure the pace of change was foreseen by Abbott (2006) in a withering paper on knowledge accumulation in sociology. The average life of a paradigm, he declares, is a mere 25 years:

> In summary, it seems that sociology is littered with research programs that are exciting for a couple of decades, then peter out into routinism and time serving. The same is probably true of methodologies. There are a number of possible mechanisms predicting this cycle. The most obvious is career structure. Twenty-five years is about the length of time it takes a single group of individuals to make up some new ideas, seize the soap-boxes, train a generation or two of students, and finally settle into late career exhaustion. Their students may keep things going, but their students' students tend to be fairly mechanical appliers of the original insights. The really creative people don't tend to make their careers by hitching themselves to other people's wagons. (2006)

The consequences, alas, are abundantly clear. Snow's (1959) two cultures have descended on social science. In one partition, much of sociology continues to drive post-haste for post-modernism, post-colonialism, post-humanism, and post-everything (Paul and van Veldhuizen, 2021). Sociology becomes the 'science of the neglected topic', with every PhD thesis and every research proposal proclaiming that it identifies a vital but previously uncharted territory. Sociology takes on cultural, emotional, critical, metaphoric, normative, and decorative turns (Abbot, 2018; Brown, 1977; McLennon, 2014; Rojek and Turner, 2000) absorbing influences from literary traditions, from cultural studies, from film studies, and from polemic. Journals turn inwards catering solely for a readership of a discipline subfield, with authors citing papers predominantly from like-minded journals. The driver of all of this is undoubtedly the precipitous and unpredictable pace of change of modern society. New wonders and new calamities arrive by the day. Rather than attempting to grasp these perturbations using a stock of accumulated concepts and theories, the assumption is that understanding them requires conceptual neologisms and perpetual paradigm shifts as above. Competition to be 'first to a discovery' goes unchecked by tradition.

Does this bode well for organised scepticism or is it a recipe for mutual incomprehension? What remains of the Mertonian norms? All depends, of course, on where you sit. Abbot himself recognised distinctly negative consequences of sociological impulsiveness for those seeking knowledge accumulation and pursuing the gradual elaboration of the words of predecessors. But he was entirely relaxed about this outcome perceiving that sociology's very purpose is to challenge, to inflame, to pose questions. Others have been less impressed. The *Journal of Classical Sociology* weeps at these developments, re-emphasising the importance of maintaining the core of the discipline of sociology and the need for constant engagement with the classical legacy (Susen and Turner, 2021).

But what of the other culture? What of those of us seeking social *science*? What of those ancients like me who came on board reading Cotgrove's *Science of Society – An Introduction to Sociology* (1969), simply assuming that a scientific approach was the very purpose. From this perspective the subsequent fragmentation of the discipline, whilst regrettable, requires little more in response than a putting up of the shutters and a redrawing of title deeds. There is no stopping the various normative and cultural turns and no need to do so, since the scientific tradition prospers under its own logic. Having shed the simplifications of empiricism and positivism, realist inquiry provides a broad foundation for a science of society. I have been at pains to describe the history to post-empiricist and realist social inquiry that stretches way back through time, emanating from the traditions of physical and clinical inquiry. Moreover, throughout the book I utilise scores of examples from across the history of social inquiry and through the spectrum of social science disciplines to exemplify the realist approach to causality, objectivity, and generality. This is no fleeting pastime, no 25-year junket.

I must be careful, of course, not to trip into aggrandisement. Elsewhere I have drawn a 'realist tree' describing many different roots and branches (Pawson, 2018). It shows that realist research has a stronger presence in some fields than others – being particularly sturdy, for instance, in the applied disciplines such as policy analysis and programme evaluation. Here it is appropriate to provide a further addendum – namely, to point out that the core ideas presented in this book bear a strong and most welcome similarity to perspectives that have been developed using somewhat different terminology. There are many, many allies. Elsewhere in the academy, the science of society is pursued as 'analytic sociology' (Bearman and Hedström, 2011), 'rigorous sociology' (Gerxhani et al., 2022), 'complexity theory' (Byrne and Callaghan, 2014: Williams, 2021), 'probability theory' (Hitchcock, 2021), 'process tracing' (Beach and Pederson, 2013) *to name but a morsel.* It is also pertinent to point out that all of these perspectives lay claim to delivering only partial and provisional truths.

This will never be to the taste of our more rhapsodic and bellicose cousins. But that is not a matter of regret – let them eat cake, let them sup wine (Smith Maguire, 2021).

KEY LESSONS

Episode 25 examines the culture driving empirical research to see how social inquiry is ordered and prioritised. If contemporary sociology could speak, it would say, 'I'm bored.' The social world undergoes constant transformation. The social world is infinitely describable. There are infinite ways of carrying out that description. Accordingly, social inquiry has become overloaded with perspectives whose main purpose is to keep pace with the schlock of the new. The upshot is that these 'decorative' approaches have no particular pedigree and go rapidly in and out of fashion. What is needed is an approach that builds upon a stock of existing theories, that seeks their applicability to emerging social trends and that refines the theories to account for those changes. This in turn requires a research culture that seeks constantly to cross-reference and mutually criticise whole bodies inquiry. This notion of 'organised scepticism' persists stubbornly in realist-inspired social science. It needs to be nurtured further and celebrated more widely.

Episode 26. Postscript: post-empiricism versus post-truth

Who says that sociologists cannot predict the future? Here is de Tocqueville in 1835 describing President you-know-who and the embryonic stirrings of what is now called the post-truth era. I have already described the symptoms. Experts are ignored. Technocrats are berated. Feelings have taken over and a new emotional politics has become normalised. As Davis (2017) puts it, 'Lies and deception, exaggeration and euphemism, flannel and waffle, spin and the selective use of the facts, artifice and gibberish: bullshit is everywhere you look.'

Part II has consisted of an attempt to reset the debate on objectivity *within* social science in favour of a realist interpretation – put simply, empiricism and constructivism have given way to post-empiricism. The question for this final episode in this part concerns the extent to which the various methodo-logical strategies outlined in Episodes 21 to 25 can also shield us from the all-pervasive bullshit. Can they be utilised to preserve a sense of objectivity in wider public discourse? I have not gone crazy. It sounds a preposterous suggestion. The methodological struggles I have described are tucked away quietly in university corridors and academic libraries. Moreover, as I noted in Episodes 18, 20, and 25 a large chunk of 'social science' is against science, being designed to pursue normative or emotional standpoints. Academic talk is often tough, but it is only talk. Generally speaking, the millions of learned words are faint whispers in the political power play.

So how might, repeat might, post-empiricism get a wider hearing? We will follow a rather circuitous route. The first point to make is that sociological and political science has been rather good at explaining the coming of the post-truth era. A number of promising hypotheses have been forwarded – financial crisis, austerity policies, stubborn inequality, elitist governance, population shifts, changing media and social media consumption, and so on (e.g., Ball, 2017; Farkas and Schou, 2019; Kalpokas, 2018; McIntyre, 2018). Any respite from emotional politics will involve charting, challenging, and countering several if not all of these considerable forces. The institutional checks and balances designed to prevent any power bloc claiming control of public discourse require urgent revision and renewal. Social science may thus point to a resolution without, of course, having the means to deliver it.

But is there a more modest role for realist thinking? Its one weapon is reasoning, a rather blunt instrument if no one is listening and public discourse is fragmenting. A key facet of the current crisis concerns the inability to distinguish 'news' and 'fake news', 'facts' and 'alternative facts'. Where in this babble of exhortations might reasoning get a hearing? How might it be possible to patch the tattered flag of enlightenment? The most likely source lies within the mainstream media, in investigative journalism and, more specifically, in the response to the new politics undertaken in the name of 'fact-checking'. We have already encountered a couple of significant misconceptions in the response for these agencies. The very terminology, 'fact-checking', sometimes betrays an empiricist inclination that particularly clear-sighted journalist are able to 'see' the overt difference between sacred facts and political embroidery (Episode 17). The cherished notion of impartiality also founders under the weight of attempting to balance a thousand views (Episode 19). Accordingly, what is investigated in this postscript is whether the more encouraging strategies developed in Part II, namely, (i) 'excavating evidence', (ii) 'theory adjudication', (iii) 'weaving evidence networks', and (iv) 'organised scepticism' have their counterparts in public discourse and in journalism.

EXCAVATING EVIDENCE

I made the case in Episodes 21 and 22 that scientific evidence gained its spurs using a process of data excavation, inspecting for the independence of theory and evidence. Scores of broadcasters, news agencies, institutes, and charitable bodies have developed fact-checking capabilities and websites, all attempting to hold the line for sound evidence. Yet fact-checking is something of a misnomer. Consider a couple of run-of-the-mill definitions: (i) 'fact-checking is the process of attempting to verify or disprove assertions made in speech, print media or online content', (ii) 'the objective is to check that all the facts in a piece of writing, a news article, a speech, etc. are correct'. The pervading impression still seems to be about separating facts from opinions, truths from lies.

This would be all well and good if the exercise consisted of checking claims on simple events and singular properties. Thus, if someone was to make the assertion that Elvis wore size 12 boots, we could hunt down his stage costumes and indeed 'fact-check' the claim. Alas, as argued endlessly above, science and social science test complex, many-sided, and provisional theoretical propositions using complex, many-sided, and provisional bodies of evidence. The requisite first task is to ensure that there is a degree of independence between the assumption in the former and the latter. And this is managed through a process, which I've termed 'excavating the evidence'. Exactly the same procedure is required for assessing political claims which are complex and convoluted and made on the basis of evidential claims which are also complex and convoluted. Their independence needs to be checked and I would argue this is the first remit of investigative journalism. Fact-checking is better described as 'data excavation'.

I will rely on one example to make the case, though there are a thousand others. I return to a famous controversy I mentioned earlier, namely, the battle cry of the leave campaign during the UK referendum on EU membership: 'We send the EU £350m a week – let's fund our NHS instead.' As pointed out in Episode 20, this figure was often described as 'contested' in timid BBC attempts to remain impartial and present 'both sides of the argument'. But this was not always the case. In Cushion and Lewis's (2017) article we come across an important exception abridged here from a Channel 4 report:

> Leave campaigners say the membership bill is £350 million a week. That would be 0.6% of national income. Or one seventh of UK health spending (13.9%). That's £252 a year per person in the UK. They estimate this because last year the UK gave £18.5bn to the EU. But what they leave out is that we get quite a lot of money back. There is a rebate every year, negotiated by Margaret Thatcher. Billions are given to the UK to spend on things like farming (£9.8bn). Even more money comes back in grants for universities and business (£5.7bn) – IFS. Bringing the total cost from £252 to £89 a year.

In a one-minute utterance we are able to see data excavation in action. Note that the exercise was repeated across the media, often in the rather fuller detail that newsprint allows (Guardian, 2016). These reports in turn encouraged a rebuke from the UK Statistics Authority (2016) though one has to search the soberly worded appendix A for the analysis. The point stressed here is that these exercises do not replace a false figure with the correct one. They interrogate the many different costs and benefits associated with EU membership, moving from the closely audited to the almost intangible. The crucial point is that is there is elbow room within public discourse to begin to spell the assumptions built into the data. The same applies in countless other examples.

I should temper enthusiasm for journalistic data excavation, however, by noting a sad end to the Brexit costs debate. A charge of misinformation went to court but claims of 'misconduct in public office' were rejected by the UK Commission on the grounds that such misconduct does not include 'false statements in relation to publicly available statistics' (Huffington Post, 2019). All is fair, it would appear, in love and war and political campaigning.

THEORY ADJUDICATION

I made the case in Episodes 21 and 23 that scientific objectivity is approached in a process of 'theory adjudication'. It is usually the case that there are rival explanations for any phenomenon or regularity and in the face of this, empirical research becomes the process of discovering evidence that will help decide on their respective merits. This is a subtle, not to say erudite, revision of the way that empirical inquiry is customarily conceived. Is there a shadow, some sort of counterpart, in public discourse? I think there is, and it is evident in miniature in the best political interviews.

I make my case, once again with the single illustration, which takes us back to the research I conducted on the potential effectiveness of a ban on smoking in cars carrying children (Episode 24). There was considerable journalistic interest at the time in the feasibility of potential legislation. Pundits arose from all sides of the argument and the proposed ban was a hot broadcast topic for a couple of months. I recall one interview, which so impressed that I published a commentary on it with the somewhat tongue-in-cheek title: 'The Today Programme's contribution to evidence-based policy' (Pawson et al., 2010). This particular *Today* programme is a flagship BBC early-morning radio news review. There is a stable programme format in which a policy protagonist is cross-examined by the presenter, acting as antagonist. Experts and their big ideas are introduced and given a brief say. The body of the interview is then given over to a well-briefed probing for potential weak links in the said policy reform. It is the nature of this questioning that is of interest, for in the best examples it takes the form of competitive cross-validation. That is to say, the interviewer confronts interviewee with *rival theories* about the policy reform and thus about its unconsidered antecedents and unintended consequences. The well-prepared guest will have anticipated the onslaught and come armed with counter evidence to support their proposals. The point is to get beyond the empty slogans that pervade many interviews. The point is to make the protagonist *work* – by requiring them to know the evidence that counters the counter arguments.

Such a cross-examination is exemplified in a *Today* interview between the advocate, Professor Stephenson of the Royal College of Paediatrics and Child Health, and the presenter, Sarah Montague. The interview began with the debate on toxic risk and closely mirrored the rival claims discussed above (Episode 24) on length of exposure, ventilation, etc. But to make the same point on a different issue I summarise a tiny section from later in the interview in which Montague raises an ethical problem, namely, that such a ban would face resistance as lawmakers are generally reluctant to intrude on 'private spaces'. Stephenson is ready, reminding us that 'a car is not a private place.

The United Kingdom has introduced legislation to stop the use of mobile phones in cars.' Montague is also ready: 'But mobile phone usage endangers other road-users' lives, whereas here we are talking about the drivers' own children.' Stephenson knows this one too: 'We have had for many years UK legislation to make children wear car seatbelts, so the state already intervenes in what parents can do in cars.'

Light sparring of this type continues throughout the interview, and I refer the reader to the original paper for fine details. The significance of the tale is not about the relative merits of the interviewer or interviewee. For the record, Stephenson was much more sure-footed on toxicity than enforceability. The point is that the interview is a miniature form of theory adjudication. The above 'evidence' on private spaces does not turn on any decisive fact but mirrors classic legal argument on establishing a precedent. Taken as a whole, the interview subdivides the policy proposal into a series of sub-hypotheses, each one being interrogated by raising a rival hypothesis and then another and then another. Whilst the formal review of the evidence mentioned above took about a year to complete and this interview lasted three or so minutes, methodologically speaking they are the same.

WEAVING EVIDENCE NETWORKS

I made the case in Episodes 21 and 24 that scientific objectivity was approached by a process of building explanatory networks. Explanations build and build on complex causal networks, each stanchion accounting for a different component of the phenomenon under investigation, each stanchion reinforcing the others. Is there an equivalent in public discourse? The answer, of course is 'no'. What is described in the idea of explanatory networks is the steady historical unfolding of scientific inquiry. Public discourse unfolds frantically, waywardly, and unpredictably. Some political discourse does, of course, claim to provide universal explanations – but without having to do the donkey work. The same ideological conviction will explain everything that is wrong in the world and provide solutions to all ills. The same normative theory explains life, universe, everything. Science is less confident.

ORGANISED SCEPTICISM

I made the case in Episode 21 that the scientific method was projected through and protected by a culture of organised scepticism. I noted in Episode 25 that this culture featured only weakly and selectively in social science. What can be said about the public realm? What price organised scepticism in the rampant outpourings of social media? What price organised scepticism in the farrago of viewpoints that constitute contemporary politics?

I can hardly bring myself to ponder the former question. But let me quote from a source that tells us that

> the average American spends 7 hours and 4 minutes looking at a screen every day. This is slightly below average and around 45 minutes longer than the British who average 6 hours and 12 minutes of screen time per day. But it is nearly four hours less than the biggest screen-time consumers, South Africans, who average around 10 hours and 46 minutes a day. (Comparitech, 2023)

Then there is the issue of content. Who provides it and what do they have to say? The modern incarnation of the opinion leader is, of course, the 'influencer'. As a fully accredited old curmudgeon, I must own up to utter ignorance. But I am led to believe that expertise extends to either themselves or the glittering array of modern consumer products. When influencers do turn to the political, it appears that the same priorities hold – namely, self-promotion, wish-fulfilment, and instant gratification (Riedl et al., 2021).

Next is the matter of how such social media truths are communicated onwards. Consider in this respect the 'like button', the smiley icon, which its inventors saw as 'a feature that lets users express their instant approval of a specific idea or item and share it'. Dean (2016) reports that within months of its first usage it became a feature of 350,000 websites. For a more recent, despairing commentary, see Kariuki (2022). What are the overall implications for public knowledge in 'screen world'? Enthusiasts see the coming of an edgy, effervescent, and empowered public. Detractors satirise the change as follows: 'the average American's base knowledge has crashed through the floor of "uniformed", passed "misinformed" on the way down and is now plummeting to "aggressively wrong"' (Nichols, 2017). Take your pick.

But what about institutional knowledge? What about the practices, rules, traditions, memories embedded in the organisations in which life is conducted. Have feelings taken over at this level? Do we have a post-truth polity, a post-truth economy, a post-truth health service, a post-truth education system? At this level post-truth pessimism simply runs out of steam. It is reminiscent of a much earlier theory of cultural hegemony. Many Marxist scholars borrowed Engels's ideas on 'false-consciousness' to describe how ideological forces are cunningly marshalled to mislead the masses into thinking that capitalism is in their interest and provides for their needs (Lukács, 1967). Turkeys, apparently, vote for Christmas – the subordinate class unthinkingly embrace the messaging of the ruling class. Post-truth thinking updates the thesis with a different set of turkeys and a daily dose of Christmases.

Both versions of the theory fail by ignoring the possibility of 'resistance' – the resolute defiance of the working-class organisations in the first episode and the subtle institutional barricades against populism in the second. The good news is that it is quite possible to acknowledge the recent dumbing-down of political discourse without conceding that it is ubiquitous or irreversible. Much of the analytic problem here stems from the fact that the empirical ammunition for post-truth politics is taken almost entirely from the narratives that surround campaigning, elections, and referendums. Politics, it is conveniently over-looked, is about action as well as words and about policies as well as promises.

Moreover, as any elementary text on governance teaches, policymaking is undertaken within a system of checks and balances. The idea of the separation of powers goes back to ancient Rome with the Senate, the Consuls, and the Assemblies providing a system of mixed government. Most modern democracies separate the legislature, the executive, and the judiciary to the same end. More specifically in the UK, the implementation of any policy passes into the hands of civil servants in many different departments in Westminster, their work being overseen by a range of Commons and Lords select committees. Upon implementation, policy evaluations and audits are produced by analysts in government departments, by academics, consultancies, quangos, and other independent organisations commissioned by government. Thereafter the broadcast media take over scrutiny with some agencies promising 'impartiality and balance' (and some not!).

Much of the above is the natural territory of 'organised distrust'. At this late stage I am not about to embark on an evaluation of the effectiveness of institutional checks and balances, merely to claim that the ethos is not yet vanquished. There are vestiges of post-empiricism and organised scepticism in public discourse – though the pompous terminology and epistemological back-drop go unacknowledged. In the previous episodes I have located examples of data excavation and theory adjudication in the mainstream journalism, and I conclude with a final quotation on objectivity from a senior BBC journalist. It bears a remarkable resemblance to Popper's redoubtable swamp metaphor:

> Judgement always plays a part in our decisions as to what is fact and what is true, or possibly true in some contexts but irrelevant on others. I think of them like beams used in construction: that a beam is made of steel is important, but when inserting one to support a building the question is not simply what material it is made of, but whether it is capable of bearing the weight that is loaded upon it. Debates over which interpretation of the facts is the right one are often less about truth and more about the proportionality of the facts cited in making the case set out. (Davis, 2017)

KEY LESSONS

Episode 28 makes a brief foray into public discourse and pits post-empiricism against post-truth. It is not a fair fight. McLuhan (1964) once said that the 'medium was the message' and today's daily diet of messages is composed of memes, emoticons, tweets, smisshers, and influencers. Glance across the warring wasteland of international relations and one sees that hopes for the 'civilising process' (Elias, 1982) and the 'new age of enlightenment' (Nikolajew, 2013) are dashed by the day. At both micro and macro levels post-truth sentiments prevail. By contrast, post-empiricism locates the quest for truth in the slow, tentative process of competitive cross-validation. Truths fight for survival with ideas being pitted systematically against each other and being subjected to detailed scrutiny of their underlying assumptions. Indubitably, it is not a fair fight but, thankfully, vestiges of such processes can be recognised in sturdy corners of institutional discourse and investigative journalism. Amen to that.

PART III

How to think about generality

Introduction to Part III

An idea is always a generalisation, and generalisation is a property of thinking. To generalise means to think. (Hegel, 1896)

All generalizations are false, including this one. (Twain, attributed in Baillargeon, 2007)[1]

History doesn't repeat itself, but it often rhymes. (Twain, attribution in Quote Investigator, 2014)[2]

We enter discussion of the third classic debate in social science methodology. What does it mean to generalise? Of the three methodological challenges tackled in this book, this one is the most obtuse. As per usual, noviciates face a messy tangle of concepts to describe the issue. In the high peaks of meta-theory, we discover the terms 'ideographic' and 'nomothetic' describing two distinct approaches to knowledge acquisition, two separate intellectual tendencies, each one corresponding to a different branch of academia. Ideographic disciplines argue that social understanding is confined to the local and the contingent. Sensemaking is specific to each human encounter and the very notion of generalisable explanation is dismissed. If this principle was accepted Part III would be very short indeed. We thus concentrate on the nomothetic branch line which assumes that social science can make generalisations; it can make legitimate comparisons from situation to situation. Social regularities are patterned, a degree of order extends across the world, and it is possible to make statements having general rather than specific validity.

Our topic in Part III speaks for itself. The thirst for generality is omnipresent in science. A study is conducted on a specific problem, by a specific team, using specific methods and specific materials, in specific settings, at a specific time. Intrepid investigators rarely wish to speak only of these frozen fragments and, with few exceptions, attempt to address their findings to a wider set of problems, investigations, measures, settings, and times. They do so in remarkably different ways. Different methodological terms are used to describe its goals – generalisability, external validity, replicability, representativity, universality, transferability, confederation, extrapolation, abstraction, scaling up, etc. As we shall also see, there are an extraordinary number of different interpretations about what is specific to a study and on the nature of the general lessons that it might inspire. Specificity may involve a study's samples, methods, data, concepts, designs, findings, hypotheses, theories, localities, language, and narrative structures. Generality may involve the search for laws, empirical generalisations, universals, comparisons, configurations, ideal types, pivotals, typicals, abstractions, sensitising concepts, middle-range theories, and so on.

Moving on to practicalities, a whole range of research methods are proposed to achieve these ambitions. Two broad strategies do the donkey work – sampling and case selection, but within these we will come upon further variations. Samples may be random, representative, quota, theoretical, stratified, purposive, convenience, snowball, and so on. Case selection, which also tends to be purposive may be small-n or large-N, may employ most-similar and most-different designs, may contribute to theory building, or may even seek implicit generalisation on the basis of a single study.

Already, alarm bells might be ringing. Tracing and illustrating all of these highways and byways is a gargantuan challenge. So how will I proceed? I commence by retreating into conceptual neutrality. At least to begin with, I am going to avoid plumping for any of the above-mentioned usages, since they betoken profound disagreements about how to bestride the one and the many. So let us commence by referring to the big idea scrutinised in Part III as 'generality' and use as a starting point its dictionary definition – 'a statement or principle having general rather than specific validity or force'. This choice provides me with a neat rhyming triplet for the three parts of the book – how to think about causality, objectivity, and now generality.

Hereafter, I limit Part III's ambitions by concentrating closely on the *logic* by which an inquiry or set of inquiries begins to make general claims. What are the guiding principles? As usual, I will fill the ensuing narrative with example after example, drawn from across social science, not to mention brief forays into physical, biological, clinical, and behavioural science. On that journey we will encounter very many of the above-mentioned technical methods. But in each case, rather than aiming for a practical manual, I will seek the model, the rationale, the logic of what it means to generalise.

Part III employs the customary format of the book, once again being organised in 'episodes', each one concluding with a summary of its key lessons.

I commence with a list of the 11 episodes and then a brief summary of where the argument will take us.

Episode 27: Two modes of generality: simple and extensional
Episode 28: Generality in the spoken word: indexicality versus abstraction
Episode 29: Generality in behavioural science: universal subjects or WEIRD samples
Episode 30: Generality as typicality: the simplifications of sampling
Episode 31: Generality in medical science: how representative are clinical trials?
Episode 32: Case studies and generality: transcending the single case?
Episode 33: Incremental steps to generality: within-case comparisons
Episode 34: Middle-range theory and the confederation of explanation
Episode 35: Populating, testing, and scoping middle-range theory
Episode 36: Research synthesis as generalisation
Episode 37: Comparison, complexity, and the specification of ignorance

Episode 27 introduces two opposing perspectives on generality – 'simple' (or part-to-whole) generalisation versus 'extensional' (or one-to-many) generalisations. Both models feature widely in social research. Realist inquiry favours the latter. Episode 28 dismisses the ideographic tradition and its inspiration in linguistic philosophy. Episode 29 rejects the claim found in some branches of psychology that there are universal behavioural laws. Episode 30 examines the basic rationale of simple generalisation, namely, that a random sample of individuals can speak for a population as a whole. Alas, the statistical associations uncovered in the sample survey are acontextual and atemporal, they have no enduring explanatory scope. Episode 31 examines the paradox of generality in clinical science. Clinical trials of a treatment take place in a rigorously controlled setting, whereas the delivery of that treatment in the real world covers widely different conditions. Is there a bridge? Episode 32 begins exploration of whether case study methods have the capacity to provide generalisable findings. Notions like 'naturalistic generalisation' and 'critical case analysis' are found wanting. Episode 33 furthers the exploration of case studies pointing to the importance of within-case explanation. Within-case analysis has potential to become cross-case analysis and thus carries the potential for creating generalisable explanations. Episode 34 celebrates the potential of middle-range theories as the carrier of generalisation in social science. Their role is to explain similarities and differences, both within and between cases. Episode 35 examines the practical development of middle-range models with an extended example on reference group theory. Episode 36 discusses the need to incorporate many existing studies in creating generalisable explanations. The potential of realist synthesis is illustrated. Episode 37 summarises all the steps required to conducting realist, middle-range, multi-method, within-case, and cross-case synthesis. Particular attention is paid to limitations of the middle-range models.

NOTES

1. The Wikiquote attribution is: *Anonymous remark; widely quoted, but with no definite source located as yet, sometimes attributed to Alexandre Dumas Père, Aristotle and Mark Twain* (https://en.wikiquote.org/wiki/Generalization).
2. Wikiquote notes: *This is very often attributed to Mark Twain, but the earliest published source yet located is by Joseph Anthony Wittreich in Feminist Milton (1987) where he writes: 'History may not repeat itself but it does rhyme, and every gloss by a deconstructionist need not be a loss, pushing us further into an abyss of skepticism and indeterminacy'* (https://en.wikiquote.org/wiki/Talk:History#:~:text=This%20is%20very%20often%20attributed,into%20an%20abyss%20of%20skepticism).

Episode 27. Two modes of generality: simple and extensional

As foretold in the Introduction to Part III, the methodological literature on generality is an angry swarm of bees. It may help to simplify matters if I make bold and suggest that there are two broad and markedly different models of generalisation found in the science and social science literature. This episode sketches out that basic distinction. I begin with a specification I first came across in Kaplan (1964), which itself has been adapted and reformulated many times (e.g., Burchett et al., 2011; Polit and Beck, 2010). Kaplan refers to a distinction between simple and extensional generalisation, which I summarise in Figure 27.1.

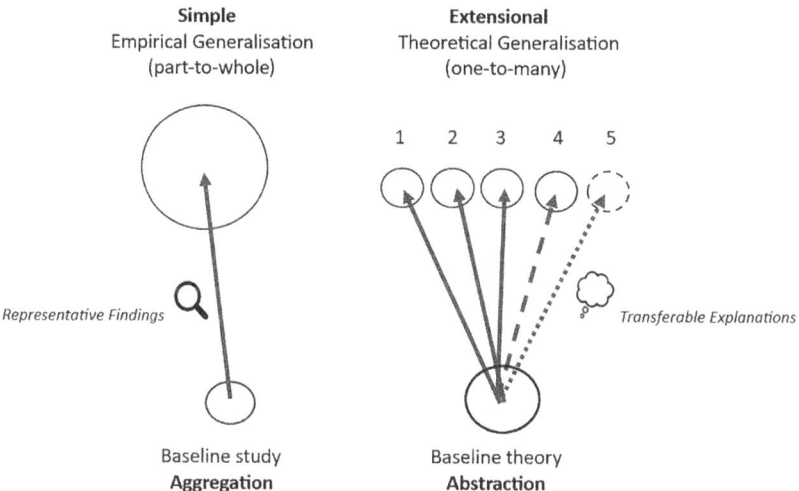

Simple	Extensional
Empirical Generalisation	Theoretical Generalisation
(part-to-whole)	(one-to-many)

Representative Findings

Transferable Explanations

Baseline study	Baseline theory
Aggregation	**Abstraction**

Figure 27.1   Two modes of generalisation: simple and extensional

As can be seen this is a very busy diagram, so let us work through the contrasts point by point. Commencing on the left we have simple generalisation, whose first characteristic, as noted in the text at the top of the figure, is the empirical domain. The core aim is to produce 'empirical generalisations'.

The raw materials of inquiry are thus considered to be regularities, properties, patterns, relationships, associations, or in some versions simply 'facts'. The second characteristic, depicted in the lower circle is that generalisation begins at baseline in a small-scale study, conducted with a limited sample or a specific prototype or a given case or a circumscribed trial or a finite test in which the said empirical regularities are detected. The third characteristic, denoted by the upper circle, is the target of generalisation, namely, the wider population beyond those specific studies. That domain is also composed of regularities, properties, patterns, relationships, associations, or facts. But there is no prior reason to believe that this pattern of observations in this wider universe will occur in the same way as those uncovered in the specific study. This brings us to the fourth characteristic, identified at the bottom of the figure, which represents the basic objective of simple generalisation, namely, one of aggregation. The aim is to scale up or extrapolate the observations in a smaller study to the unobserved wider universe. To generalise is to move from the *part to the whole*.

This brings us to the next feature, the connecting arrow, which signifies the key challenge and the defining feature of simple generalisation. There needs to be some way of justifying the transfer from the specific to the general. There needs to be some way of conducting the smaller study to ensure its findings are representative of the totality. Simple generalisation is thus founded upon and embodied by specific research strategies making this precise claim. The samples, the case studies, the prototypes, the projects, the experimental trials must have a rock-solid claim to be *representative* of the wider population. And this brings us to the final feature, depicted perhaps unimaginatively by the magnifying glass, namely, that when this full package of assumption is assembled, we end with a portfolio of empirical findings that will transfer unproblematically from the part to the whole.

Moving to the right of Figure 27.1, we follow the same sequence as it operates in extensional generalisation. Everything changes. The headline characteristic is that this strategy deals in theories. The baseline raw materials are thus conjectures, hypotheses, hunches, models, mechanisms, and explanations. These are represented in the lower circle as a body of theory that has the potential to explain many different empirical entities, many different cases. The upper circles reveal the goal, the objective, the target for generalisation. Again, the difference is absolute. The target for generalisation is not some given whole or aggregate. The objective is to discover where the theory holds. Empirical studies are conducted to investigate the wider applicability of the core theory. These further inquiries are represented in the diagram as a numbered series of case studies. The contrast is clear. The aim is not to generalise to a larger population of identical entities. The goal is to generalise across distinct cases – does the theory hold in case 1, case 2, case 3, and so on? Extensional generalisation moves from *one to many*.

Here we reach the core ontological assumption. The social world is not simply an aggregate of identical entities, nor is it composed of an infinite number of chaotic, unconnected entities. By 'entities' I simply mean the cases, events, phenomena, experiences, situations, processes, policies, organisations, individuals, societies, and so on, as studied across social science. We connect cases by a process of abstraction – policy A resembles policy B, social uprising C is comparable to social uprisings D and E, community F is like communities G, H, and I, and so on. Research proceeds by identifying a chosen entity for research with many instances. These entities are always internally complex. Examined closely, each case will have similarities and differences, and the basic task for generalisation is to account for those similarities and differences.

Translated into research terms the quest for generalisation turns from the single study to a series of studies, actual and potential, labelled 1 to 5. These are investigations of outwardly related entities postulated to have similarities and differences. The expectation is that the baseline theory will apply to some but not all investigations. In Figure 27.1 the upper circles 1, 2, and 3 represent studies of other situations where the baseline theory is found to have explanatory purchase. Circle 4 represents another situation where the putative explanation is found wanting (represented by the dashed line). It is further assumed that there are many other potential inquiries, which relate abstractly to the emerging theory, but they are yet to be conducted (dashed circle 5). Some of these future inquiries (dotted line) are expected to affirm and develop the working theory, whilst others might have explanatory shortcomings. In short, the act of generalisation moves inquiry from one study to the many. It indicates when an explanation is transferable and when it is not. Extensional generalisation, represented rather meagrely by the thought bubble, is an emergent property and the product of multiple investigations.

My overall plan for Part III is to assess these two models, to sort out their strengths and their weaknesses, to distinguish the myths and the reality. Despite my best efforts, I acknowledge that these initial sketches are hugely compressed, diagrammatically challenging, and unrelievedly abstract. Accordingly, it may assist the reader if I continue this opening episode with a skirmish or two in order to bring to life some key contrasts between the two strategies. The following five vignettes unpeel some points of contention and provide a taste of things to come.

Many readers will have recognised that the supreme exemplification of simple generalisation is none other than the sample survey. Because individuals are selected on a random basis, they are considered to provide a representative sample of the aggregate population. The behaviours, attitudes, correlations, and relationships uncovered in the part will hold for the whole.

Statistically speaking, this is entirely uncontentious. The problem lies in the way that this extrapolation is expressed. The findings are sometimes made to speak for 'the society' rather than an 'aggregate of individuals'. The former is a complex adaptive system. The latter is a snapshot in space and time. There is no reason to confuse the *population* and the *society*, but it happens all the time as research findings are presented and discussed. Much more on this follows in Episode 30.

There are many other research strategies close to the model of simple generalisation. They follow closely the plan of investigating a small part or specific instance or limited quantity in order to reveal what the whole is like. In engineering and product design, building a prototype is a customary first step (McElroy, 2016). The prototype aims to reveal the optimal set of characteristics in the item being developed. Close scrutiny of the model, which may be a material mock-up or a design blueprint, is thought of as a 'proof of concept', an affirmation of the viability of the full-scale product. Although prototypes are essential and ubiquitous, their limitations are widely recognised. The prototype remains an approximation in that it cannot capture every detail of the final product and, most especially, it cannot be trialled in every possible situation in which the product may eventually find use. Differences can be expected to emerge in the full picture and always require explanation.

A similar logic is applied with the idea of pilot projects used widely in public policy to assess the viability of new interventions or organisational reforms (Checkland et al., 2023). Pilot projects enable organisations to trial new programmes and services without committing to them too quickly. They are seen as miniature versions of real-world applications, enabling policy makers to iron out kinks in their eventual delivery. In this case the limitations of that logic are considerable, and all too well known. Pilot programmes suffer what is known as the 'showcasing effect'. The enthusiasm and novelty surrounding an intervention in its first throws are unlikely to continue as it is absorbed into the everyday routine of service provision. More precariously, intervention effectiveness is now widely understood as being particularly sensitive to context. This assumption has a slogan, namely – 'What works in Wigan on a wet Wednesday will not necessarily work in Thurso on a thunderous Thursday.' It is precisely this inevitability that has led to a switch to extensional thinking. The 'same' intervention will vary in both implementation and effectiveness as it is applied across space and over time. Extensional theory is needed to explain why. The simple lesson of the first three vignettes is that simple generalisation is not so simple and that the more complex the 'whole', the harder it is to represent it in the study of a single 'part'.

The next vignette turns to generality in physics, often characterised as the search for physical constants and the universal laws of nature. Does this involve usage of the logic of simple generalisation? For instance, if one wanted to measure the Earth's gravitational acceleration one could utilise a gravimeter (Herring, 2010) across the globe, seek a random sample of readings and no doubt find a tight cluster of results around a mean. But this bears no correspondence to how gravitational attraction is actually researched. The gravimeter actually turns up with slightly different findings, often rather minute, and these differences constitute the real scientific puzzle. Investigation turns to the extensional. Theories gain wider traction by accounting for differences within phenomena and we rely on theory to explain why the gravitational 'constant' will be different from the poles to the equators, from Mount Everest to the Dead Sea, on Earth and Mars, and so on. There are always exceptions and anomalies, and generalisation is a matter of explaining them. In the case of the varying gravitational attraction on Earth, it is the differences in centrifugal force between the equator and the poles and the non-spherical 'bulge' of the Earth that are the crucial explanatory mechanisms (Gravity of Earth, 2023). Exceptions are the rule. Even in the study of the fundamental forces of nature, generality is the craft of coping with difference.

My final vignette begins to explore the role of abstraction in extensional generality. There is a maelstrom of conceptual abstraction in social science. Many of us will have started with Durkheim (anomie, collective consciousness, social solidarity, etc.), Weber (bureaucracy, legitimacy, authority, etc.), and Marx (capitalism, materialism, alienation, etc.). Thousands of neologisms have followed. Concepts spark the sociological imagination but in themselves cannot explain similarities and difference across a range of phenomena. For that one needs abstraction of a different kind, at the level of the explanatory model or mechanism. There are familiar examples in other sciences. Darwin's evolutionary theory begins with an abstract mechanism – natural selection. This posits that species develop with favourable biological variations being preserved and unfavourable ones becoming extinct. The empirical extensions are legion across hundreds of different species – finches, earthworms, barnacles, climbing plants, and great apes – but not humans (Ayala, 2009)! The kinetic theory of gases is based on an abstract model that depicts a gas as a large number of colliding microscopic particles in constant rapid motion. It was used by Maxwell (1867) to explain the relationship between the volume, pressure, and temperature of a gas in an enclosed container. This underlying mechanism becomes the basis of the whole discipline of thermodynamics, extending to the explanation of other properties such as viscosity, thermal conductivity, and diffusion. In the remaining episodes I go in search of such abstract explanatory mechanisms in social science.

The reader will not have failed to notice a marked preference for the benefits of extensional generalisation across the five thumbnail sketches. This is no accident, no subterfuge. Realists think about generality as the business of extending and testing the reach of substantive theories.

KEY LESSONS

Episode 27 starts with first principles and identifies two contrasting models of generality, the simple and the extensional. Simple generalisation samples a part in the expectation that the regularities uncovered will apply to the whole. Extensional generalisation builds a theory that will account for the similarities and differences across a large number of cases. The former is aggregative, the latter is abstractive. At this stage, only a meagre set of examples and some heavy hints are dropped confirming that realists think about generality according to the extensional model. The remaining episodes unpick that thesis.

Episode 28. Generality in the spoken word: indexicality versus abstraction

This episode examines the appeal of the ideographic – the argument that the social disciplines cannot penetrate beyond the specific and the local. My aim, of course, is to put a wretched idea out of its misery. We shall not hear of it again in future episodes, but by understanding and reversing its fundamental flaws, it is possible to make some headway in understanding generality. According to ideographic thinking, the only way to understand people's action and reasoning is to study them in their own local contexts. Human thought is considered to be immediate and spontaneous. Sensemaking is specific to each encounter and thus cannot be explained under more general propositions. These precepts were uttered in their most radical form in ideas emanating from the philosophy of language (Wittgenstein, 1953) and from ethnomethodology (Garfinkle, 1967). Wittgenstein (1958) was contemptuous of philosophy's 'craving for generality', arguing that it is 'purely descriptive'. Ethnomethodology made a significant entry into the literature in the 1960s and 1970s promising a 'revolution in sociology' (Benson, 1974; Goldthorpe, 1973). It offered a new research programme that studied everyday reasoning, routine practices, tacit knowledge, folk methods, and so on. As previously, no attempt is made to explore the entire repertoire here; the aim is to decipher what was claimed about generalisation and to reveal basic errors in those pronouncements.

The spotlight on specificity in this episode originates in insights about the everyday usage of language. Everyday talk is something of a marvel; we make sense of each other spontaneously and effortlessly. This, despite the fact that many of the terms we use have potentially numerous, ambiguous meanings. Consider this injunction, 'Stay in your crease.' It was issued recently to the UK prime minister, Rishi Sunak, by his Australian counterpart, Anthony Albanese. What on earth does it mean? The rebuke followed an escalating row over the dismissal of a cricketer in England's defeat in the second Ashes test. An English batsman, Johnny Bairstow, left his crease innocently thinking that the ball was dead leaving him open to being stumped by the Australian wicket-keeper Alex Carey. Diplomatic furore ensued, Sunak chipping in considering that the ploy infringed the 'spirit of cricket'. Albanese responds, deliberately echoing the said phrase to indicate that Sunak should stick to politics. As can be seen, much, much more is understood than is actually said. The tiny phrase captures a lengthy public spat. Alas, this encounter with ambiguity also applies to my explanation. If the reader happens to know their cricket all is intelligible, especially the clever insult. If you have never encountered the sport, then I am afraid I have left you completely mystified by terms such as 'crease', 'stumped', 'wicketkeeper', and 'dead'. And what has any of this to do with 'Ashes'?

This little whimsy is merely an exotic example of the perfectly familiar. The recipient of any utterance always understands much more than is actually spoken. This process of filling in additional meaning became known in ethnomethodology as the 'etc principle' (Garfinkle, 1967). It is a remarkable feature of ordinary language. It applies to everything that is said. We automatically fill the gaps. We are rescued from any potential ambiguity by linguistic resources that are instantly adapted to the occasion and the context.

In the study of language, the proposed referent of an utterance is known as the 'index' and expressions that have potentially ambiguous usages are termed 'indexical'. This terminology then takes us to the generic concept of 'indexicality', namely, the idea that the significance of any linguistic expression is always contingent on the circumstances of its use. With this concept a root and branch critique of social science is proposed. Especially censured is sociology's ambition to provide explanations that are transferable across time and space. The origins of the perceived contradiction lay in treating discourse about human actions as a 'resource' for inquiry rather than its 'topic' (Sacks, 1963). His argument proceeds as follows. Sociological reasoning, regardless of how it is packaged and presented, is conducted in ordinary language. It is thus treated as an unproblematic resource for inquiry rather than the puzzling topic. There is a routine use of common-sense terms throughout social inquiry, without acknowledgement that these terms are indexical. The upshot, according to radical ethnomethodology, is that social science thus endlessly reproduces ambiguity in what it purports to explain.

How and where does this unintentional, invisible ambiguity creep in? Read any document in social science (including this one) and it is written in ordinary language. Admittedly, there are many neologisms and invented terms. And, perversely, obscurity often seems to be valued. But by and large, we write using words and phrases that are part of the common tongue. Consider, by contrast, the bulk of physical and natural science. If a botanist chooses to name the parts of a flower the 'peduncle', the 'receptacle', and the 'sepal', then that flower is unlikely to differ. If clinicians name a cancer 'acute lymphoblastic leukaemia', then the affected 'white blood cells' are unlikely to protest. Accordingly, for the ethnomethodologist, formal scientific terminology escapes the problem of indexicality. Explanations build upon a common core of uncontested concepts.

By contrast, the argument continues, social science as a matter of routine pulls in terminology that one finds in everyday usage. Moreover, since those everyday users are also the very subject of inquiry, there is a genuine prospect of perpetual misunderstanding on meaning. One can find many examples in routine social inquiry, closely inspected in Cicourel (1964). Consider a standard interview question using a rating scale to measure the subject's opinion on, say, government immigration policy. The tick boxes often use vague, ordinary language terms like 'agree' and 'strongly agree', which cannot have a set meaning and are therefore indexical. What is more, 'government immigration policy', being endlessly faceted, will mean quite different things to different people, not to mention being an utter mystery to many people whose opinions emanate solely from the small world encased in their small screens. Nevertheless, as ethnomethodology teaches us, people are able to deal with the shadowy question by applying the 'etc principle'. Research subjects will generally stump up with an answer, regardless of whether it is fired by feeling, fervour, politeness, indifference, or complete mystification. The researcher may go on to aggregate the answers to produce a measure of 'public opinion' – but that measure is based on fleeting, shifting sands. The researcher imposes spurious order onto unavoidable ambiguity.

Further examples of terminological disarray can be found in the standard repertoire of social science concepts like class, gender, race, and so on. Let us take 'social class' as a prime example. It is the venerable subject of analysis for sociology, political science, and history, yet every student learns that there is no broad consensus on its meaning, some read that it is an 'essentially contested concept' (Gallie, 1955). I will not attempt a detailed trawl through the glossary, simply mentioning without references the classic antagonism between Marxist and Weberian perspectives, the debate on whether class takes its meaning in societal powers or individual agency, the analysis of whether class society is undermined or anchored by social mobility, measurement disputes on the number and composition of class positions, the debate on whether class positions are maintained through economic, cultural, knowledge or affective advantage, the debate on the decline of class conflict, the disagreement on whether other social cleavages have become more prominent, returning finally to the conundrum of what is a classless society.

We arrive at the ethnomethodologist's charter:

i. Terminology in science is agreed and factual. It is not indexical. Conceptual exactitude permits the discovery of precise empirical findings. Inquiries can be replicated with the same operational precision providing universal laws that apply throughout the physical world.

ii. Terminology in social science, being drawn from ordinary language, is profoundly indexical and contested. People communicate effortlessly, but sensemaking is immediate and local. Since conceptual closure is impossible, there can be no cross-situational, cross-societal generalisations.

This manifesto was immensely significant in sociology – for a short period. But both propositions are entirely mistaken. No account of the history of science would recognise the former. Hopefully, I have said enough about error, anomalies, disagreements in science, and the constant revision and repair of concepts to dispel any notion of conceptual fixity. Garfinkle and followers lapse into an antiquated, empiricist view of science's certitude, namely, that evidence is beyond dispute, based on agreed operational definitions, and gleaned directly in real-world observations. This parody allows them to draw a sharp contrast with social science where none of these preconditions apply.

But neither do they apply in physical science. Realism, as we have seen in Episode 21, turns this crude empiricism on its head. Theory furnishes the basic language of science. Physical properties are measured in dozens of different ways all connected by networks of theories. Each theory is tested using evidence based on pre-existing theories. Theories gain wider traction by accounting for a growing range of phenomena. There are always exceptions and anomalies to any purported law. Explanatory scope is widened by the process of error elimination and theory adjudication. The whole process is sustained by dispute and competition. In short, one might say at any given point that conceptual contestation is the norm. It provides the challenge. Scientists would never use the term, but this is indexicality incarnate. The real process is that conceptual contestation gives way gradually to conceptual revision and clarification. Theory adaptation is the lifeblood. Conceptual fixity is a myth.

Relieved of this burden the science of the social lives on. I have argued in Episodes 22 to 25 that the above suite of explanatory processes can, with some modification and a dose of humility, be transferred across to social science. The vocabulary of social research, contra Cicourel, is not plucked directly from ordinary language. Theory furnishes the basic language of social science. Social research does not trade on facts, nor on opinion, but on evidence, whose conceptual assumptions are carefully 'excavated'. Social science does indeed throw up rival conceptual frameworks but testing them is not a matter for local happenstance or stubborn partisanship but depends on a process of 'theory adjudication'. Theories are not tested using whatever operationalisation is handy and immediate, but by examining multiple 'networks of propositions'. Social scientists strive for 'organised scepticism', which seeks to eliminate the casual construction of evidence marooned in folk wisdom and native wit.

In short, it transpires that social science terminology is not incarcerated in everyday language. The quest for causality and objectivity is not undermined by the threat of indexicality. Now let us return to the construction of a specific model for generality in social science research. I have already noted that an important ingredient lies in the idea of 'abstraction'. There is a sweet paradox in this particular saviour of social science, for much of what we know about abstraction comes from linguistics. In the remainder of this episode, I want to show that conceptual abstraction provides a starting point (but only a starting point!) on the pathway to generality in social science. Think of sociological concepts like bureaucracy, anomie, status, power, protest. Think of economic concepts like supply, demand, scarcity, surplus value. Think of policy concepts like incentivisation, legislation, prohibition, devolution. Each of them denotes a concept with many instances and many common properties. There is a distinct glimmer of generality every time these notions are used.

As noted, abstraction is itself a topic of study in linguistics. What might be learnt? Abstraction pervades every corner of ordinary language (Lupyan and Winter, 2018). A first glimpse of its potential for generalisation is found in terms that refer to classes of objects. Let me burst into traditional song:

Oh, the oak and the ash and the bonnie ivy tree,
They flourish at home in my own country.

The everyday concept 'tree' immediately connects three examples and would seem to be a passport to a thousand further examples. But is this generalisation? The answer, of course, is 'no', because ordinary language does not place any boundaries on what a tree might be. It is no basis for species classification in biology and botany. Accordingly, the creation of taxonomies in these disciplines begins with theory, a theory selecting the crucial attributes that should be used to classify the species types and subtypes (Ritchie, 2022). Again, there are many, many different organising principles. The Wikipedia entry (Taxonomy (biology), 2023) distinguishes classifications based on morphology, physiology, molecular structures, behavioural differences, ecological characteristics, geographical location, each having numerous subdivisions. Padial and De la Riva (2021) provide an engaging review of historical and contemporary shifts in the preferences for different systems. Classification systems are also used with a similar frequency throughout social science (Bowker and Star, 2000). The lesson is clear. Ordinary language will furnish us with dozens and dozens of types and subtypes of peoples, places, processes, policies, populations, and performances. Avoid the temptation of importing them directly into research. Social classifications must have a basis in theory. That theory should be extensional, explaining the reasons for similarities and differences from case to case.

Another remarkable feature of ordinary language is that it appears to furnish us with enduring explanations of daily life. Common sense captures all.

Proverbs provide a fine example here and I leave it to Christensen (n.d.) to supply the idea and its limitation.

> Proverbs are beautiful and complex things. They appear, on the surface, to be time-tested nuggets of wisdom which have been passed down through the ages. When a proverb is offered as an explanation, heads nod, and it is accepted without further discussion. But what doesn't cross anyone's mind is that if the exact opposite event had occurred, an opposite proverb would be offered up, heads would nod, and it would be accepted without further discussion.

Christensen goes on to supply a list of contradictory proverbs, two of which are sufficient to convey the superficiality of this form of abstraction:

- Is it wise to 'look before you leap' or is it the case that 'he who hesitates is lost'?
- Does 'absence makes the heart grow fonder' or is 'out of sight, out of mind' the norm?

The customary lesson applies: generalisation in social science must avoid loose, open-ended abstraction, otherwise explanations stumble off haphazardly and may eventually lapse into proverbial contradictions. Generalisations must specify clear boundary conditions stating when an explanation applies and when it does not.

Alas, sociology has long feted the power of these simple forms of conceptual abstraction. The most famous celebrant is Blumer in a 1954 paper, which introduced the idea of 'sensitizing concepts'. He made the contrast with 'definitive concepts' or what are sometimes called operational definitions. The latter are used routinely in empirical research – for example, the concept 'educational attainment' is captured by the operational measure 'years of schooling'; 'extreme poverty' is measured as living on 'less than US$1.90 per day'; 'crime rates' are measures using official 'police incidence' records, and so on.

By contrast, Blumer hails the power of sensitising concepts.

> A sensitizing concept lacks such specification of attributes or benchmarks and consequently it does not enable the user to move directly to the instance and its relevant content. Instead, it gives the user a general sense of reference and guidance in approaching empirical instances. Whereas definitive concepts provide prescriptions of what to see, sensitizing concepts merely suggest directions along which to look.

Here lies an embryonic claim for generality. Sensitising concepts 'rest on a general sense of what is relevant', when 'picking one's way in an unknown terrain ... the concept sensitizes one to the task, providing clues and suggestions' (Blumer, 1954).

What are we to make of this claim? Blumer indicates that there are hundreds of sensitising concepts – 'like culture, institutions, social structure, mores and personality'. And to be sure, they do encourage transferable thinking, moving effortlessly from instance to instance. We might, for example, begin to use the concept of 'mores' to describe the customs and conventions of any group from princes to paupers, from seafarers to landlubbers, from toddlers to geriatrics, from dwellers in the Amazonian forests to those in concrete jungles ... and so on. But so what! Just as in everyday, common-sense talk, abstract notions can be used endlessly to index a thousand local customs and conventions. Explanatory progress is a mirage as the sensitising concept advances into infinity. What we really need to learn about mores is *why* those customs and conventions are different from location A to location B, from time C to time D, and so on. Conceptual abstraction has the wondrous ability to traverse the social world but *by itself* it explains nothing. To achieve generality, abstraction needs to be properly harnessed to explanation rather than description. We await this connection in forthcoming episodes.

KEY LESSONS

Episode 28 investigates the heavily disputed role of everyday language in the quest to establish generalisations in social science. A critical proposition, derived from ethnomethodology, argues that social explanation rests on ambiguous, polysemous ordinary language, whereas scientific propositions are rooted in factual, formal terminology. This critique is summarily dismissed – there is no fixed, empirical bedrock to concepts used in either physical science or social science. Basic concepts are constantly developed and adapted in a continual, ever-enlarging stream of theory testing. There is, paradoxically, a positive case to be made claiming that ordinary language provides a springboard to generalisation. Everyday talk is deeply ambiguous, but it is also vividly abstractive. Abstract, sensitising concepts provide the initial raw material enabling the borrowing of themes to describe one social situation and another and then another. But conceptual abstraction is merely a stumbling, haphazard first step in social inquiry. Sensitising concepts provide generalisable explanations only if harnessed to programmes of theory testing.

Episode 29. Generality in behavioural science: universal subjects or WEIRD samples

There is much usage in lay and in some professional circles of the idea of the 'laws of science' or the 'laws of nature'. These expressions capture the enduring appeal of scientific certainty – laws are all powerful, deemed to apply throughout the universe. They are the epitome of generality. This imagery has met with scant support in the philosophy of science. Recall, already cited, Scriven's crushing 1961 essay, 'The key property of physical laws: inaccuracy'. Or consider Cartwright's demolition exercise in *How the Laws of Physics Lie* (1983). The idea of universal truths in methodological circles has largely given way to the idea of conditional truths.

But not everywhere. To follow the quest for universality, I take the book's one and only step into behavioural science. As a rough and ready distinction, one might say that social science takes it for granted that people's reasoning and attitudes are conditional. They change under the influence of different social structures, cultures, customs, and norms. Behavioural science, by contrast, stays within the heads of its subjects seeking to understand uniformity in cognitive process such as visual perception, spatial reasoning, decision making, moral judgement, and so on. This has proved a difficult boundary to maintain but one can say that in its earlier incarnations, behavioural science regarded these cognitive processes as human traits, as universal ways of thinking.

This imagery has led to a splendidly controversial strategy for the selection of subjects for inquiry. The ensuing dispute has much to say about how we might begin to construe the generality of research findings. Because of the supposed universality of cognitive processes, much experimental social psychology tended to be rather relaxed about its choice of research subjects. If there is little variation in the cognitive functioning of the human species, it seems sensible and parsimonious to use what are often termed 'convenience samples'.

The most convenient of these convenience samples make use of students (lured at a small price) from the investigator's own university. It is a strategy that has aroused the ire of many social psychologists. McNemar initiated the debate in 1946, arguing that 'the existing science of human behavior is largely the science of the behavior of sophomores ... [with] a waste of journal space concerning whether the findings hold for mankind in general'. The debate was still running hot in a paper by Stroebe et al. (2018) entitled 'Do our psychological laws apply only to college students?' The most famous contribution, however, comes in an acronym first used in a paper by Henrich et al. (2010a), who characterise the typical subjects of behavioural research as 'the WEIRDest people in the world'. By this, the authors claim that, quite routinely, samples drawn only from Western, Educated, Industrialized, Rich, and Democratic populations have been asked to stand as representative of the human species.

This episode provides a taste of these investigations, often labelled 'laboratory experiments'. Note, only in passing alas, that these are not remotely the same as experiments in the physical sciences or the clinical laboratory, whose designated purpose is to investigate a particular causal connection by isolating it from all other extraneous forces. In the 'psych lab', experiments consist of confronting subjects with artificial situations and simulated tasks that bring to the fore their perceptual and cognitive resources. Since these facilities are assumed to be fixed in the human brain they are then assumed to hold for mankind in general. This is a hugely ambitious conjecture and readers will have noted that it relies on the logic of simple generalisation (recall Figure 27.1). It relies on aggregation, on part-to-whole generalisation, and on claims of representativity. To be sure, it is a preposterously ambitious version of simple generalisation – but is worthy of closer inspection for that very reason.

The subject is invited to play a role in a synthetic, miniature world created by the researcher, which is supposed to reveal how the human brain functions. Two examples will introduce the drill. The basic structures of human visual perception have been investigated in a series of 'illusions', the most famous of which is the Muller-Lyer diagram (Figure 29.1). The upper and lower lines are exactly the same length, but subjects routinely perceive that the latter is longer than the former. An extension of the experiment measures the strength of the illusion in a metric called 'the point of subjective equality' (PSE). In this version the researcher manipulates the length of the lines and asks subjects to say at which points the lines become equal – to which task most respondents perceive parity when the rightward line is in fact a fifth longer than its partner. Question – are these findings indicative of some basic law of human perception?

For a second example, I call on perhaps the best-known behavioural simulation – Milgram's (1974) experiment on obedience to authority. It is often described as 'shocking', with the pun intended. As with other experiments in the psych lab it also uses deception, researching one aspect of behaviour whilst fooling the subjects into believing that another was under investigation. I omit

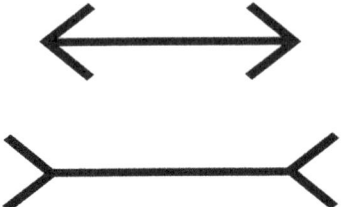

Figure 29.1   The Muller-Lyer illusion

the fiery debate on research ethics that followed, which pursued Milgram for the rest of his career. Participants took part in what they thought was an experiment to improve teaching and learning. How might punishment, delivered in the form of electric shocks, improve learning? Paid volunteers assumed they were participating in pairs, designated 'teacher' and 'learner'. Allocation was bogusly random (using fake lots) so that the learner was always a confederate of the experimenter.

The partners were located in separate rooms, connected only by a microphone. The teacher read aloud a series of word chains, which the learner was instructed to memorise. A test of recall followed. If the 'learner' erred, the 'teacher' was instructed to deliver an electric shock as punishment. The shocks were entirely fake, but the teacher was able to hear the supposed reaction of the learner as each error occurred. According to a prearranged script, successive errors were met with 15-volt increments. At '75 volts', the learner's lines called for a sharp 'ouch'. From '150 volts' to '330 volts', he was required to protest with increasing intensity. Complaints continued until at '330 volts' he fell silent and refused to participate. If the teacher faltered, the experimenter insisted that 'the experiment requires that you continue, the shocks may be painful, but they cause no permanent damage'. The findings are indeed shocking, with 65 per cent of the teachers continuing to obey instructions right up to the '450-volt' level. Question – this time posed by Greenwood (2018) – did Milgram's experiment demonstrate that humans have a universal propensity to destructive obedience or that they are merely products of their cultural moment?

What lessons might be drawn from the two studies on the capacity to generalise from these laboratory demonstrations? Let us begin with the Muller-Lyer illusion and some further insight into WEIRD subjects. Figure 29.2 reproduces Henrich et al.'s (2010a) reproduction of results from Segall et al.'s (1963) cross-cultural replication of the PSE experiment. Note American undergraduates (Evanston) at one end of the distribution, preceded by a White South African sample. These groups adhere to the classic perception noted above that the upper line in Figure 29.1 is a fifth longer than the lower line. At the other end of the spectrum, a tribe of San foragers (Kalahari) perceived no difference between the lines. It could not even be said to be an illusion from their perspective. Note in all instances significant differences between adults and children. It may be concluded that even something as basic as visual perception shows substantial differences across populations. Evidence from American students or WEIRDs more broadly is no basis for any claim about universal cognitive propensities of the human species.

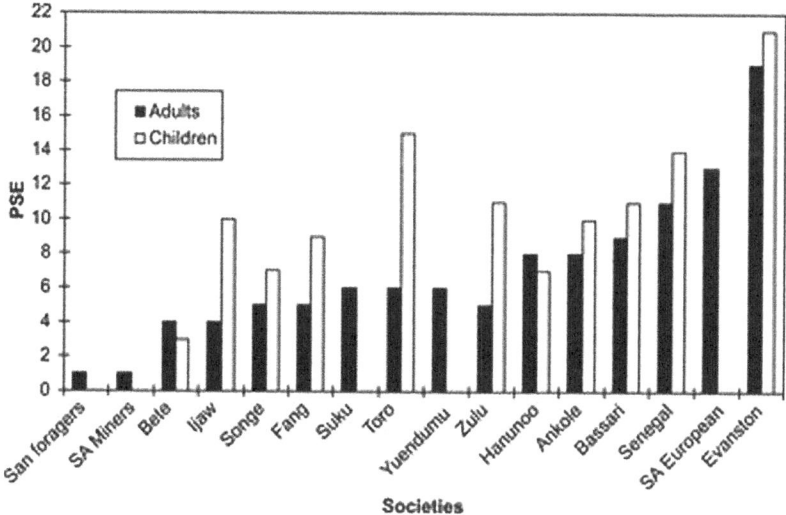

Figure 29.2   *Contrasting cross-national interpretations of the Muller-Lyer illusion*

Moving to the second example, bitter arguments about generalisability of the Milgram findings have raged on and on, beyond summary here. Milgram himself seemed confident that he had uncovered a commonplace – 'Ordinary people, simply doing their jobs, and without any particular hostility on their part, can become agents in a terribly destructive process … asked to carry out actions incompatible with fundamental standards of morality, relatively few people have the resources needed to resist authority' (quoted in Blass, 2004).

Is there any warrant in the jump from the specificity of the experiment to the generality of this conclusion? In this case, replication in other contexts has been limited – following an American Psychological Association ban on potentially harmful experiments. So let us take an alternative route to an answer. Milgram thinks that high levels of obedience follow straightforwardly from a dutiful human tendency to obey those in authority. Are there rival explanations for the high levels of conformity observed in this particular psych lab in 1961? The now committed realist reader should be shouting 'yes!' at this point, recalling Stinchcombe's dictum in Episode 2. Let me rehearse a brief selection in Box 29.1, acknowledging that further alternatives abound in the literature.

BOX 29.1 ALTERNATIVE EXPLANATIONS FOR COMPLIANCE IN MILGRAM'S EXPERIMENT

1. Does the authority of an elite university make for compliance? The study was clearly sponsored by prestigious, historic Yale University and conducted by actors presenting as high-status, white-coated, truth-seeking scientists.
2. Did the minutely scripted instructions propel high levels of compliance – 'The shocks cause no permanent damage', 'You have no other choice – you must go on'?
3. Did the subjects believe the responses were real – deception remember was at the base of the experiment? Did compliance follow from what some subjects perceived as play acting?
4. Did compliance follow from recruitment bias in using only paid subjects – 65 per cent obeyed to the end, 35 per cent refused? Might these percentages vary if the sample had been drawn voluntarily?
5. Did compliance follow from gender bias in recruitment? Only 40 out of 780 research subjects were women.
6. Did compliance follow from the unique personal demands of their task? Subjects were isolated and confronted with an immediate decision. People make real decisions over time with the support of others.
7. Might compliance by explained by factors other than obedience – attachment to a higher goal (scientific inquiry) or another motive (shame of being regarded as a failed research subject)?

To business. What do these two examples teach us about generality? The principal lesson is that these brief encounters simply do not excavate to the level of universal human traits. The findings do not and cannot apply to the whole of humanity. Even basic visual perception is influenced and is changed according to the culture and experiences of the perceiver. The same goes for complex acts of obedience – instructions are followed, declined, ignored, avoided, undermined, and forgotten under the influence of a forest of competing social forces.

So much would now be accepted – even by the die-hard behaviourist. But there remains, of course, an ongoing commitment to use psych lab methodology to reveal general patterns in people's reasoning. How might this be achieved and what do these patterns look like? Several solutions have been put forward (assessed masterfully in Stroebe et al., 2018). The first is to conduct the experimental encounters on truly representative samples. The problem here is that the universal sample – all of humanity – is a pipedream. It would need to draw participants from every walk of life in the whole world – past, present, and future. A second option proposed by Henrich et al. (2010b) is a somewhat more practical alternative – to move from convenience samples such as students to many more inconvenient samples like bus terminals, shopping centres, town squares, park benches, etc. This is exactly what Segall et al. (1963) undertook in producing the data in Figure 29.2. But even this expansion is a pin prick, a few small-scale societies in Africa. Imagine the endless histograms that would result had he been able to follow the perceptual preferences of the young and old in the far and wide.

We reach an important conclusion. Behavioural generalisation cannot be achieved by compiling more and more data from more and more people in more and more locations. To assume so is to commit the inductivist fallacy, first identified by Hume, namely, that patterns observed in a finite set of observations can never said to apply universally. The solution to the conundrum, as stressed in every episode of this book, is to rely on theory to do the job. Rather than seeking invariance, we push to more general explanations by developing theories that explain variation. In short, behavioural science needs to abandon simple generalisation and hasten to a model of extensional generalisation.

The essence of this solution can be found in a miniature example already explored in this episode. If we return again to Figure 29.2, moving from right to left one can see that the perceptual illusion bites heavily in the first three or four cases, less so in the middle section, and not at all in the final two instances. We can thus begin to name cases where the illusion holds and where it does not. We can start to place social and cultural boundaries on the perceptual regularities. But this leaves us only halfway to a solution for, to repeat, such a catalogue is infinite, never completable. Thus, what is needed is a theory of *why* some collectives are drawn into the illusion and why some are not. Such a theory exists. Henrich et al. (2010b) mention the hypothesis of 'carpentered corners' which may help explain variation. WEIRDs live in constructed environments, little boxes – surrounded by straight lines, right angles, and square corners. This may produce visual habits which may transfer across to the Muller-Lyer illusion. They may indeed – but I duck commentary of the carpentered cornered conjecture here. The methodological point is clear and foreshadowed in the notion of extensional generality – seek variation and develop theories to explain variation – keep going, establishing wider and wider patterns.

KEY LESSONS

Important lessons accrue in Episode 29, mostly negative. It is a mistake to confuse generality with universality. Pioneering behavioural scientists en-visioned an experimental study of universal forms of human cognition – for example, perceptual processes occur between the eye and the brain and so any human head could be used to decipher cognitive laws. Such hopes were dashed on witnessing the surreptitious entry of cultural influences in all lab-oratory findings. Using representative samples of subjects was then posited as an alternative requisite in uncovering behavioural laws – an impossible mission because thinking is modified in endless situations, past and present, with more to come. Early assumptions about invariance and universality are dropped in more recent work, which supposes that explaining behavioural difference is the key to producing generalisable explanations and that devel-oping theory is the starting point in that quest.

Episode 30. Generality as typicality: the simplifications of sampling

This episode examines an influential, perhaps the most influential, understanding of generality in social science. It is the supreme exemplification of simple generalisation, as discussed in Episode 27. I consider it another misadventure – an approach to generalisation that seems logical and practically feasible but has massively limited utility. Research in the social survey tradition has a singular notion of the idea of generalisation. A randomised survey study will utilise many methods of data collection and analysis but only one is considered important for providing the inquiry with wider purchase. In this tradition, the shift from the specific to the general is regarded as a matter for sampling. A well-drawn sample of individuals can speak for a population as a whole. The sample is, so to speak, a miniature society.

The goal is to locate a 'typical' or 'representative' sample of a wider population and the means to that end is known as 'probability sampling' or 'random sampling'. I depict the strategy in Figure 30.1, which readers will see at once is an elaboration of the simple generalisation model in Figure 27.1. The basic agenda remains the same – the model seeks 'empirical generalisation', enabling the transfer of findings from the part to the whole. These objectives rest on a core strategy depicted in more detail to the left of the present figure, namely, random selection – the key principle being that by a random process every potential respondent in the total population has an equal chance of being selected for the smaller sample (downward dashed pathway). This manoeuvre then protects the converse, namely, that the findings from the sample can be said to be a perfect reproduction of those in the entire population (upward dashed pathway).

In attitudinal surveys, for instance, rigorous randomisation is said to ensure that the opinion profile from a small sample will embody the views of the whole population from which it is drawn. Let us push into practicalities by examining the prototypical example of election polling and pose the classic question – will the stated voting preferences of a chosen sample reflect accurately the views as revealed in the ballot box? The crucial technical issue is to ensure that the random sample is truly 'representative' of the electorate. It transpires that this is a perilous objective.

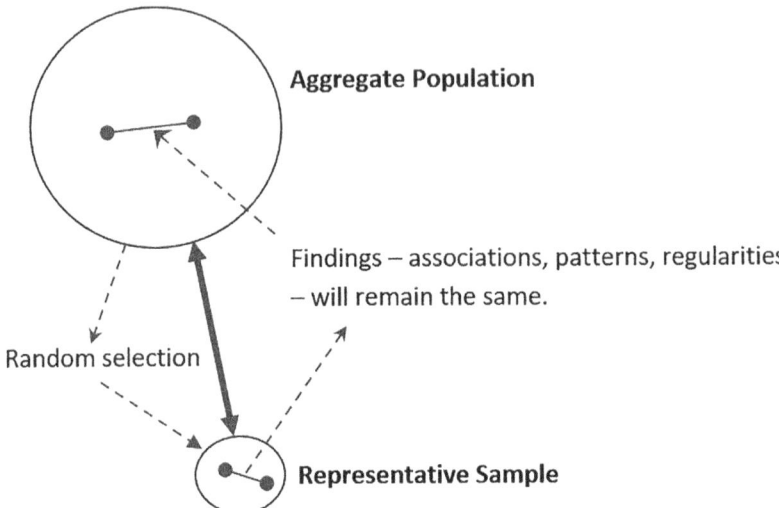

Figure 30.1   *Statistical generalisation: extrapolating from a sample to the*
                population

A full account of those pitfalls can be found in NatCen (2015), abbreviated here as follows. Firstly, there is a matter of the sampling frame, usually a list of households and their postcodes. From this it seems a straightforward matter to select a random and, hopefully, a representative sample. But who is contacted under this frame? Voting requires pre-registration and not everyone in every household will have registered. Already absent from the initial frame, moreover, are those without permanent abodes. The sampling frame becomes further strained when separate rules on eligibility are in place, for instance, for prisoners, for those in the armed forces, and for citizens living abroad. Then there is the matter of contact. Traditional person-to-person interviewing on voting preference is massively time consuming with many 'no-shows' lost to the sample. A method of selecting and locating random 'replacements' has to be established. Nowadays, samples are more likely to be traced over the phone and, increasingly, via the internet. Selection bias becomes a problem here – both methods exclude non-owners/non-users. Further statistical estimates are put in place to compensate for their loss. The so-called 'research relationship' is also important in uncovering accurate voting intentions. Modern electronic questionnaires and interviews compete by the moment alongside masses of other social media traffic and tend to over-recruit the e-chatters and the politically sensitised. Then there is a matter of 'non-response', including the undecided and those not willing to participate in the poll. Is there a reluctance to declare preferences or even to deceive? And do the willing, the reticent, and the cunning tend to favour particular parties? Then there is the tricky matter of posing the same question on preference to voters who will face different ballot papers from constituency to constituency. Should the poll leave residents to name their own preferences, and will this strategy handle the delicate preferences of tactical votes, extremist supporters, monster-raving loonies, and so on? And finally, consider turnout on the day, which is often miserable, especially if the weather is miserable. Will the polled opinion be translated in the journey to the ballot box?

It transpires that the apparently simple goal of statistical representation is often heroically complex in practice. The empirical task described above is as simple and singular as it gets in social research – namely, to provide a frequency profile in respect of one variable – voting preference. Even here we know that error is inescapable. However scrupulous, there will always be some difference between poll, exit poll, and vote. Predictions are always muted and always protected with confidence estimates.

Immediate lessons accrue. The first is that achieving randomisation is not merely a statistical exercise. If the reader looks back at the 'pitfalls' paragraph above, one sees that the challenges to random selection are understood thanks to dozens of miniature theories about the mechanics of voting, about institutional rules, about the research relationship, and about how political opinions are actually expressed. Sampling is supported; sampling is only possible on the basis of prior *excavations* of the social and behavioural processes involved. Here's a delicious paradox – statistical precision depends on theoretical insight.

The other reason to be wary of using opinion sampling as a prototype for social research is to consider its singular aim. Social surveys, of course, usually are tasked with ambitions which reach far beyond the single variable and seek patterns, associations, and regularities between many variables. Sticking with the example of voting, a sample survey could be tasked with describing voting patterns by region, class, gender, urbanisation, age, ethnicity, etc. The same claim is asserted – the findings, the regularities and associations discovered in a sample of individuals should also apply across the wider population. Let us delve into the challenges at the next level of complexity, namely, bivariate analysis. How, for instance, might one conduct a sample survey to investigate the relationship between ethnicity and voting preference in the UK?

Technical problems multiply. Let us begin with challenges of classifying ethnic background. Early empirical studies satisfied themselves with a comparison between those with 'White' backgrounds and those from 'BME' communities (Black and Minority ethnic). Later studies compiled data in five broad groups – 'White', 'Black', 'Asian', 'Mixed', 'Other'. The telling issue here is that these simple aggregates disguise considerable within-group differences. In respect of almost every potential social characteristic (employment, education, health, housing tenure, and, of course, vote) there are substantial differences in outcomes in their constituent sub-groups. If, for instance, one subdivides the 'Asian' heritage into 'Bangladeshi', 'Chinese', 'Indian', 'Pakistani', and 'Asian Other' sub-groups there is little resemblance in their opportunities and choices. The obvious plan is to continue disaggregation and indeed the UK Race Disparity Unit (GOV.UK, 2020a) now compiles data into 18 different sub-groups, with the 2021 UK census adding one more as in Box 30.1.

BOX 30.1 ETHNIC BACKGROUND CLASSIFICATIONS: MOUNTING DISAGGREGATION

Asian or Asian British
- Indian
- Pakistani
- Bangladeshi
- Chinese
- Any other Asian background

Black, Black British, Caribbean, or African
- Caribbean
- African
- Any other Black, Black British, or Caribbean background

Mixed or multiple ethnic groups
- White and Black Caribbean
- White and Black African
- White and Asian
- Any other Mixed or multiple ethnic background

White
- English, Welsh, Scottish, Northern Irish, or British
- Irish
- Gypsy or Irish Traveller
- Roma
- Any other White background

Other ethnic groups
- Asian
- Any other ethnic group

Source: Redrawn from GOV.UK (2020a).

Turning to voting behaviour in our bivariate survey, all the familiar challenges make a return. Could the sample survey reflect the dozens of parties upon which the ethnic vote may be bestowed? For practical purposes, the survey questionnaire would probably settle for tracing preferences for, say five 'named' parties, plus one for 'others' and one for 'non-voters'. Choosing the favoured five factions across the UK would cause immense difficulties, for instance, about how to include the nationalist parties in Scotland and Wales and the completely different party slate in Northern Ireland. This would probably require a separate analytic frame for four countries.

Moreover, in our study we would still have to confront the technical problems that blight the accurate detection of voting preference (ineligibility rules, registration requirements, difficulties in achieving contact and rapport, reticence and deception in revealing vote, reluctance to admit to minority preferences, turnout complacency, etc.). The crucial point in this respect is that all of these biases vary significantly from ethnic sub-group to ethnic sub-group. Let me take one example, the issue of registration – one cannot vote without formal pre-registration. An Electoral Commission (2002) report details considerable levels of non-registration in many minority ethnic groups. Yet at the same time it discovered that 'half of the non-registered voters claimed to have voted'. I curtail the review of technical problems here, noting that it would require a hugely powered survey paying great attention to response biases in order to claim 'representivity'. To the best of my knowledge, no such comprehensive survey of the ethnic vote has ever been undertaken. Survey studies that have tackled the relationship cover only limited ethnic groups and a restricted set of party preferences (Nandi and Platt, 2018).

But I now want to refocus on generality. The all-important limitation on survey findings in our working example concerns the target population to which they are said to apply. The core claim remains the same. Results are generalisable because of the random selection of respondents, the sample provides an exact replica of the population, and the part faithfully represents the whole. But let us interrogate that proposition a little more closely – what is that whole and to whom exactly do the findings apply? We return again to our putative study, which might be termed 'The Ethnic Vote in Modern Britain'. This target population, 'modern Britain', 'contemporary UK' or whatever is actually manufactured in the mechanics of research, is located in decisions about how and when the sample is drawn, which ethnic groups are included, the level of scrutiny of voting behaviour, the timeframe over which the respondents' answers apply, and so on. In summary, one might say that survey findings will be published a year or so after the survey is completed on the basis of questions to some but rarely all ethnic sub-groups on their recollections on some aspects of their voting preferences.

That is the nature of the population aggregate in survey research – located in the practicalities of sampling. The survey captures a shadowy aggregate rather than a 'society'. This in turn raises questions about the permanence of findings – just how 'contemporary' is the contemporary population supposedly represented? The survey freezes quite mechanically something that, by its very nature, is evolving constantly. If, by contrast, one assumes the realist position that those attitudes and behaviours are emergent and adaptive, then the population survey will miss the explanatory action. The population in the statistical survey is merely a transient container, a descriptive snapshot that misses the moving picture and omits to study what makes it move.

Survey findings are not, in a phrase coined by Byrne (2012), 'atemporal and acontextual'. To see this one only needs to follow some of the remarkable changes that have occurred in the UK ethnic vote. If one travels back 50 years, research by Le Lohe (1975) found that only 13 per cent of Asians turned out to vote at local elections. By the turn of the century, research by Anwar (2001) showed increasing differentiation amongst this vote with people of Indian heritage being the most likely to turn out, at a level corresponding to the White vote. Coming to more recent times transformation continues apace. Consider this summary from Duckworth et al. (2021):

> while a plurality of British Indians self-identifies with the liberal end of the political spectrum and demonstrates a preference for the opposition Labour Party over the incumbent Conservative Party, their support for Labour appears to have eroded in recent years. This shift appears to be largely driven by Hindus and Christians, many of whom have drifted away from the Labour Party, even as their Muslim and Sikh counterparts have remained steadfast supporters. If a fresh general election were called, British Indians would likely be an important swing constituency.

Even this 'contemporary' account needs updating, omitting as it does the political incorporation of members of that group by the Tory Party, and the spurt in individual Indian heritage politicians (the Prime Minister and the then Home Secretary no less) within the ruling elite.

In summary, it becomes apparent once again that the statistical associations uncovered in the sample survey are demi-regs (see Episode 7). They have no enduring power; they are material for instant punditry rather than social science. Randomised samples apply and thus misapply the idea of simple generalisation to complex systems. The alternative, the realist alternative, assumes that the target for generalisation is not the aggregates of individuals we refer to as a *population*, but the entire *system or configuration* under study. We need to understand the interplay between structure and agency that generates a demi-regularity and then transforms the demi-regularity. One can only begin to understand the durability and scope of statistical associations observed in a sample survey by providing a proper causal explanation for its contours. To do this requires the construction of evidence from a plurality of studies, a plurality of sources, using a plurality of methods, with the sample survey providing one but only one piece of the jigsaw. A study by Heath et al. (2013) provides an embryonic example of such theory-driven, multi-method research on the political integration of ethnic minorities.

I close the episode with a curious coda, which takes me back all the way to Episode 10 and Goldthorpe et al.'s (1980 [1987]) analysis of social mobility patterns in what was then termed 'Modern Britain'. In Episode 10, this inquiry was used as the pioneering example of mechanism-based explanation in quantitative sociology, and I do not budge from that endorsement. Note, however, that the study's core data are derived from a sample survey. That sample compares the class positions of fathers and sons, detailing different rates of promotion, demotion, and stability across seven class positions. The sample omits women, immigrants, the unemployed, the childless, and others. It also traverses somewhat different time periods for different families. So as with the previous example, the aggregate here is not really the population of 'Modern Britain' but something much more limited and synthetic. But let us take the study on its own terms, where there is no reason to doubt the technical rigour of the sampling procedures that furnish the basic social mobility table (Table 10.1). So let us agree, the mobility observed in the sampled fathers and sons may be considered a sound reflection of the transformation in sections of the male population in that particular time and location.

But what of the explanation? For each of the 49 potential trajectories the research team provides a generative, rational action theory of why that pathway is more or less likely. Different opportunities and barriers are postulated, and different probabilities are hypothesised for each trajectory (Table 10.2). The predictive model is then compared to the observed outcome patterns, and as noted in Episode 10 it is deemed to be a good fit. The model explains the data. There is an unheralded problem, however, if the model has only one purpose, if the explanans has only one explanandum. In such circumstances, it would be perfectly possible for the mobility researcher to fix the predictive probabilities on the basis of the observed data rather than from theory. The explanation then becomes tautologically true. So crucially, the generative theory needs independence. To have explanatory power it needs to be reusable; it must be capable of extensions to other instances. And it is this characteristic that makes rational action theory significant. It can be and has been adapted to mobility data in other societies in different periods. We don't have far to look for examples, for in Episode 11, we see Boudon applying the same rational action theory to explain educational and social inequalities across Europe. Survey data are fixed in time and place, but the explanatory materials are abstract, atemporal, and acontextual. The success of the model does not follow from sampling exactitude (simple generalisation) but lies in its agility in explaining other episodes (extensional generality).

In a much later work, Goldthorpe (2016) differs and argues forcibly that sociology should be a 'population science' on the basis that sample survey 'provides the best means so far devised of moving from the parts to the whole'. Goldthorpe's argument is that such data patterns need to be secure *before* one can proceed to the theory. Properly sampled regularities are considered the obligatory precursor to the explanatory model. He uses a little motto from Sewell to emphasise the point: 'Before you come up with some smart explanation of how the pig got into the tree, just be sure that it *is* the pig that is in the tree.' Black (1954) pointed out many years ago that 'metaphors are no argument'. But I can't resist rejoining that I would need a cunning theory even to begin to believe that unlikely evidence of my eye, and that theory would need to explain not only how the pig got up the tree but how long it might remain, how it might get down and how likely I am to find other ascending pigs in other trees.

The fact that statistical associations are drawn from a random sample does not give them privileged, immutable status. They remain demi-regs. The fact that a random sample is representative of an aggregate population does not give its findings the wherewithal to speak of societies. Societies are much more than population aggregates. We know that survey findings are impermanent, just as surely as we know the pig will descend. Generative explanations can explain stability and can explain change, and this is the first step towards generalisability.

KEY LESSONS

Episode 30 examines the venerable and powerfully expressed claim for statistical generalisation, namely, that rigorous randomisation ensures that findings from a small sample will typify the actions of the whole population from which it is drawn. This is a statistical truism but is of little help in social research because societies are much more than population aggregates; they are complex, constantly transforming social systems. The empirical relationships derived from a sample survey are fixed in time and place and, accordingly, offer no possibility of application beyond that time and place. The generative, mechanism-based explanations for these fleeting associations are not drawn from the sampled statistical associations. They are derived separately in the process of theory-building, which can be adapted to other times and places. Forthcoming episodes will pursue this pathway to generalisation.

Episode 31. Generality in medical science: how representative are clinical trials?

This episode makes a brief return to clinical research. It does so because medicine provides a spectacularly difficult example of Part III's mission of bridging the gap between the 'particular' and the 'general'. Clinical trials of a treatment take place in a rigorously controlled setting, whereas the delivery of that treatment in the real world is open to quite different regulations, norms, and beliefs. Will the results obtained in the former apply to the latter? I begin with a brief vignette to establish the prospective mismatch by comparing two patients in the two respective circumstances. Let us call the first one Archie and the second one Raymond.

Archie arrives for a potential treatment in the remarkably unusual circumstance of knowing that he may or may not get it. He is in a clinical trial and may end up in its intervention or placebo arm. The reasons for this will have already been explained and being an altruistic sort, he has agreed. He has not turned up at the clinic under his own volition, rather by having met strict eligibility requirements – pre-selected for age (not too young, not too old), pre-screened to ensure he has the particular condition at a particular stage of its development, cleared of any significant comorbidities, and having signed up to adhere to the treatment scrupulously and to expect extensive follow-up.

Into the GP's office shambles booze-loving, exercise-phobic, old-timer Raymond. He knows everyone in the surgery, knows how to wangle an appointment, chooses his favourite doctor, and comes expecting a prescription. Why else would one visit the doctor? Thanks to a previous appointment he is aware of a potential condition, but its extent has yet to be clinically determined. He comes with a considerable history, being considered a serial patient (to put it politely), with a kaleidoscope of further complaints, a heaving medicine cabinet of assorted remedies, and a penchant for skipping his medication 'on the good days'.

Forgive the reverie. The essential contrast is real enough with, for instance, one study estimating that only 7.4 per cent of patients with allergic rhinitis seen in primary care settings would be eligible for a clinical RCT (Costa et al., 2011). The gap between research and practice widens if we consider respective institutional arrangements surrounding our two heroes. The practitioners involved are likely to be different – clinical, research-oriented specialists in the former, general (or family) practitioners in the latter. The nature of the doctor–patient relationship will be different – formal, detailed, highly scripted in the former, an informal, ten-minute chat in the latter. The institutional surroundings will differ – more likely a high-status, research hospital for Archie, the familiar neighbourhood surgery in the case of Raymond.

How to bridge the gap? There is a potential resolution to our everyday drama and one that is very easy to utter, namely – make the clinical trial more responsive to real-world conditions. This idea originated in a path-breaking paper by Schwartz and Lellouch (1967) in which the authors urged a move from the classic 'efficacy trial' to the more utilisation-focused 'pragmatic trial'. For over 50 years clinical trials have pursued this mission, with mixed success. I have traced its ups and downs in three previous papers (Pawson, 2019a, 2019b, 2019c) and this episode provides the skeleton story.

I will come to the composition of pragmatic trials presently, but to begin let me pinpoint the basic objective, which will make clear the relevance to our topic of generality. Consider some early declarations. Ware and Hamel (2011) see the crucial ambition as follows: 'Pragmatic trials are designed to study real-world practice and therefore represent less-perfect experiments than efficacy trials: they sacrifice internal validity to achieve generalizability.' In Sackett's famous 'primer' (2011) on the two forms of clinical trials, he associates pragmatic trials with typicality, wanting them to answer this question: 'Does this treatment improve patient-important outcomes when applied by typical clinicians to typical patients' (underlining in the original). Sedgwick (2014) also echoes this goal in asserting that pragmatic trials are intended to 'inform routine clinical and healthcare settings'. Patsopoulos (2011), in a much-cited paper, offers: 'The research question under investigation is whether an intervention works in real-life.' The increasing reach of pragmatic research is also deemed to apply to beneficiaries. Instead of being of interest to journal subscribing research clinicians, the potential recipients of a pragmatic trial are listed by Tunis et al. (2003) as follows: 'clinical and health decision makers including patients, physicians, payers, purchasers, health care administrators and public health policy-makers'.

Laudable as they are, these declarations are imprisoned in the logic of simple generalisation. The goal is the same as in population sampling – namely, to make a particular trial more typical, more representative of usual care in the real world. This reasoning is illustrated in Figure 31.1, another reworking of Figure 27.1. A standard clinical RCT (the shaded small circle), because of its extensive controls, is representative only of a portion (shaded large circle) of the totality of treatment applications and recipients (blank large circle). The goal is to contrive a pragmatic trial (blank small circle) better to represent the totality.

Totality of the treatment application and recipients (routine care)

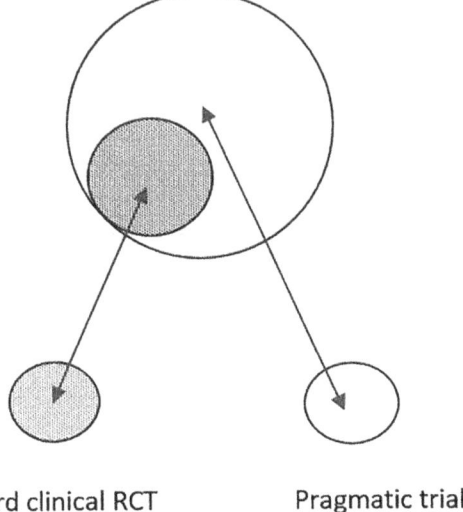

Standard clinical RCT   Pragmatic trial

Figure 31.1   Increasing the representivity of trials

How then do trials become more pragmatic? To achieve this, much research followed on the anatomy of clinical trials. What exactly constitutes the differ-ence between an efficacy trial and a pragmatic trial? There have been many attempts to define and measure the distinction, the most celebrated being the PRECIS tool (Figure 31.2) or as it is sometimes termed the 'pragmascope'. The tool (an acronym for *PR*agmatic *E*xplanatory *C*ontinuum *I*ndicator *S*ummary) has undergone considerable development but, basically, the spokes of the wheel describe the components upon which a trial may vary in its explanatory or its pragmatic orientation (Norton et al., 2021). I will not elaborate all the details, but by following the spoke labels the reader can see at a glance how the treatment parameters afforded to the Raymonds of this world differ from those demanded of Archie.

Each spoke is scored to represent proximity to real-world conditions. For example, at 12 o'clock, we have an axis which attempts to measure the degree of control on trial eligibility, which may vary from strict control to those who are considered likely to be responsive to treatment (scored 1) to open access in which trial recruits are representative of the entire cohort who may even-tually be treated (scored 5). The other eight dimensions are understood and scored in the same manner. By completing an assessment of the scoring on all nine dimensions, it is possible to compile an overall profile of the degree of pragmatism in any particular trial. Pragmatic trials have a profile linking the outer edges of the dartboard; efficacy trials have scores which cluster around the centre. For a diagrammatic compendium of trials with markedly different profiles, see the PRECIS 2 website (https://www.precis-2.org/Trials).

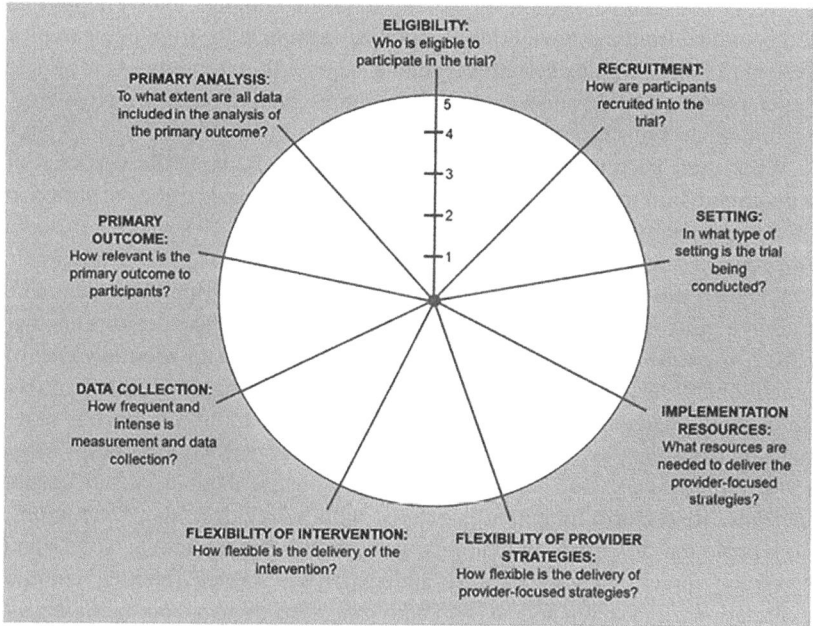

Figure 31.2   The PRECIS tool

We arrive at the crucial question. Hundreds upon hundreds of clinical investigations now bear the title pragmatic trials. Do the results obtained from these 'real-world' trials better inform the totality of real-world practice? The realist answer is 'no' and is in the negative because the whole exercise is a misapplication of population sampling. As we have seen in the previous episode, standard sampling logic seeks to justify how the findings uncovered in the sample apply to the whole population. By using the PRECIS tool, the 'sample' trial is manipulated to improve this representativity. One pragmatic treatment episode aspires to be typical of all treatment episodes.

But think more closely about what is contained in these 'episodes'. The intervention is not a simple entity. A clinical intervention is a complex biological, technical, and social system – comprised of the treatment and its causal powers, the patients undergoing the intervention, the practitioners implementing the intervention, the researchers evaluating the intervention, the institutions administering the intervention, the providers funding the intervention, the regulators approving the intervention, and the health services rationing the intervention. In short, the ability to generalise from a trial is not confined to the single dimension (e.g., some patients to all patients). All of the above-mentioned features condition trial outcomes. All of them are in a state of constant adaptation. Pragmatic trials are complex interventions and to generalise from a pragmatic trial involves extrapolating from one complex system to other complex systems. And this is not within the compass of simple generalisation. There is no such thing as a representative place in an evolving, multidimensional space.

What then becomes the claims rehearsed earlier about the capacity of a pragmatic trial to better inform usual care? Firstly, consider the construction of a pragmatic trial. Trialist A may choose to loosen RCT strictures in some respects on some of the PRECIS dimensions and it becomes a pragmatic trial (PRCT). But what is to stop trialists B, C, D configuring their pragmatic trial in a quite different fashion? For perfectly good practical reasons another PRCT might be performed on a wider patient group, by an alternative set of practitioners, using another comparison group, preferring a different proxy outcome, funded only for a shorter follow-up period, and so on. Such is pragmatism. Consider next the extrapolation to the wider real-world setting – often termed routine care. One has only to ask what is usual about usual care to spot the flaw. Real-world treatment is offered with a kaleidoscope of variations, with profound difference in treatment availability, patient beliefs, access and screening, practitioner availability and expertise, service funding, cultural expectations, and so on, and so on. There is no such thing as routine treatment in a world of contrasting treatments. In short, pragmatic trials can be designed in endless configurations and real-world settings come in countless variations. A particular manifestation of the former cannot speak for the heterogeneity of the latter.

Thus collapsed the original objective of fabricating a trial with widespread applicability. And after 50 years of endeavour came a major retreat by the leading lights of the pragmatic trial movement: 'Our conception of PRECIS-2 is that it is to be used by trialists to design a trial whose results are applicable to a context in which they, the trialists, are intending the results to be used' (Zwarenstein et al., 2017). A similar volte-face occurred when it came to ambitions on who would use the findings from pragmatic trials. The original expectation was wide-eyed – recall Tunis et al.'s (2003) formidable roll call of clients. Since the applicability of a pragmatic trial has shrunk, so have expectations about users: 'We would argue that trialists should not worry about trying to guess the various perspectives of those making decisions but should instead do all they can do to describe the context of their trial' (Treweek and Zwarenstein, 2009).

What are we left with? What are the lessons of this episode? There is a clear need for an alternative model of generality in clinical research. Pragmatic trials are marooned in the futile search for the typical case. What is the alternative? To this end, it is useful to redraw Figure 27.1 (extensional generality) as Figure 31.3 and then as Figure 31.4 in order to spot the requirements. Figure 31.3 reveals the precise and curtailed explanatory reach of a pragmatic trial. At the bottom of the figure, we have the pragmatic trial, conceived in its true colours as a complex system (as represented by the explosion symbol, mimicking the PRECIS maps). Along the top we have an unlimited number of real-world applications of the 'same' intervention (1 to N), depicted in their true colours as a varying array of complex systems. Case 1 exemplifies the direct applicability of the pragmatic trial. Research user 1 scrutinises the published configuration of ingredients in a given pragmatic trial (the PRECIS profile) and deems them close enough to those operating in her institution. She implements the treatment in the same manner and evidence utilisation becomes a reality, as represented by the solid line.

Interventions in the real world

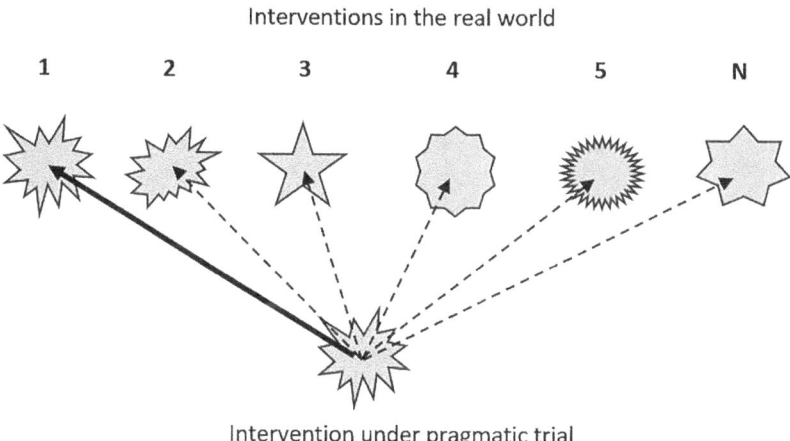

Intervention under pragmatic trial

Figure 31.3   Generalisation as the search for the representative study

But what of users 2, 3, 4, 5, … N? They decipher that a pragmatic trial's characteristics such as patient eligibility, practitioner expertise, practitioner adherence, comparator flexibility, outcomes monitored, and follow-up intensity are not the same as on their patch, and the disappointing lack of applicability is represented by the dashed lines. Where do they turn? Do they have to await the results of tailor-made pragmatic trials that match the characteristics of systems 2, 3, 4, 5, … N? Given the substantial expense of mounting trials, the trundling pace of trial results, and the competing priorities facing trial funders, it is totally unrealistic to imagine that the vast mosaic of matching pragmatic trials could ever be assembled. Clearly, real-world practitioners need to look for additional support from a different kind of evidence.

The basic elements of that mission are depicted schematically in Figure 31.4. This begins with the assumption that interventions are complex systems, whose outcomes may be expected to differ. The task of generalisation is extensional: what is it about different applications that generates different outcomes? Rather than seeking the usual, the typical, the representative, we assume differences and seek to explain them. This strategy is depicted in the figure as the process of theory-building (the thought bubble). An intervention is implemented in different ways in different locations to different populations (1, 2, 3, 4, 5). Research reveals that there are differences in outcome from case to case (A, B, C, D, E). Research is then tasked with explaining the difference between each case. Why there might be a difference between cases 1 and 2? Hypothesis A is proposed and tested. Why might there be a difference between cases 2 and 3? Hypothesis B is proposed and tested. Generalisation is the process of bringing together these hypotheses into a unified theory accounting for an ever-widening array of system differences.

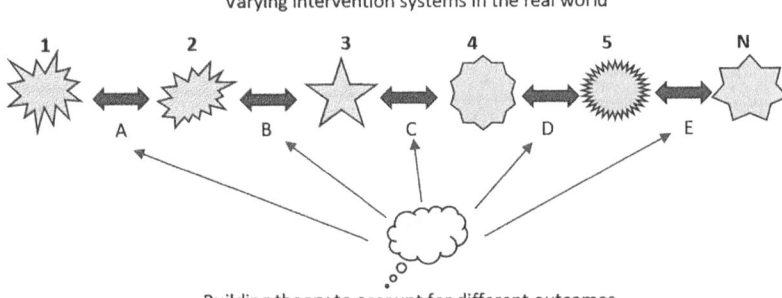

Figure 31.4   Generalisation as the explanation of case-to-case differences

Figure 31.4 is highly schematic at this stage but remains central to Part III. It depicts the universal challenge of extensional generalisation across the whole of science – not only clinical, but physical, biological, and social. All of them vie for knowledge that bestrides case after case, system after system. This quest, as we shall see, is approached in many different ways. But let me stick to topic and ponder alternative methodologies for broadening the applicability of clinical evidence.

I'm no epidemiologist, so let me close with three simplified examples about dealing with difference within the field of healthcare. Firstly, at the micro level, how should practitioners use evidence to deal with variation between individual patients? This brings me back to the Raymonds of this world. How might a GP, let us call her Dr Foster, cope with his eccentric health beliefs and his unique clinical history? What evidence might be useful? Raymond enters the surgery with his baggage of comorbidities and lifestyle foibles. On screen Dr Foster will upload the nationally endorsed, RCT-based guidelines for the suspected condition. She engages, so to speak, in a brief consultation with Archie. She then has to come to a judgement on what the differences might follow and how to deal with them. For this she needs a theory – a theory of how Raymond departs from the 'norm'.

For this she turns to tacit, internalised, experiential evidence, collected from colleagues, from experience with other patients, and from previous consultations with Raymond. There is a name for this type of wisdom, namely, 'practice-based evidence'. For an extended account, see Gabbay and Le May (2011). It is the judicious blend of formal evidence-based practice and informal practice-based evidence that enables Dr Foster to decide what to do. According to the patient who sits in front of her, she then follows, adapts, or even sets aside the formal recommendations. She aspires to contextual sensitivity, and her internal deliberations seek to cater for differences in patients in her list. See Griffiths (2009) for some revealing real-world examples of how such a balance is struck.

Secondly, this time at the biological level, consider the development of cancer treatment. Tumour heterogeneity, ranging from spontaneous regression to relentless progression, is the great bugbear of treatment guidelines. Even if an established biomarker is used as the basis for patient selection, cancer treatment trials still generate heterogeneous effects (Maris, 2005). Closely targeted treatments on specially selected patients continue to achieve both success and failure. How can research help to deal with differences at this cellular level? The solution is to go back to the drawing board and into the lab, to devise more sophisticated theories of how 'genetic and epigenetic heterogeneity affects tumour evolution' (Alizadeh, 2015). These findings are then incorporated into a revised treatment and returned to the field for empirical testing, where a different pattern of success and failure will eventuate (hopefully with a more positive balance). Recognising, understanding, and dealing with small differences in treatment efficacy, rather than pinning all hopes on all-purpose pragmatic trials, holds the key to generalisable knowledge.

Thirdly, consider health service reforms like the introduction of screening systems or of laboratory testing regimes. These are manifestations of complexity. Efficiency gains always vary, depending as they do on implementation variability and contextual differences. There is no all-purpose RCT, pragmatic or otherwise, capable of providing the decisive evidence supporting their widespread implementation. To achieve extensional generality, the methodological pathway is the same. The solution is to concentrate on the theory underlying the reform, to test it in multiple, within-site and between-sites inquiries and to emerge with an explanatory theory to account for the differences in outcomes. The methodology employed here is known as 'realist synthesis' (Pawson, 2006) and excellent examples explaining the mixed success of screening and testing regimes may be found in Duddy and Wong (2021) and Duddy et al. (2022). Full consideration of realist synthesis follows in Episode 36.

KEY LESSONS

Episode 31 takes a sidestep to examine the respective logics of simple and extensional generalisation as they operate in evidence-based medicine. Classic RCTs use randomisation, precise entry restrictions, and strict implementation controls in order to assess the efficacy of a treatment. Real-world applications of that treatment are made in the absence of such stringent constraints. Pragmatic trials relax those rigid preconditions in an attempt to make their findings more applicable to real-world conditions. This attempt to maintain the authority of simple generalisation fails – a single trial, however configured, cannot be made to represent the myriad differences in real-world applications of a treatment. Discovering and explaining heterogeneity in clinical outcomes becomes the key to the wider understanding of treatment effectiveness.

Episode 32. Case studies and generality: transcending the single case?

This episode returns to social science. It makes a leap to an alternative methodological tradition and considers how generality is conceived in case study research in social science. The case study is a familiar, sometimes dominant, starting point for empirical research in many disciplines, spanning the micro and the macro, the historical and the contemporaneous. Readers wanting to inspect the prodigious travels of the case study method should consult the major collections – Ragin and Becker (1992), Gomm et al. (2000), George and Bennett (2005), Byrne and Ragin (2009), Yin (2017). Here I stick solely to the case study's ambitions on generality. How can we transcend the single case? What can the detailed excavation of a specific case tell us about further, unresearched cases? As we are about to see, bets are hedged. There is disagreement and equivocation, so much so that I will spend several episodes tracking down alternative perspectives on how case studies may be deployed to derive generalisable explanations.

These different orientations stem from the sheer diversity of inquiries that consider themselves 'case studies' and I commence with a Cook's Tour. Let us begin in social anthropology and in case studies describing the cultures and patterns of behaviour in 'small scale' or what were then termed 'tribal' societies. The intrepid researcher was often cast off for a long duration to experience and to make an immersive record of local custom and practice. The classic example is Malinowski's *Argonauts of the Western Pacific* (1922). He found himself marooned in New Guinea during World War I and produced an account of 'life from the natives' point of view'. The account typifies this tradition – holistic in spirit and diary like. Qualitative inquiry provides the basic empirical materials. Quite literally, these are 'tales from the field', boldly going where most of us have no opportunity to go. One might even venture that there is a spotlight on the exotic and the exceptional. Accordingly, there is little or no formal attempt to draw parallels with other societies.

This approach – close-textured, rounded, memoirs of the citizens' perspectives – then transferred itself across to Western society. Notable studies include the Lynds' study of 'Middletown' in the United States (1929) and Stacey's (1960) study of Banbury in the UK. It must be said that the comings and goings in these localities were inevitably more complex than in their traditional anthropological counterparts. Accounts were correspondingly more selective and indeed both of these communities were subject to extensive restudy. But we remain unequivocally with the initial usage of the term case study, referring to geographically bound localities and communities. Once again, these modern-day anthropologies utilise lengthy, detailed narratives, taking the form of what Geertz (1973) calls 'thick description' of the actors, cultures, contexts, meanings, behaviours, and reasoning within the situation studied. This group of case studies usually disavows any claim that the chosen community is 'representative' in the statistical sense. But there is little to deny that they seek a 'sense of recognition'. The stories are homely rather than exotic. A clue to this sneaking wider ambition lies in the subtitle of the Lynds' first book, *Middletown: A Study in Modern American Culture*.

Essentially the same technical approach marks the next cluster of case studies. The research strategy stays fixed, but the empirical focus shrinks yet further. Researchers now boldly go into field locations in modern society with relatively untold stories – street-corner gangs, asylums, protest camps, hospital wards, factory floors, call centres, police patrols, care homes, nature reserves, science labs, and even submarines. I refrain from citing examples; the list is endless. These case studies hold true to the primary aim of providing an account from the 'natives' point of view'. But once again, given the familiarity of many of these locations, there is no denying that they are written with an understanding that they have the capacity for some form of conceptual transfer (e.g., from the author's account of a hospital ward to the readers' recollections of other hospital wards).

A related and substantial sub-category of case studies in modern sociology and social policy occurs in inquiries focusing on processes rather than places. The core task is to research changes in life chances as they are affected by parenthood, separation and divorce, long-term illness, disability, educational failure, unemployment, care provision, and so on. This becomes case study research when specific groups and sub-groups are chosen purposefully to portray how the particular process unfolds. A variant here is qualitative longitudinal case study, which carries these inquiries through time. Again, the core aim is to capture the unique sensibilities and experiences of those involved. Once again, these contemporary case studies tend to shy away from any strong claims on typicality. But since the topics studied are very much 'issues of the day' there is often an undeniable, embryonic claim to have explained some significant contemporary trend with clear policy implications. I examine the embryos in due course.

The next and perhaps major academic location for case study research is to be found in comparative historical research. It still bears one essential characteristic of its truncated elder, namely, 'historical research', in that its basic data depend on a deep immersion in archival data, official documents, secondary sources, recollections, autobiographies, memoirs, diaries, and in previous historical study. In this respect, it is like the anthropological case study. Thick description once again provides the raw materials, though in this instance, what is described is not bounded by space and place but by episode and process. Topics for study include social movements, revolutions, democratisation, nationalism, war, and peace. Explanations for these events reside in descriptions of collective action, coalition formation, mobilisation, struggle, propaganda, and so on as they play out in a specific period. Cases remain cases but their content consists of historical episodes. Coming to the 'comparative' in comparative historical research, we find the first clear commitment to create explanations that are valid beyond a particular time and place. These are *cross-case* companions. Generality is the express concern. Comparisons reveal similarities and differences and these are deemed to repeat themselves in further instances. There are many different approaches to this objective, and I set aside consideration of cross-case comparison to Episode 37.

The next pocket of case study research lies in social and public policy and in the field of evaluation research. Programmes and interventions are the basic coinage, with research seeking to assess 'what works?' These are not usually considered or termed 'case studies' since they employ a large repertoire of research methods ranging from the RCT to in-depth qualitative studies. But I want to include them in the inventory because each evaluative study tends to be conducted as a separate case. Accordingly, research in this field raises the classic question on generality. Will the results obtained in this case obtain elsewhere? Will an intervention that worked here work elsewhere? Many different research strategies have been proposed to answer this question. Some are dependent on choosing strategically significant cases, others dwell on within-case differences, and others attempt to synthesise many different cases. All will be considered in due course.

Our whirlwind tour ends with cases being regarded as 'configurations'. This orientation has been suggested in a characteristically restrained way by Byrne (2009). The logic here begins with the idea of causal explanation. If that is the basic task of inquiry, argues Byrne, the case study must also include the complex array of features that make up that explanation. Cases are not simply places, spaces, localities, processes, histories, interventions, and so on. Each of these, inevitably, is a complex system. Accordingly, the case study must feature material on the contexts, mechanisms, and outcomes that will feature in the causal account. It must provide evidence on the structural and agential forces that act in the system under study. The essential, empirical task covers more ground, more intricately. Methods of case study analysis are correspondingly more varied. We leave behind thick description and move to a whole family of techniques that include qualitative comparative analysis, single-case propensities, Bayesian methods, cluster analysis, and so on (Byrne and Ragin, 2009).

I pursue none of these technical details in this episode in order to reinforce the basic argument of the configurationalists. Even if our initial focus is on specific localities or specific communities or specific historical events or specific social movements or specific policies or specific programmes, the explanation for specific empirical patterns uncovered lies in a wider system in which they are embedded. Thus, rather that the case study being regarded as some natural, given boundary for inquiry, its features actually emerge in the process of inquiry. Ragin (1992) comes to this exact conclusion in reconsidering the wide range of candidates for 'casehood' already considered. Human social life is conceptually 'sliced and diced' in various ways in the process of inquiry. None of these research design decisions are proceeded by the presence of some given, natural, authentic case – rather it is the researcher's hunches and working assumption that reveal the case. He calls this process of arriving at a focus for inquiry 'casing'. A methodological revolution is predicted. In a matter of decades linear social inquiry with its starting point in 'sampling' will be superseded by complex inquiry with its organising strategy of 'casing'.

I proceed no further with the long and winding history of the case-study and leave to history the battle of the gerunds. The focus of Part III is on generality, and I move on to consider how the aforementioned portfolio of case study approaches deal with the matter of external validity, generalisability, and so forth. The big questions remain unanswered. Is it possible that knowledge of one case can inform more cases or even all cases? How do we achieve the transfer of explanation from case to case? As already noted, there is a great deal of equivocation on how and how far this is possible. I consider several strategies across the remaining episodes. My narrative moves from relative failure to relative success, from mistaken claims to promising strategies for understanding generality. All will be revealed in due course, but I might provide an enigmatic preview here by pointing out that the realist preference involves a strategy that combines within-case and cross-case analysis.

To begin, I focus on classic 'single location' case studies – the pioneering wave of case studies in the form of thick ethnographic descriptions of particular locations, be they pacific islands, townships, street corners, classrooms, or call centres. As noted, the authors of these case studies often eschew claims that their analysis can speak to locations beyond the one studied. Or do they? Examined closely there are modest aspirations for their broader relevance. These claims take on two forms which I label: (i) naturalistic generalisation and (ii) purposive sampling.

These research narratives are often likened to personal diaries. But these diaries are not private documents. They are written in order to be read by others. The case is chosen, researched, and published to provide enlightenment to the wider community of social science. The readership, who may be relatively unfamiliar with the chosen event, episode, locality, institution is invited – often very quietly – to follow, to absorb, to reflect upon the unfolding narrative ... and to take the ideas onward.

This objective has a name. Stake calls it 'naturalistic generalisation' (1995). It is an attempt to harness an everyday form of human understanding that Piaget refers to as 'schema' (1971). It bears a close resemblance to a notion already considered, namely, Blumer's 'sensitising concepts' (1954). Readers are transported to another time and place. Storyline by storyline, we come to understand the participants' reported reasoning. It makes sense because we are acquainted with at least some of its aspects. No one can deny this process, whereby an ethnographic text, especially a well-written one, 'rings a bell'. But is it a basis for generalisation? Exactly the same sense of familiarity can be evoked by novels, films, and even cartoons. Exactly the same sense of familiarity may be triggered by the Lynds' Middletown or by the Simpsons' Springfield. When and how the imagery, the schema, the message will be grasped and taken elsewhere depends entirely on the recipient. Thick descriptions of everyday life have great conceptual fecundity, but the concepts, like confetti, are blown in the wind. The ability of naturalistic generalisation to 'take you there' is simply a reflection of the abstractive nature of everyday language (Episode 28). It is wondrous but also informal, tacit, latent, short-lived, and haphazard.

So let us move on to more formal attempts to widen the explanatory grasp of case studies using methods referred to, somewhat interchangeably, as 'purposive' or 'purposeful' or 'judgmental' or 'strategic' sampling. Here, the cases chosen for research are not self-identified and bounded localities. Nor is the task one of providing thick description of the inhabitants' worldviews. Rather, the researcher actively shapes and selects the case, making formal and explicit judgements on why it has wide-reaching implications. This approach crops up thickly in the patch of contemporary case studies noted previously, especially those featuring battles with social problems and the policies that might alleviate them.

The very purpose of purposive sampling is to lay claim to generality. The ironclad contrast with statistical sampling remains. These are not considered typical or representative cases but have other significant characteristics that render them generalisable. The strategic selection of the case is the basis of the claim for wider relevance. This particular case for case studies is perhaps most comprehensively argued by Patton (2002) in a 16-fold typology of modes of purposive sampling. I refrain from assessing them all here, noting in passing many overlaps as well as one unfathomable slippage back to the idea that a 'typical case' can be manufactured. Patton's examples are drawn mainly from evaluation research, where the generality stakes are high. Does the case have wider policy relevance? Will an intervention that has worked here work elsewhere? I restrict analysis to just two subtle strategies in which the inquiry is fabricated in order to make this direct claim on generality. The case, thanks to its chosen properties, is said to possess extensional validity.

I begin with the idea of choosing a 'critical case'. Patton explains the logic with characteristic brio: 'If it can happen there, it can happen anywhere.' If some behavioural outcome is found to occur in an unlikely, unpromising locality or group, then the chances are that it will occur much more widely. In this manner the critical case allows for generalisability. For instance, in assessing the readability of patient documentation, health legislators test out materials on the critical case of those with relatively poor health literacy. In the United States, the federal Food and Drug Administration recommends that product literature and clinical documents meant for the lay public should be assessed against the reading level of an 8th grade student. No argument here. But the acid test is whether critical case logic can be applied to more complex behaviours, processes, and settings.

Let us take a more careful look at such an inquiry. Critical case logic can also apply in the opposite scenario: 'If it doesn't happen there, it won't happen anywhere.' A classic example of this proposition in British sociology was the choice of research location in the *Affluent Worker* studies (Goldthorpe et al., 1968). The thesis under test, put very simply, was that with increasing affluence in the post-war period the industrial labour force was becoming more middle class in its values and beliefs. A crucial test of the thesis was designed using the critical case of manual workers, who had moved to new industry (car assembly), in new communities (recently constructed housing estates), in a new town (Luton). It seems an exemplary critical case: these workers had uprooted deliberately in search of high wages and to 'better themselves'. But had they, as the thesis predicted, become middle class? The 'embourgeoise-ment' hypothesis was dealt an empirical blow – even under conditions that favoured it. Goldthorpe and team discovered that these workers' attitudes and beliefs were still much more closely aligned to those of the traditional working class than those of their middle-class neighbours.

But how far and for how long does the rebuttal hold? What is the durability of the critical case? Did the affluent workers' loyalties to their roots persist? Devine (1992) 'revisited' the workers in the same town and industry in the early 1990s and found that that class allegiances had shifted hither and thither. There was a strong sense of ambivalence. Indeed, in a later reflection (2016), she notes that the very idea of working-class affluence had almost disappeared with economic crises, labour market shifts, and fluctuations in unemployment. In Luton, the car plant had shrunk, manufacturing had declined, the industrial labour force diminished. The local economy was now dominated by the service sector. The town was no longer the home of the 'new working class'. It became a plural city with a White British minority. The methodological lesson here is that critical case status is rather short-lived and unavoidably local. Such studies are better conceived as assessments of claim and counter claim, rather than proving a basis for enduring and widespread generality. The notion that a particular case will always remain critical is impossible to sustain in the study of complex and evolving processes.

A second strategy from Patton's typology also seeks to burst its narrow empirical boundaries. He refers to it as the study of the 'extreme or deviant' case. Despite its dramatic name, it refers to a familiar enough research design. The idea is to study a case at the leading edge of change. Studying 'vanguard' reforms throws light on 'what could be'. Schofield (2000), for example, endorses the strategy in her studies of those pioneering schools in the American South which were the first to desegregate. Locating the unintended consequences provides intelligence for those that follow. She discovered some schools were overhasty in moving to a 'colour-blind' policy. Avoiding all mention of race had the opposite of its supposed effect. Those schools pursuing a more gradual transition were more successful. Medical research may also be driven by the discovery of outliers. In the initial, dark days of AIDS research came the discovery of a small number of cases of people infected with HIV who did not die or develop AIDS. These asymptomatic exceptions drove vital research into the mechanisms that drove virus–host interactions (Klein and Miedema, 1995).

It is possible, unfortunately, to draw a rather different conclusion from studies conducted at the vanguard. In some circumstances they may mislead. Interventions that bring novel resources and attendant publicity to a problem may fade in effectiveness after the initial wave of enthusiasm. Early practition-ers and participants may be rather proud of their pioneering status, but what of those that follow? This so-called 'showcasing' effect warns against evaluating a programme in its first flush. Indeed, one can argue that there is a typical, declining rhythm to public commitment to innovation – often moving from enthusiasm, to acceptance, to routinisation, to fatigue. This unfortunate pattern was especially pronounced in the Covid-19 restrictions when unprecedentedly severe social controls were maintained over a considerable period of time – followed enthusiastically to begin, only to be gradually circumvented and undermined (Pawson, 2023). The decreasing effectiveness of smoking cessa-tion schemes may also be explained by programme fatigue – tried, tried, and then not tried again (Heckman et al., 2018). Case selection at the leading edge may inform or it may mislead.

Patton also recommends the study of intervention failure as another form of 'extreme' case study. To be sure we can all learn from our mistakes and attempt to rectify them. This too applies at the institutional level as noted by advocates of the process of 'continuous quality improvement'. But interventions fail for a whole variety of reasons. Failure, like effectiveness, depends on context. There is no root cause of failure. There is no reason to suppose that a close understanding of the clangers, conspiracies, cockups, and cross-purposes that apply in a particular case have relevance elsewhere.

I cease my examination of Patton's typology of purposive samples here. There are other judgmental strategies claiming extensional application, such as 'maximum variation samples', 'homogeneous samples', 'intensity samples', but they are all Janus-faced. They may inform or they may mislead in wider application. There is no need to prolong the agony. A single case however purposely chosen, however subtly manufactured, can never, *by itself*, speak to all potential cases. I've put this rather bluntly here because we live to fight another day (namely, in the following episodes) to seek generality using case study methods. The problem with the subset of critical, extreme, vanguard case selection strategies considered thus far is that they offer a one-shot solution in the face of inevitable and incessant change within any case. They treat case selection as a technical decision applied at the beginning of research projects – shape the case in this way in order to have widespread application. This logic bears an uncomfortable similarity to the way that a survey researcher makes an initial, definitive choice of sampling frames and sampling fractions. Sampling and/or case selection comes first, allowing for the main business of developing definitive empirical findings. By itself, the sampling strategy, be it random or purposive, is understood to provide the warrant for generalisation. No such licence exists.

KEY LESSONS

Episode 32 begins exploration of whether case study methods have the capacity to provide generalisable findings. Some exponents of the method eschew the very idea of producing transferable lessons. Other strategies are more positive, two of which are discussed. The notion of naturalist generalisation trades on the human capacity to read a case study in an empathetic fashion and so apply its findings to other situations more familiar to the reader. Empathy, alas, is haphazard and the reach into wider episodes is entirely capricious. Purposively selected case studies are chosen on the basis that they are strategically placed to reveal lessons that apply more broadly. In practice the explanatory reach of such critical cases is always limited. The critical case ceases to be critical when it is located in a complex and evolving system.

Episode 33. Incremental steps to generality: within-case comparisons

Rather than selecting the case as the preliminary to inquiry, perhaps the shaping of such studies can be achieved incrementally? Rather than defining the case under some understanding of its outer shell, might we learn more about its explanatory powers by concentrating on within-case comparisons? These considerations herald an alternative strategy for conducting case studies, variously termed 'organic', 'dynamic', or 'theoretical' (Emmel, 2013; Mason, 2002). Here, the composition of the case studied is refined and adapted over time, during the execution of an inquiry. The very purpose of in-depth emersion on this model is to spot subtle difference within the group, or location, or processes, or case under study. These differences are unlikely to be self-evident at the start of research and they require a continual focusing and refocusing of the case inquiry. Different sub-groups, novel sub-situations, diverse actions, and unforeseen counteractions become apparent on closer inspection. Put briefly, the purpose of such organic sampling in case study research is to develop explanation with the gradual development of within-case comparisons.

Let us have a brief look at three different examples using this approach, all incidentally born and bred at the University of Leeds, UK. I begin with the 'Following Young Fathers' research project, which was discussed as an example of generative causal explanation in Episode 14. Here, I paraphrase Neale's (2021) description of the evolution of her sample as follows. The original casing consisted of an opportunistic sample of a dozen young men identified by local youthwork and welfare practitioners. Following further funding, the sample was boosted to 31 young men, and this provided the basis for the detection of the different trajectories of fatherhood for young men from 'skilled', 'semi-skilled', and 'low-skilled' family backgrounds, as discussed previously. Dynamic sampling unearthed significant cases within the case. Thereafter the sample was further adapted, in search of an understanding of the experience of fathers who had been young offenders and also those with experience of different levels of welfare support. Further iterations followed through time. The research commences with what sounds like a tightly defined case, namely, the experience of young unmarried men facing unplanned parenthood. But in order to understand the breadth of that experience, in order to trace the underlying causal forces and their disparate consequences, organic, within-case sampling proved essential.

Next take the example of research on a different system shock. How does mass redundancy impact on a community? How do individuals move on from a critical life event? This was the task in Gardiner et al.'s (2009) case study of the impact of closure of steel plants in South Wales, resulting in the loss of over 3000 jobs, which in turn prompted many local interventions aimed at redeployment. Research began with an opportunist sampling frame of participants in a retraining arm of the local trade union from which a representative sample of 175 workers was chosen for semi-structured interviews. The interview transcripts revealed a thumping diversity of response to the fateful moment. Theoretical work began at this stage seeking to trace different patterns within the career reconstructions. Eighteen in-depth interviews were conducted to this end, revealing three different trajectories, three sub-cases within the case. In brief, these were: (i) 'active career planners', who had anticipated severance and made prior use of employment services, (ii) 'triggered career changers', who accepted the forced redundancy and sought out those limited opportunities that became available, and (iii) 'career crossroaders' who stalled in some distaste of limited and ill-fitting training opportunities. Each cluster was reinterviewed, and further transcripts reveal the different configurations of resources, identities, qualifications, past experiences, and future projections that constituted each trajectory.

For a final example I return to prison and the research described in Episode 12 on the rehabilitative potential of the Simon Fraser Prisoner education programme. It is case study in one sense described earlier, namely, that evaluation research generally follows the fortunes of single interventions in a single institution. In this instance, armed with the notion that programmes always generate different outcomes for different participants, we began with interviews with the instructors, seeking their view on the types of inmates whose prospects might benefit from the programme and those who might remain untouched. In the manner of each of the previous examples this led to hypotheses on why the different sub-groups could be expected to follow quite diverse trajectories. For example: (i) capable prisoners who had missed out previous educational opportunities (the 'second chancers') and might continue to develop strongly on release; (ii) poorly qualified inmates who found the course challenging but battled through the semesters (the 'improvers'), who might be inspired to roll up their sleeves on release; (iii) previously well-educated prisoners who shone academically (the 'high-flyers') but who experienced little sense of lasting personal change. The list continues; we postulated many other disparate cases within the case. The research then evolved quantitatively, trying to substantiate the sub-group hypotheses with information on release and reconviction.

Hundreds of other inquiries could have been used to illustrate this organic, dynamic, theory-based approach to sampling within the case study. One might speculate that it is the norm in modern qualitative research (Mason, 2002). Interestingly, Emmel (2013) has also tied the knot with realist inquiry. He points out that the gradual, organic entry into the case study is emblematic of realist principles. I have no quarrel with this, though I would prefer to say that these slowly developing insights assist us with understanding causality rather than generality. As stressed throughout Part I, one common method of understanding causal forces is to trace their action at the sub-group level. Structure acts upon agency in different ways. Societal forces are interpreted differently according to the reasoning and resources of different sub-groups. Referring back to our examples, the shockwave of young fatherhood, the threat of redundancy, the opportunity for rehabilitation are all dealt with in diverse ways, producing different causal trajectories for different incumbents. Organic sampling provides an important entry point into the contours of realist explanation.

But we are still left with the question of the day. Do these iterative, internal sampling strategies provide the grounds for understanding cases beyond the situation studied? Can within-case comparisons inform cross-case comparisons? Does organic sampling permit extensional generalisation? The answer is yes and no. Let us start in the negative and with the inconceivable. If we think of a case study as a specific exploration of a generic social issue it remains impossible to extend the empirical findings of one study to many or all other potential cases. We cannot expect the unplanned experience of young fatherhood of a small group of young men in the north of England, however closely dissected, to correspond to unplanned fatherhood of young men with different backgrounds by dint of nation, race, religion, culture, and historical period. There is no reason to suppose that the trajectories discovered in a unique prisoner higher education programme in Canada would apply to all other inmate populations, to dozens of other 'correctional' programmes, and to all prison regimes. The causal trajectories discovered in those affected by the collapse of the Welsh steel industry are unlikely to be replicated in other industries, in other labour markets, in other economies. Social science has to wean itself off this ambition to stretch from one instance to all instances. We have to avoid the slippage back into the idea that it is possible to locate a case that has key characteristics of all cases. Attempting to generalise in this fashion simply opens up endless permutations of cases within cases within cases. One can never get to the end of endless.

All of this is true, but it also misses the point. Pointing out such shortfalls is to beg the impossible – single studies that cover every possible context, every possible process, every possible configuration in a complex, evolving, multidimensional space. The quest for generality has and must have more modest ambitions and must contain stopping rules. A more plausible approach has a different starting point, which begins by posing a somewhat surprising question. Ragin and Becker (1992) recommend that we might gain a clearer understanding of a case study's explanatory range by asking the prior question – 'What is this a case of?' This suggestion has caused bafflement – 'Obviously dear professors, our three cases are case studies of young fatherhood, mass redundancy, and prisoner education.'

This reluctance to look beyond the case study title, beyond the headline substantive concern, misses the key feature of organic or dynamic sampling. Under this research strategy the case study is not an exploration of some specific manifestation of a generic social issue but is actually an investigation of a range of sub-samples and internal differences within the case study as identified in a range of provisional theories. This outlook provides an alternative answer to Ragin and Becker's question. It is these provisional hypotheses that define the case study, and it is the emerging theories that capture the opportunity for generalisation.

Let us reconsider a couple of examples. One of the hypotheses tested in the prisoner education example was about the potential of 'second chancers'. They had disregarded traditional schooling for a life of crime but now grasped the slim opportunity it may provide to escape the revolving door of imprisonment. This theory appeared to have mileage in the particular prisoner education programme in British Columbia. But is also the very basis of adult education provision the world over. Many people in many walks of life for a whole variety of reasons choose to overlook, ignore, spurn, or even despise the opportunities presented in conventional schooling. With the passing of years and following a multitude of bumps in life's road, these sentiments are sometimes replaced by another, namely, regret. At that very point some form of adult education may offer a lifeline. So, to repeat the question – what is the Simon Fraser study a case of? Amongst many, many other hypotheses, it provides a case study of the theory of the 'second chance'.

For another example of the underlying, often unseen potential for generalisation from the case study let me link up two of the previous examples – young fathers and redundant steel workers. These are hardly studies of the 'same' phenomenon. What then are these case studies of? Recall that both identify sub-groups who followed different trajectories in response to fateful moments in their lives. In both examples the research locates individuals who recover from setback and others who remain mired. We might thus begin to think of both inquiries as case studies of 'resilience' in the face of abrupt changes in the life course. Both inquiries seek out the identity of 'crisis survivors' and 'crisis strugglers'.

Using this lens, what comparable lessons might be learnt? Consider in this respect the two most 'successful' sub-groups in making some form of recovery from personal crisis, namely, the young fathers with a 'skilled' trajectory and redundant workers who were 'active career planners'. In this respect it is instructive to read the transcripts of the Dominics and the Bens, and then the Jeffs and the Dereks who represent the respective groups. Differences abound; after all we are comparing young people and the middle-aged. But, read closely and commonalities also spring forth. There are common identities – the strong attachment to the role of male breadwinner. There are common levels of communal support – especially from close family who might share in the solutions. There is a common understanding and close familiarity with institutional lifelines – the availability of education and training support. There is a measure of cultural capital in the ability to foresee future opportunities. There is a common level of personal resilience – the stubborn willingness to sit through hard times in the expectation that there will be a new normal. It is these miniature theories that explain similarities and differences in causal trajectories that apply in both case studies. The within-case comparisons inspire cross-case comparisons. What we have in essence here is a different model of generality, a nascent example of extensional generalisation.

Let us examine the mechanics more closely. The first point to note is that I've made the connection between the two studies. Pawson has drawn parallels between redundancy and fatherhood that because of the atomisation of inquiry would normally lay dormant. For obvious reasons the noted equivalence could not possibly enter the heads of Neale or Gardiner. Big questions follow – (i) are such linkages feasible and (ii) do they constitute a legitimate form of inquiry? Answer 'yes' and 'yes'.

First question. The repurposing of explanation is perfectly achievable because of the social sciences' collective immersion in studies of social stratification. In all walks of life, researchers have detailed the dynamics of inequality. This shared memory provides researchers with a portfolio of guesses, a storehouse of theories that they may call upon in any new inquiry on any new fault line. So, Neale and Gardiner, Smith and Jones, Uncle Tom Cobleigh and all, know full well, at the commencement of inquiry, that different groups of people will respond to crisis situations in recognisable ways. And they know, roughly, the kinds of reasoning and resources that will propel the varied responses. Such empirical outcomes are rooted in common, underlying patterns of social entrapment and in common struggles to resist it.

These conjectural anchorages, these thematic storehouses are the very essence of academic disciplines. They are also the pathway to generalisable explanations. But the potential interconnections are often unheralded and usually left untied – to repeat, social inquiry tends to the atomised and sequential, rather than the cumulative and confederational. Any new inquiry, whilst calling tacitly on the collective memory will prefer to capture the moment, to add empirical nuance, to invent the odd neologism, and to hammer home the specifics. Collectively, there is still a preference to pile up within-case comparisons without acknowledging that they also apply cross-case. Research routinely pours old wine into new bottles but prefers not to acknowledge it. In doing so, the opportunity for seeking extensional generality is missed. Rather than remaining tacit, rather than being pulled together in the ad hoc fashion as in my fatherhood $\approx$ redundancy example, the borrowings, the connections, and the cross-case extensions need to be made formal and explicit.

The second question. Is this explanatory scrounging a legitimate manoeuvre in the cannons of research methodology? Sure is. Indeed, it has a name. It is called middle-range theory. It lies at the heart of social science's quest for generality and is the topic for the next episode.

KEY LESSONS

Episode 33 examines the internal structure of a case study. All social inquiry seeks to understand differences in outcomes and trajectories in the system under study. In a single case study, the iterative process of organic sampling allows the researcher to identify important within-case differences in these trajectories. But more significantly for present purposes, it generates theories to account for these differences. Those same theories then become the launchpad for between-case explanation. The great strength of organic sampling in case study research is that it deploys and builds realist causal explanation. Different choices made in different contexts create different outcomes. Adding further case studies provides the potential for a composite understanding of these causal configurations. This capacity to move from within-case to cross-case explanations opens up the pathway to extensional generalisation. Its realisation is pursued in the next episodes.

Episode 34. Middle-range theory and the confederation of explanation

In 2005 at an International Sociology Congress in Stockholm I gave a paper entitled, 'Whatever happened to middle-range theory?' It was delivered as a mock eulogy, a tribute to the greatest idea of the greatest American sociologist – Robert K. Merton. I did not wear a black armband, but I did look forward to a glass of brännvin at the 'wake' that followed. At the time, as I was able to show with the help of a little bibliographic snooping, the term middle-range theory had more or less disappeared from the sociological literature. I am pleased to say that there has been something of a revival in recent times. My goodness, in the title of a recent paper, Cartwright (2020) feels able to declare, 'Middle-range theory: without it what could anyone do?' Quite so.

I have written previously about the close connection between middle-range theory and realist inquiry (Pawson, 2000), about the continuities in the middle-range thinking in the work of Merton and Boudon (Pawson, 2009), and about the importance of middle-range theory in policy evaluation (Pawson, 2010). Here, I want to concentrate on the idea of middle-range theory as the pivotal device for producing generalisable explanation in social science.

Let us begin at the beginning with Merton's relatively brief paper introducing the idea of middle-range theory (reprinted in Merton, 1968b, chapter 2). They are 'theories that lie between the minor but necessary working hypotheses that evolve in abundance during day-to-day research and the all-inclusive systematic efforts to develop a unified theory that will explain all the observed uniformities of social behaviour, social organization and social change' (Merton, 1968b). This, perhaps the most famous definition, is disappointing for it only tells us what middle-range theories are not. The paper was written in response to the domination of 'grand theory' and 'piecemeal empiricism'. The culprits of his time were, respectively, 'social system theorists' and 'multivariate modellers'. Both have waned in influence over the years but many modern academic tribes remain who suppose that it is possible to theorise without empirical content or that our task is to provide endless descriptive content without the need for unifying explanation.

So what exactly is Merton striving for? Let us peruse another definition. Middle-range theories are 'sufficiently abstract to deal with different spheres of social behavior and social structure, so that they transcend sheer description or empirical generalisation' (Merton, 1968b). The second clause we know already – approaches to be avoided. The first clause is the key: what does he mean by the idea of confederating 'different spheres of social behaviour and structure'? One can gain a first grasp by thinking of three research mentalities at the beginning of an investigation. They approach some novel, contemporary happening., of which the first says, 'I have a master theory, it explains everything – watch it work again.' The second says, 'This is a grossly neglected topic, never researched before; let me provide the pioneering explanation.' The third, sitting gracefully and modestly in the middle, says, 'Here's a theory that has had some success in explaining aspects of one social situation; let us try it out on another, and then another.'

In modern parlance, Merton wants to 'repurpose' theories – to continually adapt them beyond the original formulation. A key part of his plan was to break sociology out of its disparate substantive silos – education, health and illness, organisation, crime and deviance, stratification, family, community, science, gender, development, power, race and ethnicity, culture, and so on. Each of these might be expected to contain similar social processes that might yield to broadly the same social explanation. But these time-honoured domains do not collapse into one. Middle-range theory seeks only to conjoin particular features of them, or what Merton refers to as 'delimited aspects of social phenomenon'. I illustrate this in Figure 34.1. The large 'shape' icons, all being different, represent the diverse substantive domains of social inquiry. Middle-range theory seeks to confederate explanation of delimited features therein, as represented by the smaller spheres. Note his favoured term 'confederation'. It encapsulates Merton's distinctive approach to generalisation. We do not aspire to a unified theory of everything but a middle-range theory that explains and unites specific features of quite different social phenomena. We are able to spot similarities amidst the differences.

Hopefully readers will recognise Figure 34.1 as another embodiment of the basic diagram on extensional generalisation introduced in Episode 27. This is not simple, part-to-whole generalisation. Generality on this model moves from one case to the many, it depends on the use of middle-range abstractions, and what are transferred from case to case are explanations.

I will develop a methodological script for all of these features in due course, but for now a brief example of confederation will be helpful, the obvious choice being Merton's pet middle-range theory, namely, the theory of references group affiliation. The general idea is that people take the standards of 'significant others' as a basis for monitoring their own situations. They create expectations for themselves by making comparisons (positive and negative) with other groups. Merton first used the theory to explain the sometimes-surprising loyalties and jealousies of US servicemen drafted in World War II (Stouffer et al., 1949). In the major syntheses of the theory

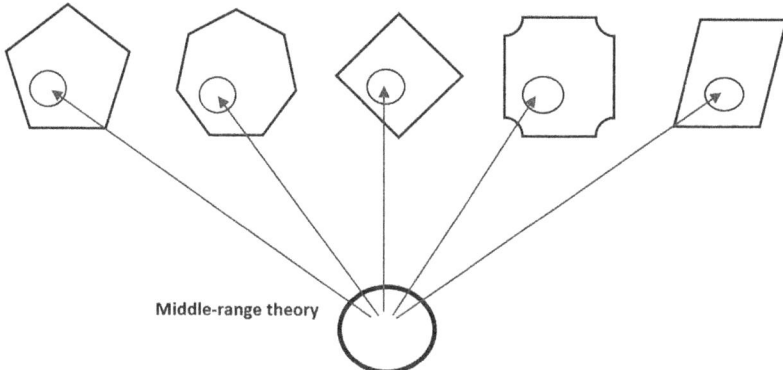

Figure 34.1   Middle-range theory: confederating different 'spheres of social behaviour'

(Merton, 1968b, chapters 10 and 11), he moved on from the peculiarities of military life to show the same underlying processes are able to 'confederate findings from disparate fields such of race and ethnic relations, social mobility, delinquency, politics, education, and revolutionary activity'.

In the years that followed the list of applications grew. In the early days of UK industrial sociology, it was used to explain why shipyard workers in the north of England measured their worth minutely and disputatiously by fighting for pay differentials from trade to trade, with never a care for comparison with wealthy southern stockbrokers (Runciman, 1966). Onwards the idea travelled, encompassing, for instance, the finding that those with Parkinson's disease were able to maintain a positive outlook about their uncontrollable symptoms by selectively comparing their plight favourably to those in a later stage of illness (Charlton and Barrow, 2002). Reference group theory arrives in the present day in explaining how anti-vaxxers were able to maintain the seditious belief that coronavirus was a biological weapon developed by the Chinese government (Romer and Jamieson, 2020). Groups that feel politically disenfranchised are more likely to use as reference groups the ideas from other sources that question the legitimacy of the entire political system. Conspiracy theorists are a tailor-made reference group. Another interesting example is the recent substantial increase in people reporting mental health problems. How much of this is due to a change in reference group affiliation? The 'prevalence inflation' hypothesis states that the huge increase in mental health awareness campaigns has led to a change in popular discourse (Foulkes and Andrews, 2022). The stigma of 'mental illness' has given way to the normalisation of 'mental health issues'. Interpreting one's difficulties as a mental health problem now has some social value. A once shameful reference group has become legitimate. Finally, consider the ultimate modern incarnation of the reference group – the 'influencer'. Not everyone is captivated (or fooled) by these role models and market research spends a small fortune in seeking out the perfect match between the particular product, the particular consumer group, and the ideal influencer (Belanche et al., 2021).

Many, many more examples could be called upon as Merton demonstrates in the mammoth chapters noted above. But even my more modest list of updates in the paragraph above exemplify the middle-range compromise between explanatory width and explanatory depth. The examples roam from rivalry in the workplace, to health beliefs, to marketing. They have limited things to say about all of them but make no pretence of being the sociology of work, healthcare, consumer behaviour, and so on. To repeat for emphasis – the *delimited* substantive focus is represented in Figure 34.1 by the smaller circles within each shape figure.

Next, an important clarification. Middle-range theory deploys middle-range abstraction, but it is not defined by nor restricted to the production of abstract concepts. Readers will recall that I have been deeply ambivalent about the power of conceptual abstraction. I have noted its haphazard role in everyday understanding (Episode 28). I have noted the superficial power of sensitising concepts (Episode 28). I have noted the bogus allure of naturalistic generalisation (Episode 32). But middle-range theory, as its name suggests, is about theorising and not conceptualisation. It is all too easy to see an idea like the 'reference group' as a conceptual gadabout, as a metaphoric echo chamber. Name any group and it is easy to locate the significant others who act as comparators, both negative and positive. Everyone but everyone looks over their own shoulders. In my teaching days I used to ask students to identify a particular social group and to name others who set standards, inspire, curb, or influence its members. It is easy, all too easy. Conceptual abstraction promises mountains but delivers a range of molehills.

Middle-range theories are theories. They are propositions, hypotheses, models, explanations. They deal in causality and the understanding of causality is realist. In the founding essay Merton goes on to describe their composition as follows: 'Limited sets of assumptions from which specific hypotheses are logically derived and confirmed by empirical investigation' (1968b). This, I think, is the key definition and it must be teased out – remaining with the example of reference group behaviour.

Causal explanations of social life begin with some significant stimulus, which might occur on a different scale – it might be a major historical turn, a pandemic, a local uprising, a policy innovation, a bureaucratic reform, a social programme, or simply a significant life event. The stimulus produces a disparate response. The uprising amplifies or peters out, the pandemic flares or declines, the policy has intended and in untended consequences, the life course change prompts mindfulness or proves a minefield. What stands between stimulus and response is the mechanism and the context. The mechanism describes the many different ways that the stimulus may be interpreted, and the context explains how those interpretations will vary from location to location, group to group, individual to individual. Accordingly, reference group theory requires much more than the naming of significant others, it must have a causal structure. It must explain why incumbents of the 'same' group behave differently. It must explain their different points of comparison. It must explain the consequences of their different choices.

In short, Merton wants us to construct causal explanations with a clear proposition structure. This mission is handled by building theories supposition by supposition. The basic task is to provide a 'set of assumptions' lying behind the observed associations and from which they can 'be derived' (Merton, 1968b). It 'introduces a ground for prediction which is more secure than mere empirical extrapolation from previously observed trends' (Merton, 1968b). In different terminology, one can say that middle-range theories utilise predictive, probabilistic models. Figure 34.2 adapts Figure 34.1, inserting model building between the conceptual framework and the empirical instances.

The middle-range theory (large circle, bottom of the diagram) assembles a set of component properties that constitute its core conceptual framework. These are made up of the key mechanisms and contexts that will provide the causal explanation. They are developed at a level of abstraction having the potential to cross substantive boundaries. Key concepts are represented using a token three smaller circles within the core middle-range theory. Moving upward via the large arrow we come to the model. Middle-range models take the form of 'if-then' propositions. In realist terminology they take the following form. If this configuration of mechanisms and contexts is in place, then a particular outcome pattern is more likely to follow ... if a different arrangement of mechanisms and contexts applies, then the outcome will be altered. Different explanatory configurations are developed in the centre of the figure (depicted by variations of the three basic concepts). The explanatory structure takes the form of predictions about how different configurations will generate different outcomes. The model proceeds organically identifying a range of potentially significant within-case and between-case trajectories. The predictions are tested in a range of empirical cases and instances (the many upward arrows).

Alas, this model-building feature of middle-range theory had been overlooked in the literature. It is the means by which it 'transcends sheer description'. It is high time for an empirical example. The pivotal importance of middle-range models can be grasped by returning to their usage in reference

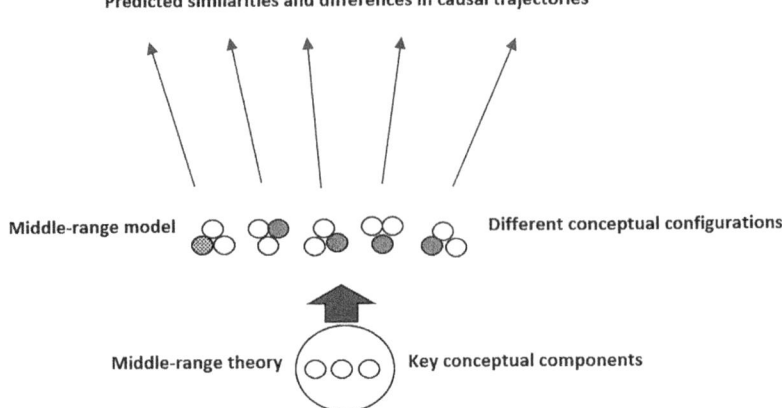

Figure 34.2   Middle-range models: from concepts to explanations

group theory. Merton produces an array of different models in his 'contributions' and 'continuities' in reference group theory (1968b, chapters 10 and
11). One of them examines in much more detail the simple distinction between
membership and non-membership of a social group. As far as the individual
is concerned, life is sometimes lived on the inside and sometimes outside and
sometimes on the margins of the plethora of existing groups. You may be
a wife, a mother, a Catholic, a yoga enthusiast, a cricket supporter, etc. But you
may want to be a feminist, a novelist, an actor, an influencer, a cricket umpire,
etc. Each station, actual and potential, ascribed and proscribed, will carry different meanings and quite different possibilities of being realised. Table 34.1
examines 'outsiders' and posits a more complex set of possible affiliations to
group membership.

Table 34.1, the initial casing, focuses entirely on 'non-members' of a group
and considers how they might perceive 'membership'. A model, a series
of explanatory propositions, is created hypothesising that there are some
significant distinctions *within* this 'outsider' station. First of all, it is feasible
to differentiate between those who (by dint of resources or qualification or
characteristic) are simply ineligible for the in-group and those who are potentially eligible thanks to the possession of the appropriate requirements but
who continue to remain unaffiliated. This simple contrast between entitlement
to and disqualification from in-group membership is represented in the two
columns to the right of the table. The model also takes into consideration the
question of attitude to group membership of these non-members. Do they want
to belong to the in-group? An approximate three-fold distinction in this respect

Table 34.1   Outsiders: a typology of aspirations to group membership of 'eligibles' and 'non-eligibles'

Attitude toward membership	Eligible for membership	Ineligible for membership
Aspire to belong	1.Candidate for membership	2. Marginal member
Indifferent to affiliation	3. Potential member	4. Detached non-member
Motivated not to belong	5. Autonomous non-member	6. Antagonistic non-member

Source: Redrawn and relabelled from Merton (1968b, p. 344).

(aspiration, indifference, opposition) is depicted moving down the three rows of the table. As always in realist inquiry, resources and reasoning, structure and agency, capacities and choice carry the causal punch.

Putting the two factors (eligibility and attitude) together forms the model as depicted in the middle section of Figure 34.2. The model generates a repertoire of abstract, if-then propositions about different forms of reference group dispositions, according to the group's location within the six constituent cells. In cell 1 we have non-members who both aspire to and are eligible for in-group membership. Reference group theory posits that they are likely to choose that in-group as a yardstick for their behaviour, to act in ways that closely resemble the behaviour of the in-group and, eventually, to benefit from doing so. Cell 2 members, by contrast, may want to and attempt to copy the values and behaviours of the in-group but the model advises that they are more likely to remain shunned and on its margins because of the lack of some crucial membership attribute. Merton actually used the label 'marginal man' for this cell, borrowing it from a celebrated study of his era (Stonequist, 1937). In modern, gender-free parlance we might now regard them as 'wannabes' who remain unwanted.

Moving to the second row, cells 3 and 4 locate sub-groups who are deeply ambivalent about in-group membership. 'They are entirely indifferent to its orbit. It constitutes no part of their reference group' (Merton, 1968b). In everyday life, neither of these two groups is likely to reach out to or take cognisance of the in-group. The main difference is that those in cell 3 may simply be more adjacent to its ambit; they are potentially qualified for membership and are aware of its role expectations. But they have other ambitions. Those in cell 4 are equally detached from the in-group but less likely to receive any contact with or overtures from the inside. As a result, they remain in limbo – unqualified for and indifferent to the slim opportunities to join it.

The bottom row identifies outsiders who deeply oppose membership of an in-group. Indifference turns to resentment. The model differentiates them according to whether they are eligible (cell 5) or non-eligible (cell 6) to join that group in the first place. Both regard the in-group with some hostility. But the eligibility distinction raises the Simmelian hypothesis, that the qualified individuals who expressly reject membership are more likely to pose a threat to that group than are the antagonists automatically disbarred from membership. The 5's self-chosen autonomy provides the conditions for direct hostility. The 6's opposition is likely to remain more diffuse and unfocused.

In this manner, the table builds a formal explanatory model supplying a degree of predictive power about what will happen in encounters between in-group and out-group members. Causal hypotheses are provided forecasting significant qualitative differences in behavioural outcomes for different sub-groups. According to the precise location of out-group actors in the conceptual matrix of eligibility and attitude, one can expect a whole range of dispositions to the in-group ranging from chummy acquiesce to downright hostility. So here in a nutshell is how Merton intends social inquiry to proceed. Social life will continue to throw up many instances in which a group is cast into 'outsider status'. Rather than treat them afresh and describe the multifarious ensuing reactions, he wants inquiry to be led by pre-existing hypotheses about the precise affiliations within the group studied. In any 'new' study, what are the outsider sub-groups? Are they 'membership candidates', 'marginal members', 'antagonistic non-members', and so on? Over which cells (1 to 6) in Table 34.1 are these outsiders distributed? Extensional generalisability is achieved as more and more primary studies utilise and extend the model across different social spheres.

We now have a template and an example of the construction of predictive, probabilistic, middle-range causal hypotheses. But how are they populated and tested? This is the topic for the next episode.

KEY LESSONS

Episode 34 celebrates the manufacture of middle-range theories as an exemplification of the idea of extensional generalisation. Theory has the task of confederating findings in empirical study after empirical study. This absorptive, synthesising function captures the very meaning of generality. Middle-range theories have a distinctive structure. They are causal propositions pitched at a level of abstraction that allows them to make explanatory connections between different spheres of social behaviour. They begin by differentiating between the sub-groups/sub-situations that comprise a particular class of behaviours. For each sub-group, hypotheses are constructed on their respective reasoning and resources. These are combined into a model which makes probabilistic predictions about the different consequences of these choices and capacities. They take the form of if-then models, having the explanatory potential for explaining similarities and differences, within and between many empirical cases.

Episode 35. Populating, testing, and scoping middle-range theory

Attention turns to the later stages of middle-range explanation. How do we utilise and test the abstract models? How do we populate the models with findings from empirical research? How do we draw boundaries on where the models apply? In short, how do we execute and complete a middle-range study? Merton's own strategy is perhaps eccentric. Picture him striding from the sociology department to the university library at Columbia (no internet in those days). His goal is to push to the limit the idea of confederating explanation of 'different spheres of social behaviour'. He searches the shelves for examples, for case studies. And these come thick and fast (Merton, 1968b, chapter 10). He finds examples in contemporary research on 'renagadism, treason, the assimilation of immigrants, class mobility, social climbing' that fit the bill. He works across the library classification and finds reference group behaviour in the 'sociology of military life, race and ethnic relations, social mobility, delinquency, education, politics and revolution'. He recalls parallels in sociological classics, such as in the reference groups identified in Durkheim's subtypes of suicide. Example after example is chewed over in paragraph after paragraph, and deposited, somewhat randomly, in footnote after footnote.

His method, in short, is to ransack the existing literature. He is a plunderer. This brings us to the remaining characteristic of middle-range theory, which again, alas, is largely ignored and unexplored in the literature. Interestingly, paradoxically, it is about the perils of plundering. Merton (1968b) recognises this as a problem and adds a final methodological rule as follows: 'The middle-range orientation involves the specification of ignorance. Rather than pretend knowledge where in fact it is absent, it expressly recognizes what must still be learned in order to lay the foundations for still more knowledge.' The danger, Merton warns himself, is to find empirical instances galore and to assume that the theory applies everywhere. Plunder at your peril. Middle-range theory is extremely proficient at linking different spheres of social behaviour but there must be stopping rules and there must be scope conditions. It is important to locate and stipulate the exact family of instances where the theory has genuine explanatory power.

It is instructive to apply this imperative to the model of outsider behaviour in Table 34.1 and I illustrate the predicament with a little plundering of my own. Think again of the characters in that table, that medley of outsiders – (1) the candidates, (2) the marginals, (3) the potentials, (4) the detached, (5) the autonomous, and (6) the antagonistic. It is possible and indeed quite inspiring to find instances galore that follow the predictions in the model. In the previous episode I drew instant parallels between two sub-groups who experienced some form of recovery from personal crisis, namely, the young fathers with a 'skilled' trajectory and redundant workers who were 'active career planners'. They belong to very different walks of life but demonstrate how it is perfectly possible to confederate diverse 'spheres of social behaviour'.

Moreover, with a little more scrutiny of the same examples, it is possible to further extend the middle-range theory on the behaviour of outsiders. Both of the two sub-groups in the previous paragraph can be conceptualised as 'marginal members' (category 2). Redundant workers become outsiders thanks to unemployment. Young freewheeling men lose their previous identity due to unplanned, unexpected fatherhood. But both sub-groups are also 'aspirational'. So, as the theory predicts for sub-group 2, both do all in their powers to establish a new insider identity – in different employment spheres in the case of the former and as traditional breadwinners in the case of the latter. The theory holds good and confederates two seemingly disparate cases.

The model gains more spurs if we proceed further to the behaviour of other sub-groups into the same substantive examples. Gardiner et al. (2009) introduce us to a redundant cluster at the 'career crossroads'. They had difficulty finding and had little interest in the new opportunities that became available in the area (IT training, welfare work, etc.). Lifestyles were significantly crushed by loss of earnings. Family life developed disruptions and tensions. As a result, this group tended to drift, they remained uncertain of where to turn. In reference group terms, they are 'detached non-members' (category 4). Their behaviour is mired in ambivalence.

Consider next the 'low-skilled' trajectory in Neale and Davies's (2015) study. These young men were outsiders. They had negligible qualifications and intermittent work histories, and were dependent on out-of-work benefits. Most of them had tenuous and volatile relations with their families. Unplanned parenthood creates a further crisis. Even though many of the young men tried to create positive relationships with the mother and child, their meagre resources and chaotic lifestyles prevented any possibility of achieving traditional breadwinner status. They drifted from benefit to benefit, lodging to lodging, training placement to training placement. They were marooned in inactivity and ambivalence. Accordingly, aspirations to parental responsibility simply came and went. One can say that they typified the behaviour of 'detached non-members' (category 4). Over time, a fraction of this group drifted into drugs and petty crime, completely abandoning their families and children. They deliberately vacated all concern for insider status and became 'antagonistic non-members' (category 6).

Moving to the prison estate, we encounter the outsiders of all outsiders – inmates, incarcerated out of harm's way. Yet their reference group affiliations vary immensely. Duguid and Pawson's (1998) study of prisoner education is easily recast in the corresponding terminology. There are many 'marginal members' (category 2), prisoners with poor education and work records who have gradually shifted from petty to more serious crime. Yet some of them remain aspirational; they find prison life intolerable and grasp any opportunity of going straight. Success in education in prison may provide that slim second chance of approaching insider status and they grasp it. Other inmates are content to remain 'antagonistic non-members' (category 6). Prisoner education can provide a pleasant pastime, especially for those high-flyers already well qualified. But it has no impact on their identity and future ambitions, except perhaps to harden their identity and make them cleverer criminals.

The explanatory fecundity of the outsider typology begins to reveal itself. I have simply added contemporary examples to the dozens provided by Merton. Note, again, that these empirical extensions are the mark of genuine explanatory power and do considerably more work than in the repeated, static applications of 'sensitising concepts'. Here is the crucial difference. Middle-range theory extends both inwards and outwards. The middle-range model is able to explain similarities and differences *between cases* (e.g., redundant workers and young fathers) but also similarities and differences *within cases* (e.g., marginal and antagonist inmates). It is thus able to differentiate and predict a range of behaviours in different environments. The model is dynamic. It is capable of growth and such explanatory cumulation is what makes a discipline.

There is, however, a flipside to the coin of explanatory fertility in middle-range theory. An adequate test of a model requires much more than trawling for new examples, for examples are a little too easy to plunder. A good theory always makes clear its scope conditions. For instance, in the above I have corralled together some actions of some redundant steelworkers, some young fathers, and some prisoners as typifying the role of 'marginal outsiders', 'detached non-members', 'antagonistic non-members', and so on. No doubt these placements could be extended to many other spheres of behaviour – health beliefs, educational opportunities, political preferences, and so on. And no doubt sociology would be all the better for such explanatory cumulation rather than endless neologism and redescription.

But before one jumps immediately to the idea of instant explanatory unification, we also have to contemplate what lies unexplained in the growing list of examples. This is what Merton means by the 'specification of ignorance' – acknowledging what lies unacknowledged in the network of between-case and within-case comparisons. So let us return to the typology of outsider aspirations (Table 34.1) and consider potential omissions. The model explains outsider activity on the basis of two mechanisms – eligibility and attitude. What is missing?

Consider but two plausible omissions. An out-group's perception of an in-group might also depend upon: (i) the degree of closure and self-protection of the in-group, and (ii) the longevity of membership in the out-group. These two factors separate the cases that we have previously conjoined. In respect of the former, there are rather solid economic and cultural barriers extending throughout society that limit the rehabilitation of prisoners, whilst the return to employment presents practical barriers rather than closed shops, and admission to fatherhood is, on the whole, more of a norm than an obstacle. In respect of the second hypothesis on longevity of group membership, prisoners serve 'time' as it is often put, and its passage tends to cement their identity as 'ex-cons'. By comparison, imminent redundancy and impending fatherhood are relatively unexpected, short-term conditions, and, accordingly, these identities are not so indelible.

In short, one sees how middle-range models can explain many similarities and differences within a case and many similarities and difference between cases but, of course, cannot cover all permutations in all cases. Like all scientific theories, the explanatory model only works up to a point. There is nothing untoward in that and the solutions are the same as they have always been. In a single study, the researcher explains variation via a chosen set of case comparisons and then specifies ignorance. Potential omissions and potential extensions to a study are acknowledged in its conclusions. If, however, like Merton, one has a couple of decades to explore further, one can add 'continuities' to the theory. Merton (1968b, chapter 7) thus continued to build the theory of reference group behaviour through a series of other formal extensions to the model. One of these covers the issue mentioned above about the varying levels of closure of different in-groups. Another tackles more complex behavioural choices when there are multiple, competing reference groups. Extensional generalisation is not infinite. Its boundaries extend and ignorance diminishes, but never disappears.

A puzzle remains. In my introduction to middle-range theory I acknowledged that it came close to extinction for many decades. Somewhat teasingly, may I offer an explanation of near-death by way of reference group theory? In my discipline one becomes an accredited insider by way of expertise in 'theory' or 'methods' or a 'substantive' domain. Merton wants to supersede these traditional substantive domains of social inquiry if only in respect of 'delimited aspects'. But what defines the scope of those limited interconnections? What is the 'something' that binds them together? In the working example, dilemmas presented by fatherhood, redundancy, and prisoner rehabilitation are conjoined. What binds them together? What gives them identity? I've suggested that the adhesive concerns 'life crisis', 'identity dilemmas', 'resilience', etc. Middle-range expertise is thus forged when one becomes a sociologist of 'life crisis', 'identity dilemmas', 'resilience', and the like. The problem is that such specialities do not crop up in the library classification or on the undergraduate curriculum. Middle-range theory remains an aspirational outsider – easily overlooked.

I must not over-exaggerate. Nursing science, by contrast, is thickly populated by middle-range theories. It is a staple of journals and textbooks (Meleis et al., 2000; Smith et al., 2024). What are the delimited but cross-cutting themes that are explored? There are, for instance, theories of: 'symptom management', 'self-reliance', 'cultural marginality', 'caregiving dynamics', 'life transitions', 'story-centred practice'. For a full list, see the Smith volume. I have no space here to describe them; perhaps the titles alone are sufficient enough to give an impression of cross-cutting themes. These are aspects of nursing that are instantly recognisable and apply generally. Take the idea of assisting the patient to build 'self-reliance'. This process is not specific to the condition being treated, nor the rank of the practitioner, nor the characteristics of the patient, nor the type of healthcare facility, and so on. Middle-range theory pounces on such generic practices and much is to be learned by comparison of their outworkings across many different healthcare domains.

KEY LESSONS

Episode 35 examines the process of testing middle-range theory. How do we gather evidence to support its development? Middle-range models take the form of if-then models, which explain when, where, and why empirical regularities might and might not hold. In general terms, the models predict differences in the behaviour of sub-groups and sub-situations of those involved in a particular sphere of social behaviour. These predictions are traced, tested, and deepened in between-case and within-case investigations of the postulated sub-groups and sub-situations. They gain wider traction, they increase in generalisability, if they are able to explain similarities and differences in outcomes across more and more cases. Expansion into ever-widening domains is the aim. But middle-range models are never all-embracing, they need boundary rules. Like all theories their scope has to be carefully delimited, otherwise the coveted explanatory expansion becomes haphazard.

Episode 36. Research synthesis as generalisation

This episode explores an alternative practical route to building generalisable explanations in social science. I have bestowed upon middle-range theory the function (and the glory) of confederating inquiry. Many inquiries are brought together over time. Accordingly, the requisite growth, the gradual consolidation is the function of a discipline rather than a property of an individual inquiry. It requires collective, collaborative imagination. Merton began his work on reference-group theory well before World War II. Case examples were added over a long period in the various editions of *Social Theory and Social Structure* (see the preface to the 1957 and 1968 editions for the timeline). Applications have been added to this day. Reference group theory can be considered a ready-made, up-and-functioning example of a middle-range theory. It is prepackaged and ready to go. But what if the researcher enters the fray without an off-the-peg theory in mind? How might connections be made to other inquiries. There is another strategy of synthesising inquiry, which involves reversing the protracted timeline.

I have argued throughout Parts I and II that all inquiry starts with theory. We do not build up from observational data for sensory observation is infinite and needs something to guide it. Accordingly, the research process proceeds back and forth from theory to evidence. The guesses and conjectures at the starting of inquiry are gradually tested, refined, adapted, and hardened. This is the organic, incremental process described in Episode 33, as when an individual case study is probed to discover internal differences. On close inspection, the particular case is found to comprise different collections of agents with different agendas. How might this theory refinement process move from one case to another, from one study to a collection of studies? The requisite iterative strategy is presented in Figure 36.1 in a deliberately idealised form.

Begin in the middle with any current inquiry. It will move organically between theory and evidence. At T_1 we have the initial hunches and conjectures. Different pieces of evidence (E_A and E_B) are assembled over time and the explanatory theory is refined by stages (T_2) with a temporary resting point at T_3. In our idealised world, this 'present inquiry' will have been informed by 'previous inquiries' which have tackled the same, delimited family of substantive issues but not covered every angle (they will have specified ignorance).

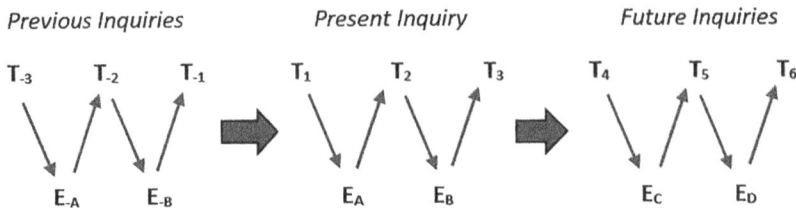

Figure 36.1   *Research synthesis: building on and building onwards from inquiry*

They will, however, have utilised the same investigatory zigzag, pictured to the left of the figure. The theories leading these previous inquiries are depicted with minus subscripts indicating that they are earlier incarnations of similar conjectures. Likewise, the evidence chains have minus signs indicating their chronological place. We then move to 'future inquiries', depicted to the right. Ideally, these should be informed by the previous sequence of investigation and so explanatory power builds. Theories T_4, T_5, T_6, with the support from E_C and E_D, increase the depth and the breadth of understanding. Collected together, the sequence of investigations becomes a middle-range theory. The emerging theory has a large number of consequences which are supported with a growing evidence base. Progress through the whole sequence is depicted by the larger, block arrows, which represent the key goal of the gradual confederation of inquiry.

   In real as opposed to idealised inquiry, such interconnections may be sought, overlooked, or ignored. But if a discipline makes claim to 'progress', if there is a 'growth of knowledge', then such lines of inquiry must be decipherable. Indeed, Figure 36.1 deliberately mimics Popper's famous (1992) depiction of the evolutionary process whereby scientific theories progress by gradually eliminating gaps and errors in what came before. But does social inquiry look like this? Some of its present-day features mitigate against this model. Substantive silos remain powerful – criminal justice scholars do not read public health research, and so on and so on. And then there is the relentless pursuit of originality – the race to be the first to research a novel public issue (of which there is an endless supply). Put in a nutshell, I suppose that it would be a rare paper indeed that begins, 'Here is an unprecedented issue. This study will tackle it using a theory that has been around for many a year in many a field.'

   I must not over-exaggerate, some important conventions remain – bibliographic citations to previous research, oversight in journals by specialists in the same field, the publication of replies and rejoinders, and so on. One might say that in social inquiry, the process illustrated in Figure 36.1 operates in fits and starts. The process in full fledge is, however, a fundamental requirement in the production of middle-range theory. It is often said that a discipline that forgets its founders is lost. More mundanely here, I vouch for the idea of tackling new issues using old theories. Such a process is a prerequisite of extensional generalisation. How can it be simulated? How can it be brought to life?

For once we have a straightforward answer. We can work backwards! We can run the process retrospectively. This is the task for 'research synthesis' or 'research review'. Modern research output is prolific and unplanned. New investigations tend to ignite haphazardly, disconnectedly. Even if connectivity was an expectation, any new investigation is unlikely to have the time, the resources, and the warrant to seek significant wisdom from previous studies. One helpful solution is to rethink that warrant. Rather than firing off inquiries ad nauseum, let us stem the tide of new investigations and seek to discover what existing research has to say. Let us weave backwards to locate the vital zigzag of theory and evidence. This strategy may be envisioned by running all arrows in Figure 36.1 in reverse.

This radical but simple idea was my inspiration for developing the methodology of 'realist synthesis' (Pawson, 2006). It is a particularly apt strategy for the 'small batch' production that typifies social inquiry, none more so than in the arena of public policy research. Policy makers unleash programmes and interventions in huge volleys. This is the era of evidence-based policy, so each of these initiatives is likely to have been put to research under the auspices of 'evaluation research'. This 'cottage industry' model has been a recipe for knowledge fragmentation. By and large, evaluation research is contract research, so each inquiry is handled separately by different teams applying disparate methodologies. The result is that there is little or no linkage between studies. No zig and zag. No middle-range output.

All of this is so despite the fact that in the humdrum of policymaking there is a constant borrowing of ideas and huge connectivity between interventions. Policy interventions are if-then theories – 'If we apply these resources in these situations, it should bring about significant change in behavioural outcomes.' These 'programme theories', dare I say because of the limited imagination of policy makers, carry huge similarities. Faced with a fresh crisis or a stubborn social problem, they offer a similar diet of 'carrots or sticks or sermons'. This catchy, caustic phrase was used by Bemelmans-Videc et al. (1998) to emphasise how the same programme theory, give or take a few tweaks, will have been tried in many different times in many different places. Carrots include financial incentives, grants, loans, subsidies, support packages, seed corn funding, vouchers, premium payments, free trials, and so on – as found across healthcare, crime prevention, transport, training, housing, education, and so on. I won't elaborate on the two alternatives other than to note that analysis of a particular 'sermon' is coming up. The important consequence is that we already possess many different empirical investigations of the causal potential of most programme theories. The frequent policy borrowings and their evaluation histories provide the opportunity to develop and refine the programme theories retrospectively. They cry out for joined-up analysis, and the adhesive is provided in the form of middle-range theory.

Such is the rationale for realist synthesis, and it is high time to move to an example. I omit all technical details here as well as discussion of the difference with other approaches to 'systematic review'. These may be obtained from the above-mentioned volume. For a working example, I summarise a review I carried out on youth mentoring (Pawson, 2004). Mentoring, at the time, had taken a grip on the imagination of the policy community. It was based on a simple programme theory – creating a close, one-to-one relationship with a knowledgeable, experienced guide was seen as an all-purpose resource to surmount all kinds of deprivations and disaffections. The pioneering and still most famous intervention of its kind was the Big Brothers Big Sisters of America programme. Since its inception in 1904 it has been imitated the world over.

As a consequence, research studies on youth mentoring are piled high and analysing this agglomeration is an opportunity for research synthesis. We already have a ready-made portfolio of case studies with which to pursue within-case and between-case analysis. Existing studies cover mentoring programmes large and small, aimed at different groups of young people with different types and levels of disengagement. They employ all manner of research methods (qualitative and quantitative) and draw in all manner of evidence (administrative and anecdotal). One feature, however, is completely familiar. Outcomes are mixed – youth mentoring sometimes works and sometimes fails. The core task for synthesis is to develop a generic theory that will explain similarities and differences in these causal trajectories.

I omit the many months of work involved in locating, reading, quality appraising, and extracting evidence from the available studies, and move to the synthesis. The explanation for within-case and cross-case differences begins with tentative theories on how mentoring might work. What goes on within the mentoring relationship that brings about change in the mentee's aspirations and behaviours? What provides the causal powers? As ever in realist analysis, the starting point is to gather hypotheses on the generative mechanism which might bring about the desired changes. The literature revealed some telling differences. It transpired, on close inspection, that the commonsensical but rather amorphous programme theory about the benefits of mentoring relationships turned on quite different mechanisms (Box 36.1).

BOX 36.1 MENTORING MECHANISMS

- **M_1 Befriending**: creating bonds of trust and sharing new experiences, so that the mentee recognises the legitimacy of other people and other perspectives.
- **M_2 Direction Setting**: promoting self-reflection through the discussion of alternative lifestyles leading to a reconsideration of loyalties, values, and ambitions.
- **M_3 Coaching**: coaxing and cajoling the mentee into acquiring the skills, credentials, and testimonials required to move beyond the disaffections of street life.
- **M_4 Sponsoring**: advocating and networking on behalf of the mentee to gain the requisite insider contacts and placements to take up new opportunities and lifestyles.

These initial theoretical insights change the research question. Rather than trying to discover if youth mentoring works, the synthesis turned to the question, 'What specific form or blend of mentoring is applied in any particular intervention and in what circumstances will it work or fail?' The search for evidence thus turned to context. What kind of skills and attributes must the mentor possess to deliver each or all of these mechanisms? What kind of characteristics must the mentee have to respond to them? What kind of relationship must exist between mentor and protégé to achieve the desired end? How does this relationship develop, and can it be sustained over time? What are optimal opportunities, timeframes, meeting places to develop the requisite rapport? Can the developing mentoring relationship withstand rival influences from peers and communities? What additional resources, beyond close interpersonal contact, must the programme have to achieve significant change? It is only by answering this network of questions that the diverse intervention outcomes can be explained. Evidence on all of them was available. Substantive details are omitted here other than to mention a single example on the issue of the questionable sustainability of the relationship between mentor and mentee. Evidence on its fragility was subject to much discussion (and handwringing) in qualitative studies that focused on the intricate mechanics of 'befriending'.

Finally, we come to evidence on intervention outcomes, the conclusions reached in this study. The usual mixed picture of programme success and failure pertained but the permutations are numerous and intricate. I summarise a mere handful of the disparate findings here, each with a snippet of the accompanying evidence, in order to reveal the bare bones of the synthesis (Box 36.2).

BOX 36.2 A MINIATURE, MIDDLE-RANGE MODEL OF MENTORING MEDIATIONS

• Mentor–mentee relationships were often delicate and combustible. Both parties came together on a voluntary and unrehearsed basis. To work optimally relationships required careful matching, with mentors who had very similar beginnings to their charges being more successful.
• The implementation of all programme mechanisms (M_1 to M_4) was rare – few mentees made it from disaffection to life change. Individual mentors rarely had the experience and resources to inculcate all of the change mechanisms.
• The programme theory was often confused. Failed programmes often had ambitions for significant change in lifestyles, envisioning the sustained journey via mechanism M_1 and M_4. Most lacked resources, depending on sporadic contact providing little more that befriending, M_1.
• Mentoring was often aimed at the disaffected and the antagonistic. But passage to and beyond befriending (M_1) mostly applied mentees that were not entirely disengaged. They were often selected (and self-selected) for clear signs of some level of preparedness for change.
• Programmes that succeeded at the higher levels went significantly beyond mentoring. They supplied considerably more that one-to-one contact, including support to the mentees' families, networking opportunities, training provision, and so on.

Box 36.2, delivered at a very high level of compression, only begins to express the explanatory reach of the middle-range theory of youth mentoring. Middle-range models are multifaceted, and it is important to express the explanatory range using diagrams, flowcharts, change maps, etc. These may be found in the original research (Pawson, 2004). The crucial point here, however, is that even this simplified summary articulates the core idea of developing an explanation that spans many different cases and is able to explain within-case and between-case differences. It exemplifies the multi-propositional structure of a middle-range model (recall Figure 34.2). It embodies the idea of extensional generalisation.

One further comment on the conclusions to this particular study may be instructive. Middle-range theories are comprehensive – but by nature they are also fertile. Think again about the differential effectiveness of youth mentoring programmes. Many young people proved difficult to budge, some less so. The precise reasons for the lopsided outcomes are uncovered, sometimes directly from the horses' mouths, across the very many empirical studies under review.

The review has precise, practical boundaries: the case studies are all youth mentoring programmes.

But can we extend the emerging middle-range theory beyond youth mentoring? Can we explain the explanation? Indeed, we can and in more than one way. To see this, it is useful to return to Ragin and Becker's (1992) question, 'What are these case studies of?' Three expansions come immediately to mind. Perforce, the interventions reviewed above are also instances of the broader case of 'mentoring programmes'. A more ambitious programme theory about the wise, experienced councillor has also found its way into the workplace, healthcare systems, business, childcare, breastfeeding to name but a few. Many of the same dynamics on the difficulties of matching, on programme overambition, on unreachable subjects, on the need for supplementary resources, and so on, also apply.

The youth mentoring initiatives are also cases of programmes aimed at 'outsiders'. The protégés belong to an 'out-group' receiving overtures from the 'in-group', as represented by the mentor. Some mentees turn out to be unreachable – perhaps we should think of them as 'antagonist non-members'. Some respond to befriending but without shifting lifestyles – perhaps we can consider them 'detached non-members'. Some may ponder new directions but remain unqualified – 'marginal members' perhaps? And just a few benefit from gaining insider contacts and qualifications, thus representing 'candidate members'. Hey presto – at a stroke the middle-range model of youth mentoring exemplifies the broader model of reference group theory.

Finally, it can be said that mentoring programmes are 'sermons'. The basic ingredient is solid advice, wise counsel, authoritative information. A significant proportion of all policy interventions consist of analogous attempts to advise, to inform, to reason, to point to the benefits of behaviour change. One example is perhaps sufficient. The year-long pre-vaccination Covid control interventions depended basically on the presumed power of messaging – 'stay home, stay alert, save lives', 'remember hands, face, space', etc. The success (or otherwise) of such sermons depends on a similar body of mechanisms and contexts noted above. Who's advising, who's listening? Do they share the same motivations and belief systems? Will wise counsel work without further support or sanctions? Will any change be sustained?

Middle-range theories have this nested, organic character. The middle-range theory of youth mentoring sits inside middle-range theories of institution-based mentoring, of out-group behaviour, and of sermonising. One application inspires another, with the potential of confederating a widening diversity of substantive fields. This explanatory intersection carries the very aim of generalisable social inquiry, consolidating existing inquiry rather than starting from scratch. It is exactly what constitutes the 'sociological imagination' (Wright Mills, 1959).

KEY LESSONS

Episode 36 argues that the method most likely to succeed in creating generalisable explanations will involve some form of research synthesis. Realist synthesis is one such approach, widely used in the evaluation of social and public policies. Similar interventions based on similar programme theories are widely implemented with widely varying outcomes. By developing middle-range theories it becomes possible to explain the chequered history of within-programme and between-programme variations. Generalisable explanations follow from researching the repetition of social processes. In other forms of inquiry, family resemblances between similar processes often go unrecognised, and the opportunity for confederation explanations is often missed. The realist remedy? Explanatory progress demands the combination of retrospective and prospective inquiry.

Episode 37. Comparison, complexity, and the specification of ignorance

In the preceding ten episodes I have steered around some significant methodological potholes and then gradually assembled a realist, middle-range platform for producing generalisable explanations in social science. It may be useful to summarise the basic ingredients (Box 37.1) before introducing some final caveats. Students of the history of sociology might like to compare this effort with the pioneering model (Merton, 1968b).

BOX 37.1 A REALIST, MIDDLE-RANGE PLATFORM FOR PRODUCING GENERALISABLE EXPLANATIONS

- The aim is to study causal processes that repeat themselves throughout society. Societies evolve but have recognisable order because of the recurrence of similar underlying mechanisms.
- Social inquiry is normally organised by substantive field – education, healthcare, crime, race, etc. Middle-range theories sit between them, seeking to explain some aspects of many of them.
- The ability to confederate these diverse substantive spheres begins with the processes of abstraction. Middle-range theory occupies a conceptual space between whole systems theories and operational definitions.
- Causation is understood in realist terms. Causal patterns emerge as agents respond to structures. The causal trajectories explored in middle-range theory are produced by the action of underlying generative mechanisms acting in context and over time.
- Middle-range theories take the form of if-then models. If this configuration of mechanisms and contexts is in place, then a particular causal pattern is more likely to follow. If a different arrangement of mechanisms and contexts applies, then the causal outcome will be altered.
- Middle-range models are thus comparative and probabilistic. They chart the circumstance in which a particular causal trajectory is more likely and less likely to follow. The ability to generalise begins with such probabilistic comparisons.

- Middle-range explanation is case-based. Testing the models involves assembling a set of cases to evaluate whether the if-then predictions apply. Comparisons are made within and between the chosen cases and theory is gradually refined to account for a widening array of differences.
- Some form of research synthesis is required to locate and select the various cases for comparison. Synthesis can be prospective or retrospective.
- Within-case and between-case analysis is potentially limitless. Comparisons cannot be organised on all aspects of all cases. The scope and boundary of the emerging middle-range explanation must be carefully specified.
- The assembled evidence must be sensitive to the ingredients of causal explanation. Case by case, the data must inspect both structure and agency, both mechanism and context. A multi-method evidence base is prerequisite.
- There is no limit to the number and scope of middle-range theories. They may overlap, expand, and swap findings from one to another.

We now have a logistical overview, a method for synthesising studies, and some practical examples building towards an understanding of generalisation in social science. How can the model be extended and what are its limitations? These are the questions for this concluding episode.

To begin with the pivotal product – middle-range theories. I must re-emphasise that they come in far more shapes and sizes than in core examples I have stalked throughout the previous episodes. I have concentrated on one illustration, reference group theory, in order to explain the full platform summarised as Box 37.1. There are, of course, countless other middle-range theories, which have been assembled across different disciplines and substantive areas. I have already noted one hotspot in nursing science (Smith et al., 2024). Let me continue an eccentric list here – restorative criminal justice (McCold, 2000); management theory (Sanchez et al., 2017); spatial demography (Howell et al., 2015); migration (Engbersen et al., 2016); social work (Loewenberg, 1984); and even archaeology (Smith, 2011).

Merton was abundantly clear that the 'middle' in middle range did not refer to research conducted at the interpersonal level, as typified by reference group theory. Accordingly, there have been other attempts to develop a micro middle-range outlook in psychology (e.g., Friedman, 2015). The main omission from the previous account, however, is the research conducted in the domain of comparative historical research in sociology and political science. The substantive scale is decidedly macro, what Tilly (1984) refers to as the study of 'Big Structures, Large Processes, Huge Comparisons'. Such comparisons by their very nature are extensional; they seek to draw together and explain patterns that apply globally.

The methodological repertoire is equally huge, so let me begin with a highly truncated catalogue. Different comparativists prefer 'small-n' and 'large-N' designs, most-similar and most-different comparison, theory-building, process tracing, qualitative comparative analysis, and so on. Not all of these have an interest in generalisation, some being content with providing narrative historical accounts. Some favour an approach described earlier as naturalistic generalisation. Some, large-N methods, take a statistical approach: many different nations are surveyed in the expectation that the sample findings will apply worldwide.

I have no space to re-engage in a critical assessment of all of these branch lines here. Instead, I will follow the route that most clearly resembles the realist platform developed to this point. Most disciplines have their trailblazers, and the methodological transformation of comparative historical research is often associated with the work of Charles Tilly. Tilly's work spans many of the aforementioned traditions, the relevant point being that these were gradually forsaken (Hogan, 2004: Maiz, 2015) for an approach based on generative mechanisms (Tilly, 2001). The 2001 paper introduces his methodology of 'relational realism'. One of his long-standing interests is in episodes of collective violence (everything from bar-room brawls to genocide) and he goes on to announce the significance of a mechanism-based approach as follows:

> Although I still deny the existence of general laws from which we can deduce all particular cases of collective violence, I now believe that a fairly small number of mechanisms and processes recur through the whole range of collective violence – with different initial conditions, combinations and sequences producing systematic variation from time to time and setting to setting in the characteristics, intensity and incidence of collective violence. (Tilly, 2003)

Here in one long sentence is the comparative historian's version of realist causal analysis developed at length in Part I – mechanisms acting in context and over time generate different causal trajectories, which can be charted systematically. This core axiom has been extended by many of Tilly's colleagues. I mention two contributions here. Tarrow's methodological writings (2010, 2019) carry forward the repertoire of relational realism. Particularly wise are his 'words for the young' in the 2019 paper.

Then there is the celebrated monograph, *Dynamics of Contention*, which adds a further member to the team (McAdam et al., 2001). The subject matter is indeed huge – all forms of political struggle such as protests, strikes, wars, revolutions, ethnic conflict, nationalist movements, and so on. To explain the patterning and variation therein the authors deploy a middle-range model, specifying the recurrent mechanisms and processes that generate similarities and difference between cases. The model is complex, combining many mechanisms such as 'brokerage' (creating links between contending factions), 'threat attribution' (collective focusing on the cause of discontent), and 'commitment' (building solidarity, avoiding backsliding). The model is then tested and refined using pairwise comparisons across 18 contentious episodes drawn from many different parts of the world, including the Mau Mau revolt, the 1989 Tiananmen crisis, US civil rights, Swiss unification, Hindu–Muslim conflict, and so on. Regular sequences and patterns are found to recur across these disparate crises. By definition, such an inquiry trades on previous research on selected episodes in the history of selected nations. The inquiry utilises another realist requirement, namely, 'research synthesis'. Evidence on each episode is not created afresh by the authors but draws on previous inquiries of area specialists, who have burrowed more single-mindedly into the cases in question.

I outline the bare bones of this study to affirm once again the scholarly breath of middle-range realism. A little motto, 'thinking without comparison is unthinkable', is often used to herald this field, affirming yet again that relational generalisation, confederating case after case, is the proper aim in social science. But there is another sneaking motivation for this glimpse of *Dynamics of Contention*. It is often celebrated as a paradigm changer in comparative historical research. But it has also raised the critical ire of area specialists who claim that team McAdam committed the sin of overambition – a failing described artfully in the quip 'Big Structures, Large Processes, Huge Comparisons and Enormous Headaches'. The butt of criticism is this – in hastening from case to case to case the authors overlooked significant features of each specific episode, which had contributed significantly to its particular trajectory. They had flitted rather than burrowed. Quite disarmingly, in a later reflection McAdam and Tarrow (2011) confess that they had 'tried too much' and they indeed fell short in the face of such complexity.

I confess complete ignorance of the Sandinistas revolution in Nicaragua, the anti-Marcos revolt in the Philippines, etc., etc., so will not replay the particular critiques or the ensuing confessional here. I use the example in order to re-emphasise a final piece in the middle-range jigsaw, namely, Merton's notion of the 'specification of ignorance'. He argues that one builds middle-range models by piecing together previously disconnected fragments of evidence – but that building has to stop with a clear indication of the boundaries and scope conditions of the resultant models. In a nutshell, it transpires that it was this lack of clear stopping rules that created the methodological contention on *Dynamics of Contention.*

So let us conclude by examining that challenge in a little more detail. It occurs in the attempt to strike a balance between cross-case and between-case analysis. In the words of another comparativist, 'The multimethod scholar wants to get the individual case right, whilst at the same time being interested in causal mechanism the travel and have widespread relevance' (Goertz, 2017). Striking this balance always involves a significant trade-off and recognising its inevitability is key to articulating middle-range theory. Describing the precise trade-off applied in a study is the final and essential component of realist thinking. I close with such an example from my own research on the Covid pandemic (Pawson, 2021, 2023; Serrano-Gallardo et al., 2022)

Let us begin with some comparative data. Figure 37.1 displays selected European statistics on Covid-19 incidence rates. Note that the period refers specifically to the pre-vaccination period, when so-called non-pharmaceutical interventions (aka lockdowns) were the only interventions available to halt the spread of the virus. Note, moreover, that is a highly selected and visually simplified version of the available data, being a tiny sample from the Johns Hopkins University 'dashboard' with its worldwide coverage. It is instructive to explore the perpetual trade-off between within-case and cross-case comparison using this visual example.

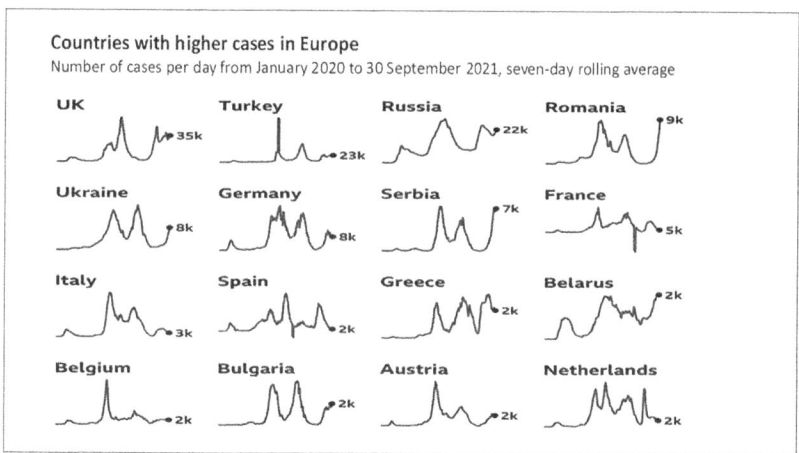

Source: BBC Covid-19 map, https://www.bbc.co.uk/news/uk-58783591; derived from the Johns Hopkins University Covid-19 dashboard, https://coronavirus.jhu.edu.map.html.

Figure 37.1   *Covid-19: some comparative data*

My own meagre efforts to understand lockdown started in a paper that compared expectation and reality in the UK (Pawson, 2021). Policy at the time was driven by epidemic modelling, predicting the likely course of the outbreak. This begins with the standard epidemiological assumption about the 'natural' bell-shaped curve of the rise and fall of a disease (known colloquially as the 'do nothing' curve). Statistical estimates were then applied predicting how the various lockdown measures would be able to 'flatten the curve'. As can be seen in the UK graph in Figure 37.1 (and indeed in all others), the expectation that lockdown measures would steadily and gradually force down transmission proved hopelessly optimistic. The 'do something' curves look rather more like a mountain landscape. Indeed, we do not know to this day how the world would have fared in the absence of vaccination.

Is it possible to explain the perturbations? In attempting to do so in the UK case I compiled seven causal hypotheses that might account for the bedraggled lockdown trajectories (Pawson, 2023). For the sake of wordage, I merely list them here, considering a couple in a little more detail. (i) cross-institution incompatibilities, (ii) the free-rider problem, (iii) contextual heterogeneity, (iv) implementation drift, (v) guidelines ambiguity, (vi) novelty and routinisation effects, (vii) problems with 'unlocking'.

The first refers to the fact that 'lockdown' includes a large set of restrictions applied simultaneously to a large range of institutions. Controls applied in one sector can have a knock-on effect in other sectors. In the first wave of the UK virus, the high risk of hospital-acquired infection led to a programme of discharging elderly patients to care homes. This strategy succeeded in its primary, numerical aim but failed to include a testing programme to accompany transfer and so displaced the problem causing a substantial surge in care home transmission. Such emergent, unanticipated interactions also occurred between other sectors, with details in Pawson (2023).

The free-rider problem refers to the benefit that the uncommitted may receive because of the actions of the committed. People who ignore the lockdown rules still gain if the majority comply. The significant problem occurs when free-riding becomes conspicuous. In the UK, outrage followed when Dominic Cummings, the prime minister's then senior adviser, broke lockdown rules with a 500-mile round trip to a family estate. A torrent of media abuse was ignited – 'one rule for those in charge and one rule for everyone else'. Goodwill plummeted; compliance took a blow. Further blows continued to be inflicted in the infamous Downing Street drinks parties.

I omit example of the other hypotheses here; they refer to standard programme deficits like the inevitable loss of enthusiasm for long-term restrictions. I return to the key methodological question. Is it possible to explain the perturbations in Figure 37.1? Does the seven-mechanism, middle-range model explain the dynamics of the UK graph? The answer is yes and no. These hypotheses are additive. They explain why the lockdown regime was so prolonged, why it continually fired and misfired, why it kept escaping from intentions. But they cannot explain every contour in the transmission curve. They cannot plot its exact month-to-month trajectory. As a matter of fact, the two processes above are discernible in the data. The care home bulge and the

Cummings effect are clearly detectable (GOV.UK, 2020b; Fancourt et al., 2020). But the overall transmission curve results from the combined effect of many mechanisms acting on different communities and institutions and it is only the broad, wayward flux that may be explained.

What of cross-case analysis? In another paper, with Spanish colleagues, we attempted to utilise the same model to explain the transmission curves in that national regime (Serrano-Gallardo et al., 2022). The Spanish incidence landscape is also pictured in Figure 37.1. It proved relatively easy to locate good evidence on all the causal mechanisms as above and the same conclusion follows. This lockdown regime was prolonged, it continually fired and misfired, and kept escaping from the policy maker's intentions. The contours, the peaks and troughs of transmission, are again present, though their profile is, of course, completely different, depending on the intensity and timing of controls and their infractions.

Examined in more detail, the Spanish case revealed some subtle differences in these processes. I mention just two here. Spain is administratively divided in 17 autonomous communities. Accordingly, the Covid-19 command-and-control systems varied significantly. Other than in national 'state of alarm' periods, lockdown measures varied widely, and so did the graphical data on incidence and mortality. Spain has a welfare model that relies heavily on family responsibilities, and different generations co-habit together for longer than anywhere else in Europe. Although incidence and death rates were high in the Spanish care home sector due to the frailty of residents, none of this was 'imported' from other sectors. So, whilst there are clear communalities between the two cases, there are also features quite specific to each one. It is possible to anticipate a widespread irregular response but not to explain every precise contour in every country in Figure 37.1. This eventuality is not a failing of middle-range thinking, it is the basic condition of all middle-range explanation. And the solution is glimpsed in this tiny example. Use the middle-range theory to pull together the important commonalities, but also make clear comparisons that are beyond its scope.

We reach a conclusion on extensional generalisability. In both of the examples examined in this episode (contention and Covid), there is an explanatory trade-off in terms of explanatory power. By working at a middle range of abstraction, a causal model can explain similarities and difference between a wide range of cases. But at the level of the individual case, and because of the complexity of any particular case, key within-case differences will necessarily be overlooked and will require further analysis. These precise boundaries need to be explained in any application of middle-range realism. Ignorance needs to be specified.

It is perhaps appropriate to end on the gravest global crisis in public health in recent years. There will be another pandemic and vaccination will not always be available to quell it. We know that applying strict controls on a population's movements, actions, and beliefs is fraught with difficulties. But we do have a middle-range map indicating some likely points of slippage. Some, if not all, of the pitfalls can be anticipated. History will not repeat itself, but it will rhyme.

KEY LESSONS

Episode 37 completes the full case for extensional generalisation in social science. All the steps in realist, middle-range, multi-method, within-case, and cross-case synthesis are specified. Particular attention is paid to limitations of the middle-range models. It is perfectly possible to extend explanations from one case to another, one historical episode to another. The parallels drawn are never perfect and can never capture all the nuances of any single case. Boundary conditions must be carefully specified about what is and is not included in the comparisons. Further middle-range inquiry can continue to 'plug the gaps' in a process that is never complete. Partial knowledge is better than none.

Afterword

Dear Reader,

This is a long book. I have battled with the methodological puzzles herein since I began doctoral studies in the early 1970s. Accordingly, one might say that the present effort occupied somewhere between three and fifty years in the writing. So, let's keep this conclusion snappy.

I dispense with the grand summary. I have concluded each episode with a resumé of lessons learnt and, hopefully, these constitute the condensed case. Moreover, I have already applied the ultimate compression in the Preface. Here it is again:

> *Realism provides the optimal methodology for social science, providing objective and generalisable causal explanations. Causality is understood through the action of generative mechanisms. Objectivity is approached by adjudicating between contending theories. Generality is captured in middle-range theories. Realism embodies the science in social science. But it is imperfect.*

Let us turn instead to my subtitle, which proclaims rather grandly that the book provides a 'methodology for social science'. Ever since the term 'social science' was first coined, intrepid authors have attempted to write the rule book. There have been hundreds and I mean hundreds of efforts. I mention two. Many, many years ago Durkheim's *Rules of Sociological Method* (1895) found its way onto my undergraduate reading list. I found it baffling; it addressed problems that I never knew existed. Many years later, along came Giddens's *New Rules of Sociological Method* (1976). By then I had embarked on empirical research, and I found it of little help.

What chance this poor effort? I make just one small plea on my own behalf. What I've come up with here might well be entitled *The Old Rules of Sociological Method*. I have attempted to extract and justify some realist principles for conducting social research on the back of a generous portfolio of existing examples. Those illustrations reach across many research domains and a broad portfolio of practical methods. But they remain a pinprick; I could have called upon a thousand others. Accordingly, there is another way of perceiving my efforts. The book is no more and no less than an attempt to codify and formalise *existing practices*. I have tried to capture a tradition.

So, just as Monsieur Jourdain spoke prose without knowing what it was, it may well be that you, dear reader, have been thinking like a realist without knowing it! I thus call to the aid of the party what I might call the 'craft tradition' in empirical research (Alford, 1998). It starts with a puzzle, makes headway with some creative guesses, constructs data to test those hypotheses, recognises errors, chases them down, and ends up with refined theory. It is possible to walk this walk without knowing the formalities of mechanisms, contexts, time-dependent demi-regularities, stopping rules, theory adjudication, middle-range theory, boundary conditions, and so on. It begins in doctoral research when students realise that their task is to make a small contribution to an existing body of research. This pragmatic tradition in inquiry means that investigation never starts from scratch. Each study seeks to make a useful empirical contribution but also solidifies into a collective understanding of good research practice. Robust explanations build when this craft tradition is repeated over and over.

Realist inquiry, as I have attempted to show, has deep roots in the philosophy of science. But it has a complementary seedbed in this bottom-up, utilitarian hunch that 'this is how inquiry is supposed to proceed'. Methodological rules are both the medium and outcome of empirical research. If you have come this far, I trust that you have not been baffled and that the realist rules are not too recondite. I place my faith in the idea that these 'gentle guidelines' are adaptable and sturdy enough to inform all manner of social research. They may even withstand the march of time.

References

Abbott A (1998) 'The causal devolution'. *Sociological Methods and Research* 27(2), 148–81.

Abbott A (2006) 'Reconceptualising knowledge accumulation in sociology'. *American Sociologist* 37(2), 55–66.

Abbott A (2018) 'Varieties of normative inquiry: moral alternatives to politicization in sociology'. *American Sociologist* 49, 158–80. https://doi.org/10.1007/s12108-017-9367-8.

Adam B (1994) *Time and Social Theory*. London: Wiley.

Alford R (1998) *The Craft of Inquiry*. Oxford: Oxford University Press.

Alizadeh A (2015) 'Toward understanding and exploiting tumor heterogeneity'. *Nature Medicine* 21(8), 846–53.

Andrews J (n.d.) 'Does the claim of "1.9 million more children in good or outstanding schools" stack up?' Education Policy Institute. https://epi.org.uk/wp-content/uploads/2018/07/EPI_-1.9m_Good_outstanding_schools_analysis.pdf (accessed September 2023).

Anstead N (2015) 'Televised debates in parliamentary democracies'. *London School of Economics and Political Science Media Policy Brief 13.* http://eprints.lse.ac.uk/66293/ (accessed September 2023).

Anwar M (2001) 'The participation of ethnic minorities in British politics'. *Journal of Ethnic and Migration Studies* 27(3), 533–9.

Archer M (1995) *Realist Social Theory: The Morphogenetic Approach*. Cambridge: Cambridge University Press.

Archer M (1998) 'Realism in the social sciences', in Archer M, Bhaskar R, Collier A, Lawson T and Norrie N (eds), *Critical Realism: Essential Readings*. London: Routledge, pp. 189–205.

Archer M (2020) 'The morphogenetic approach: critical realism's explanatory framework approach', in Róna P and Zsolnai L (eds), *Agency and Causal Explanation in Economics. Virtues and Economics*: Cham: Springer, pp. 137–50.

Atkins P (2010) *The Laws of Thermodynamics: A Very Short Introduction*. Oxford: Oxford Academic Press.

Ayala F (2009) 'Darwin and the scientific method'. *Proceedings of the National Academy of Sciences of the United States of America* 106(suppl 1), 10033–9.

Baillargeon N (2007) *A Short Course in Intellectual Self-Defense*. New York: Seven Stories Press.

Ball J (2017) *Post-Truth: How Bullshit Conquered the World*. London: Biteback Publishing.

Barnes B and Bloor D (1982) 'Relativism, rationalism and the sociology of knowledge', in Hollis M and Lukes S (eds), *Rationality and Relativism*. Oxford: Blackwell, pp. 21–37.

Barnes B, Bloor D and Henry J (1974) *Scientific Knowledge: A Sociological Analysis*. Chicago, IL: University of Chicago Press.

BBC Royal Charter Archive (1927–2017) https://www.bbc.com/historyofthebbc/research/royal-charter (accessed September 2023).

Beach D and Pedersen R (2013) *Process-Tracing Methods: Foundations and Guidelines*. Michigan, MI: Michigan University Press.

Beach D and Pedersen R (2016) *Causal Case Study Methods: Foundations and Guidelines for Comparing, Matching, and Tracing*. Michigan, MI: Michigan University Press.

Bearman P and Hedström P (eds) (2011) *The Oxford Handbook of Analytical Sociology*. Oxford: Oxford University Press.

Becker H (1951) 'The professional dance musician and his audience'. *American Journal of Sociology* 57(2), 136–44.

Becker H (1967) 'Whose side are we on?' *Social Problems* 14, 239–47.

Becker H (1973) *Outsiders*. New York: Free Press.

Beeken R, Simon A, von Wagner C, Whitaker K and Wardle J (2011) Cancer fatalism: deterring early presentation and increasing social inequalities? *Cancer, Epidemiology Biomarkers & Prevention*, 2127–31. doi: 10.1158/1055-9965.EPI-11-0437.

Belanche D, Casolo V, Flavian M and Sanchez S (2021) 'Understanding influencer marketing: the role of congruence between influencers, products and consumers'. *Journal of Business Research* 132, 186–95.

Bell, D (1974) *The Coming of Post-Industrial Society*. New York: Harper.

Bemelmans-Videc M-L, Rist R and Vedung E (eds) (1998) *Carrots, Sticks, and Sermons: Policy Instruments and Their Evaluation*. New Brunswick, NJ: Transaction Press.

Bennett A (2010). 'Process tracing and causal inference', in Brady H and Collier D (eds), *Rethinking Social Inquiry: Diverse Tools, Shared Standards*. Lanham, MD: Rowman & Littlefield, pp. 207–20.

Bennett W (1990) 'Toward a theory of press-state relations in the United States'. *Journal of Communication* 40(2), 103–25.

Benson D (1974) 'Critical note: a revolution in sociology'. *Sociology* 8(1), 125–9.

Berger P and Luckman T (1966) *The Social Construction of Reality*. New York: Anchor Books.

Berger V, Bour L, Carter K et al. (2021) 'A roadmap to using randomization in clinical trials'. *BMC Medical Research Methodology* 21, 168. https://doi.org/10.1186/s12874-021-01303-z.

Bhaskar R (1975) *A Realist Theory of Science*. Brighton: Harvester.

Bhaskar R (1979) *The Possibility of Naturalism*. Brighton: Harvester.

Bhaskar R (2002) *Reflections on Meta-Reality*. New Delhi: Sage.

Bikker A, Atherton H, Brant H et al. (2017) 'Conducting a team-based multi-sited focused ethnography in primary care', *BMC Medical Research Methodolology* 17, 139. https://doi.org/10.1186/s12874-017-0422-5.

Black M (1954) 'Metaphor'. *Proceedings of the Aristotelian Society* 55, 273–94.

Blackwood B, O'Halloran P and Porter S (2010) 'On the problems of mixing RCTs with qualitative research: the case of the MRC framework for the evaluation of complex healthcare interventions'. *Journal of Research in Nursing* 15(6), 511–21.

Blass T (2004) *The Man Who Shocked the World: The Life and Legacy of Stanley Milgram*. New York: Basic Books.

Blumer H (1954) 'What is wrong with social theory?' *American Sociological Review* 19(1), 3–10.

Blumer H (1986) *Symbolic Interactionism: Perspective and Method*. Berkeley, CA: University of California Press.

Blunt A (1938) 'Blake's "Ancient of Days": the symbolism of the compasses'. *Journal of the Warburg Institute* 2(1), 53–63.

Borchers A (2007) 'The history and contemporary challenges of the US Food and Drug Administration'. *Clinical Therapeutics* 29(1), 1–16.

Borenstein M, Hedges L, Higgins J and Rothstein H (2021) *Introduction to Meta-Analysis*. New York: Wiley.

Borjas GJ (2014) *Immigration Economics*. Cambridge, MA: Harvard University Press.

Bothwell L, Greene J, Podolsky S and Jones D (2016) 'Assessing the gold standard – lessons from the history of RCTs'. *New England Journal of Medicine* 374, 2175–81.

Boudon R (1974) *Education, Opportunity and Social Inequality*. London: Wiley.

Boudon R (1980) *The Crisis in Sociology*. London: Macmillan.

Boudon R (2013) *Sociology as Science*. Oxford: Bardwell Press.

Bowker J and Star S (2000) *Sorting Things Out: Classification and Its Consequences*. Cambridge, MA: MIT Press.

Breur T (2016). 'Statistical power analysis and the contemporary "crisis" in social sciences'. *Journal of Marketing Analytics* 4(2–3), 61–5. doi:10.1057/s41270–016–0001–3.

Brown R (1977) *A Poetic for Sociology: Toward a Logic of Discovery for the Human Sciences*. Chicago, IL: University of Chicago Press.

Brown R (ed.) (2016) *The Changing Shape of Work*. London: Springer.

Buckley W (2007). *Sociology and Modern Systems Theory*. Englewood Cliffs, NJ: Prentice-Hall.

Burchett H, Umoquit M and Dobrow M (2011) 'How do we know when research from one setting can be useful in another? A review of external validity, applicability and transferability frameworks'. *Journal of Health Services Research & Policy* 16(4), 238–44.

Burns PB, Rohrich RJ and Chung KC (2011) 'The levels of evidence and their role in evidence-based medicine'. *Plastic and Reconstructive Surgery* 128(1), 305–10. https://doi.org/10.1097/PRS.0b013e318219c171.

Byrne D (2002) *Interpreting Quantitative Data*. London: Sage.

Byrne D (2009) 'Complex realist and configurational approaches to cases: a radical synthesis', in Byrne D and Ragin C (eds), *The Sage Handbook of Case-Based Methods*. London: Sage, pp. 101–112.

Byrne D (2012) 'UK sociology and quantitative methods: are we as weak as they think? Or are they barking up the wrong tree?' *Sociology* 46(1), 13–24.

Byrne D and Callaghan G (2014) *Complexity Theory and the Social Sciences*. London: Routledge.

Byrne D and Ragin C (2009) *The Sage Handbook of Case-Based Methods*. London: Sage.

Campbell D (1974) 'Evolutionary epistemology', in Schilpp PA (ed.), *The Philosophy of Karl R. Popper*. LaSalle, IL: Open Court, pp. 412–63.

Campbell D (1988) *Methodology and Epistemology for the Social Sciences*. Chicago, IL: University of Chicago Press.

Cartwright N (1983) *How the Laws of Physics Lie*. Oxford: Oxford University Press.

Cartwright N (2020) 'Middle-range theory: without it what could anyone do?' *Theoria* 35(3), 269–323. https://doi.org/10.1387/theoria.21479.

Centers for Disease Control and Prevention (2010) 'How tobacco smoke causes disease: the biology and behavioral basis for smoking-attributable disease: a report of the Surgeon General. Atlanta'. https://www.ncbi.nlm.nih.gov/books/NBK53010/.

Charlton G and Barrow C (November 2002) 'Coping and self-help group membership in Parkinson's disease: an exploratory qualitative study'. *Health & Social Care in the Community* 10(6), 472–8. doi:10.1046/j.1365–2524.2002.00385.x. PMID: 12485134.

Checkland K, Hammond J, Coleman A, Macinnes J, Mikelyte R, Croke S, Billings J, Bailey S and Allen P (2023) '"Success" in policy piloting: process, programs, and politics'. *Public Administration* 101(2), 463–80. https://doi.org/10.1111/padm .12790.

Cherkaoui M (2005) *Invisible Codes: Essays on Generative Mechanisms.* Oxford: Bardwell Press.

Chilton P (2004) *Analysing Political Discourse.* London: Routledge.

Christensen D (n.d.) Blog: 15 pairs of contradictory proverbs. https:// www .derekchristensen.com/15-pairs-of-contradictory-proverbs/ (accessed March 2023).

Cicourel A (1964) *Method and Measurement in Sociology.* Glencoe, IL: Free Press.

Coleman C and Moynihan J (1996). *Understanding Crime Data: Haunted by the Dark Figure.* Maidenhead: Open University Press.

Coleman J (1986) 'Social theory, social research, and a theory of action'. *American Journal of Sociology* 91, 1309–35.

Collier D (2011) 'Understanding process tracing'. *Political Science and Politics* 44(4), 823–30.

Collin F (2011) 'Harry Collins and the empirical programme of relativism', in Collin F (ed.), *Science Studies as Naturalized Philosophy.* Synthese Library v348. Dordrecht: Springer, pp. 83–108.

Collins H (1985) *Changing Order: Replication and Induction in Scientific Practice.* London: Sage.

Collins H (2004) *Gravity's Shadow and the Search for Gravitational Waves.* Chicago, IL: University of Chicago Press.

Collins H and Evans R (2017) *Why Democracies Need Science.* Cambridge: Polity Press.

Comparitech (2023) 'Screen time statistics: average screen time in US vs. the rest of the world'. https://www.comparitech.com/tv-streaming/screen-time-statistics/ (accessed February 2024).

Contributors to Wikimedia projects (9 April 2021) Generalization. Wikiquote. https:// en.wikiquote.org/wiki/Generalization.

Corr P and Williams D (2009) 'The pathway from idea to regulatory approval', in Lo B and Field M (eds), *Conflict of Interest in Medical Research, Education, and Practice.* Washington, DC: Institute of Medicine. Ebook at: https://www.ncbi.nlm .nih.gov/books/NBK22930/ (accessed February 2024).

Corry O and Jorgensen D (2015) 'Beyond "deniers" and "believers": towards a map of the politics of climate change'. *Global Environment Change* 32, 165–74.

Costa D, Amouyal M, Lambert P (2011) 'How representative are clinical study patients with allergic rhinitis in primary care?' *Journal of Allergy and Clinical Immunology* 127(4), 920–6.

Cotgrove, S (1969) *The Science of Society – An Introduction to Sociology.* London: George, Allen and Unwin.

Curtis J, Stoelwinder J and McNeil J (2009) 'Management of waiting lists needs sound data'. *Medical Journal of Australia* 191(8), 191–2.

Cushion S and Lewis J (2017) 'Impartiality, statistical tit-for-tats and the construction of balance: UK television news reporting of the 2016 referendum campaign'. *European Journal of Communication* 32(3), 208–33.

D'Amato R, Loughnan M, Flynn E and Folkman J (1994) 'Thalidomide is an inhibitor of angiogenesis'. *Proceedings of the National Academy of Sciences of the United States of America*, 91(9), 4082–5.

Davis E (2017) *Post-Truth*. London: Little Brown.

Dean M (2016) 'Political acclamation, social media and the public mood'. *European Journal of Social Theory* 20(3), 1–18.

Dennis N, Henriques F and Clifford Slaughter C (1956) *Coal Is Our Life*. London: Eyre and Spottiswode.

Department of Health, NHS Clinical Services Team (2012) 'Referral to treatment consultant-led waiting times: Rules Suite'. Overview at: https://www.england.nhs.uk/statistics/statistical-work-areas/rtt-waiting-times/rtt-guidance/ (accessed June 2023).

Department of Health & Social Care (2022) 'Referral to treatment consultant-led waiting times: Rules Suite' (October). https://www.gov.uk/government/publications/right-to-start-consultant-led-treatment-within-18-weeks/referral-to-treatment-consultant-led-waiting-times-rules-suite-october-2022,

Devine F (1992) *Affluent Workers Revisited*. Edinburgh: Edinburgh University Press.

Devine F (2016) 'The working class, middle class, assimilation and convergence' [Online]. *The Sociological Review Magazine*. https://t hesociolog icalreview .org/journal-collections/past-and-present/the-working-class-middle-class-assimilation-and-convergence/ (accessed June 2023).

Dex S, Ward K and Joshi H (2008) 'Changes in women's occupations and occupational mobility over 25 years', in Scott J, Dex S and Joshi H (eds), *Women and Employment: Changing Lives and New Challenges*. Cheltenham, UK and Northampton, MA, USA: Edward Elgar, pp. 33–50.

Diderot D and D'Alembert J (1751–1766) *Encyclopédie: Dictionnaire Raisonné Des Sciences, Des Arts et Des Métiers*. Paris: André Le Breton.

Doll R and Hill A (1964) 'Mortality in relation to smoking: ten years' observations of British doctors'. *BMJ* 1, 1399–410.

Douglas J (1967) *The Social Meanings of Suicide*. Princeton, NJ: Princeton University Press.

Doust J and Del Mar C (2004) 'Why do doctors use treatments that do not work?' *BMJ Clinical research* 328(7438), 474–5. https://doi.org/10.1136/bmj.328.7438.474.

Duckworth C, Kapur D and Vaishnav M (2021) *Britain's New Swing Voters? A Survey of British Indian Attitudes*. Washington, DC: Carnegie Endowment for International Peace. https://carnegieendowment.org/2021/11/18/britain-s-new-swing-voters-survey-of-british-indian-attitudes-pub-85784 (accessed July 2023).

Duddy C and Wong G (2021) 'Efficiency over thoroughness in laboratory testing decision making in primary care: findings from a realist review'. *BJGPOpen*; 5(2), doi: 10.3399/bjgpopen20X101146.

Duddy C, Gadsby E, Hibberd V, et al. (2022) 'Understanding what happens to attendees after an NHS Health Check: a realist review.' *BMJ Open* 12, e064237. doi:10.1136/bmjopen-2022-064237.

Duguid S and Pawson R (1998) 'Education, change and transformation: the prison experience'. *Evaluation Review* 22(4), 470–95.

Durkheim É (1895, reprinted in 1982) *The Rules of Sociological Method*. New York: Free Press.

Durkheim É (1897, reprinted in 1951) *Suicide: A Study in Sociology*. New York: Free Press.

Edo A (2019) 'The impact of immigration on the labor market'. *Journal of Economic Surveys* 33, 922–48. https://doi.org/10.1111/joes.12300.

Ekblom P (1997) 'Gearing up against crime: a dynamic framework to help designers keep up with the adaptive criminal in a changing world'. *International Journal of Risk, Security, and Crime Prevention* 2(4), 249–2.

Electoral Commission (2002) 'Voter engagement among black and minority ethnic communities'. https://www.electoralcommission.org.uk/sites/default/files/electoral _commission_pdf_file/ Ethnicfinalreport_11586-6190__E__N__S__W___.pdf (accessed June 2023).

Elias N (1982) *The Civilizing Process, Vol. II: State Formation and Civilization.* Oxford: Blackwell.

Elizabeth J (2014) 'Who are you calling a fact-checker?' American Press Institute, May. https://www.americanpressinstitute.org/fact-checking-project/fact-checker-definition/ (accessed September 2023).

Ellis C (1999) 'Heartful autoethnography'. *Qualitative Heath Research* 9(5), 669–83.

Ellis C, Adams T and Bochner A (2011) 'Autoethnography: an overview'. *Qualitative Social Research* 12(1), Article 10.

Emirbayer M and Mische A (1998) 'What is agency?' *American Journal of Sociology* 103(4), 962–1023.

Emmel N (2013) *Sampling and Choosing Cases in Qualitative Research: A Realist Approach.* London: Sage.

Engbersen G, Snel E and Esteves A (2016) 'Migration mechanisms of the middle range: on the concept of reverse cumulative causation', in Bakewell O, Engbersen G, Fonseca ML and Horst C (eds), *Beyond Networks: Migration, Diasporas and Citizenship.* London: Palgrave Macmillan. Ebook at: https://doi.org/10.1057/ 9781137539212_10.

Falleti T and Lynch J (2009) 'Context and causal mechanisms in political analysis'. *Comparative Political Studies* 9(3), 1143–66.

Fancourt D, Steptoe A and Wright L (2020) 'The Cummings effect: politics, trust, and behaviours during the COVID-19 pandemic'. *Lancet* 396, 464–5.

Farkas J and Schou J (2019) *Post-truth, Fake News and Democracy.* London: Routledge.

Farrell G, Tilley N and Tseloni E (2014) 'Why did crime drop?' *Crime and Justice* 43, 421–90. See also the full report at: http://irep.ntu.ac.uk/id/eprint/26190/ 1/3652_Tseloni.pdf (accessed September 2023).

Felson M (1986) 'Linking criminal choices, routine activities, informal control and criminal outcomes', in Cornish D and Clarke R (eds), *The Reasoning Criminal: Rational Choice Perspectives on Offending.* New York: Springer-Verlag, pp. 118–30.

Fenby J (1986) *The International News Services.* New York: Schocken Books.

Feyerabend P (1975) *Against Method.* London: Verso.

Feyerabend P (1994) *Killing Time.* Chicago, IL: University of Chicago Press.

Fielding N (2008) 'Analytic density, postmodernism and applied multiple method research', in Bergman M (ed.), *Advances in Mixed Method Research.* London: Sage, pp. 37–52.

Filippo D and Sanz-Casado E (2018) 'Bibliometric and altmetric analysis of three social science disciplines'. *Frontiers in Research Metrics and Analytics.* https://doi .org/10.3389/frma.2018.00034.

Foulkes L and Andrews JL (12 October 2022). 'The prevalence inflation hypothesis: are mental health awareness efforts contributing to the rise in mental health problems?' *New Ideas in Psychology* 69. doi:10.1016/j.newideapsych.2023.101010.

Fowler P (2003) 'Evidence-based everything'. *Journal of Evaluation in Clinical Practice* 3(3), 239–43.

Friedman, H (2015) 'Further developing transpersonal psychology as a science: building and testing middle-range transpersonal theories'. *International Journal of Transpersonal Studies* 34(1–2), 55–64.

Fuller S (2018) *Post-Truth.* Cambridge: Cambridge University Press.

Gabbay J and Le May A (2011) *Practice-Based Evidence for Healthcare.* London: Routledge.

Gallie W (1955) 'Essentially contested concepts'. *Proceedings of the Aristotelian Society* 56, 167–98.

Gardiner J, Stuart M, MacKenzie R, Forde C, Greenwood I and Perrett R (2009) 'Redundancy as a critical life event: moving on from the Welsh steel industry through career change'. *Work, Employment and Society* 23(4), 727–45.

Garfinkle H (1967) *Studies in Ethnomethodology.* Englewood Cliffs, NJ: Prentice Hall.

Geertz C (1973) 'Thick description: toward an interpretive theory of culture', in Geertz C, *The Interpretation of Cultures: Selected Essays.* New York: Basic Books, pp. 3–30.

Genetic Science Learning Center (2020) 'When cell communication goes wrong'. https://learn.genetics.utah.edu/content/cells/badcom/ (accessed September 2023).

George A and Bennett A (2005) *Case Studies and Theory Development in the Social Sciences.* Cambridge, MA: MIT Press.

Gerring J (2008) 'The mechanismic worldview: thinking inside the box'. *British Journal of Political Science* 38(1), 161–79.

Gerring J (2010) 'Causal mechanisms: yes, but....'. *Comparative Political Studies* 43(11), 1499–526. https://doi.org/10.1177/00104140103.

Gerxhani K, De Graff N and Raub W (2022) *Handbook of Sociological Science: Contributions to Rigorous Sociology.* Cheltenham, UK and Northampton, MA, USA: Edward Elgar.

Giddens A (1976) *New Rules of Sociological Method: A Positive Critique of Interpretative Sociologies.* London: Hutchison.

Giddens A (1984) *The Constitution of Society.* Cambridge: Polity Press.

Goertz G (2017) *Multimethod Research, Causal Mechanisms, and Case Studies.* Princeton, NJ: Princeton University Press.

Goffman E (1961) *Asylums.* New York: Anchor Books.

Goldthorpe JH (1973) 'Book review: a revolution in sociology?' *Sociology* 7(3), 449–62.

Goldthorpe JH (1997) 'Current issues in comparative macrosociology'. *Comparative Social Research* 16(1), 1–26.

Goldthorpe JH (2016) *Sociology as a Population Science.* Cambridge: Cambridge University Press.

Goldthorpe JH and Hope K (1974) *The Social Grading of Occupations.* Oxford: Clarendon Press.

Goldthorpe JH, Lockwood D, Bechhofer F and Platt J (1968) *The Affluent Worker: Industrial Attitudes and Behaviour.* Cambridge: Cambridge University Press.

Goldthorpe JH, Llewellyn C and Payne G (1980, reprinted in 1987) *Social Mobility and Class Structure in Modern Britain.* Oxford: Clarendon Press.

Gomm R, Hammersley M and Foster P (2000) *Case Study Method.* London: Sage.

Gouldner A (1971) *The Coming Crisis of Western Sociology.* London: Heineman.

GOV.UK (2020a) 'Ethnicity data: how similar or different are aggregated ethnic groups?' https://www.gov.uk/government/publications/ethnicity-data-how-similar -or-different-are-aggregated-ethnic-groups (accessed September 2023).

GOV.UK (2020b) 'COVID-19: number of outbreaks in care homes'. https://www.gov .uk/government/statistical-data-sets/covid-19-number-of-outbreaks-in-care-homes -management-information (accessed September 2023).

Gravity of Earth, Wikipedia (2023) https://en.wikipedia.org/wiki/Gravity_of_Earth (accessed October 2023).

Greenwood J (2018) 'How would people behave in Milgram's experiment today?' *Behavioural Scientist.* https://behavioralscientist.org/how-would-people-behave-in -milgrams-experiment-today/ (accessed June 2023).

Griffiths F (2009) 'The case in medicine', in Byrne D and Ragin C (eds), *The Sage Handbook of Case-Based Methods.* London: Sage, pp. 441–61.

Guardian (2016) 'Does the EU really cost the UK £350 million a week?' https://www .theguardian.com/politics/reality-check/2016/may/23/does-the-eu-really-cost-the -uk-350m-a-week (accessed September 2023).

Guardian (January 2022) 'Women 32% more likely to die after operation by male surgeon, study reveals'. https://www.theguardian.com/society/2022/jan/04/women -more-likely-die-operation-male-surgeon-study (accessed September 2023).

Hammersley M (2008) 'Troubles with triangulation', in Bergman M (ed.), *Advances in Mixed Method Research.* London: Sage, pp. 22–36.

Hansen P, Larsen E and Gundersen C (2022) 'Reporting on one's behavior: a survey experiment on the nonvalidity of self-reported COVID-19 hygiene-relevant routine behaviors'. *Behavioural Public Policy* 6(1), 34–51.

Hanson N (1958) *Patterns of Discovery.* Cambridge: Cambridge University Press.

Harding P (2017) 'Remember that facts are sacred'. *British Journalism Review* 28(3), 17–22.

Harding S (1976) *Can Theories Be Refuted? Essays on the Duhem-Quine Thesis.* New York: Springer.

Hares J (2017) 'Death or brain damage from anaesthesia'. https://patient.info/treatment -medication/anaesthesia/death-or-brain-damage-from-anaesthesia #: ~: text = The %20risk%20of%20dying%20in,not%20been%20put%20into%20numbers (accessed June 2023).

Harré R (1972) *The Philosophies of Science.* Oxford: Oxford University Press.

Harré R (1986) *Varieties of Realism: A Rationale for the Natural Sciences.* Oxford: Basil Blackwell.

Harré R (2002) *Great Scientific Experiments.* New York: Dover.

Hayes D and Guardino M (2010) 'Whose views made the news? Media coverage of the march to war in Iraq'. *Political Communication* 27(1), 59–87.

Heath A, Fisher S, Rosenblatt G, Sanders D and Sobolewska M (2013) *The Political Integration of Ethnic Minorities in Britain.* Oxford: Oxford University Press.

Heckman B, Dahne J, Germeroth LJ, Mathew AR, Santa Ana E, Saladin M and Carpenter M (November 2018) 'Does cessation fatigue predict smoking-cessation milestones? A longitudinal study of current and former smokers'. *Journal of Consulting and Clinical Psychology* 86(11), 903–14. doi:10.1037/ccp0000338.

Hedström P and Swedberg R (eds) (1998) *Social Mechanisms. An Analytical Approach to Social Theory.* Cambridge: Cambridge University Press.

Hegel G (1896) *Philosophy of Right.* London: G. Bell.

Henrich J, Heine SJ and Norenzayan A (2010a) 'The weirdest people in the world?' *Behavioral and Brain Sciences* 33(2–3), 61–83.

Henrich J, Heine SJ and Norenzayan A (2010b) 'Beyond WEIRD: towards a broad-based behavioral science'. *Behavioral and Brain Sciences* 33(2–3), 111–35.

Herring T (2010) *Treatise on Geophysics* (Vol. 3). Amsterdam: Elsevier.

Hesse M (1974) *The Structure of Scientific Inference*. London: Macmillan.

Hitchcock C (2003) 'Of Humean bondage'. *The British Journal for the Philosophy of Science* 54(1), 1–25.

Hitchcock C (2021) 'Probabilistic causation', in Zalta EN (ed.), *The Stanford Encyclopaedia of Philosophy* (Spring 2021 edn). https://plato.stanford.edu/archives/spr2021/entries/causation-probabilistic/ (accessed September 2023).

Hogan R (2004) 'Charles Tilly takes three giant steps from structure toward process: mechanisms for deconstructing political process'. *Contemporary Sociology* 33(3), 273–7.

Holmes C and Mayhew K (2012) 'The changing shape of the UK job market and its implications for the bottom half of earners'. Resolution Foundation. https://www.resolutionfoundation.org/app/uploads/2014/08/The-Changing-Shape-of-the-UK-Job-Market.pdf (accessed June 2023).

Hout M (1983) *Mobility Tables*. London: Sage.

Howell F, Porter J and Matthews S (eds) (2015) *Recapturing Space: New Middle-Range Theory in Spatial Demography*. Dordrecht: Springer International.

Huffington Post (2019) 'Lying about statistics is not misconduct, judges in Boris Johnson case rule'. https://www.huffingtonpost.co.uk/entry/boris-johnson-court-bus-claim_uk_5d1c9bc0e4b082e55372c5d0 (accessed June 2023).

Hume D (1748, reprinted in 2007) *An Enquiry Concerning Human Understanding*. Oxford: Oxford University Press.

Husserl E (1952) *Ideen zu einer reinen Phänomenologie und phänomenologischen Philosophie. Zweites Buch. Phänomenologische Untersuchungen zur Konstitution.* The Hague: Martinus Nijhoff.

Hyde M (2019) 'Column: of all the hills to die on, why on earth has Labour chosen Chris Williamson?' *Guardian*, 29 June.

Hyman H (1960) 'Reflections on reference group theory'. *Public Opinion Quarterly* 24(3), 383–96

Jary C and Bryant-Smith L (2015) *Working with Ministers: A Practical Handbook on Advising, Briefing and Drafting* (6th edn). Civil Service Learning. https://www.civilservant.org.uk/library/2015_Working_with_Ministers.pdf (accessed June 2023).

Johnson R, Onwuegbuzie A and Turner L (2007) 'Toward a definition of mixed methods research'. *Journal of Mixed Methods Research* 1, 112–33. doi:10.1177/1558689806298224.

Jordan A and Adelle C (2012) *Environmental Policy in the European Union: Contexts, Actors and Policy Dynamics.* London and Sterling, VA: Earthscan. ISBN 9781849714693.

Kalpokas I (2018) *A Political Theory of Post-Truth*. London: Palgrave Macmillan.

Kaplan A (1964) *The Conduct of Inquiry: Methodology for the Behavioural Sciences.* Aylesbury: Chandler.

Kariuki P (2022) 'How the like and share buttons ruined social media'. https://www.makeuseof.com/how-like-share-buttons-ruined-social-media/ (accessed September 2023).

Karlson J (2011) 'People can not only open closed systems, they can also close open systems'. *Journal of Critical Realism* 10(2), 145–62.

Karyotis G and Rüdig W (2018) 'The three waves of anti-austerity protest in Greece, 2010–2015'. *Political Studies Review* 16(2), 158–69.

Katz R (2004) 'FDA: evidentiary standards for drug development and approval'. *NeuroRx: The Journal of the American Society for Experimental NeuroTherapeutics* 1(3), 307–16. https://doi.org/10.1602/neurorx.1.3.307.

Kennedy H (2021) *Kennedy Report on Diversity.* London: Royal College of Surgeons. https://www.alsgbi.org/2021-kennedy-report-on-diversity/ (accessed June 2023).

Kent D and Kitsios G (2009) 'Against pragmatism: on efficacy, effectiveness and the real world'. *Trials* 10, 48. http://doi.org/10.1186/1745-6215-10-48.

Kent D, Rothwell P, Ioannidis J, Altman Dr and Hayward R (12 August 2010) 'Assessing and reporting heterogeneity in treatment effects in clinical trials: a proposal'. *Trials* 11, 85. doi:10.1186/1745–6215–11–85.

Klein M and Miedema F (1995) 'Long-term survivors of HIV-1 infection'. *Trends in Microbiology* 3(10), 386–91.

Knorr-Cetina K (1981) *The Manufacture of Knowledge: An Essay on the Constructivist and Contextual Nature of Science.* Oxford: Pergamon Press.

Koyré A (1968) *Metaphysics and Measurement.* London: Chapman Hall.

Kravitz R, Duan N and Braslow J (2004) 'Evidence-based medicine, heterogeneity of treatment effects, and the trouble with averages'. *The Milbank Quarterly* 82(4), 661–87. http://doi.org/10.1111/j.0887–378X.2004.00327.xrages.

Krippendorff, K (2018) *Content Analysis: An Introduction to Its Methodology.* London: Sage.

Krajick K (2019) 'Scientists track deep history of planets' motions, and effects on Earth's climate'. https://news.climate.columbia.edu/2019/03/04/geological-orrery-solar-system-chaos/ (accessed February 2024).

Lakatos I (1970) 'Falsification and the methodology of scientific research programmes', in Lakatos I and Musgrave A (eds), *Criticism and the Growth of Knowledge.* Cambridge: Cambridge University Press, pp. 91–196.

Lamers H, Van Hal T and Clercx S (2020) 'How to deal with scholarly forgetting in the history of the humanities: starting points for discussion'. *History of Humanities* 5(1), 5–29.

Lasky N, Fisher B and Jacques S (2017). '"Thinking thief" in the crime prevention arms race: lessons learned from shoplifters'. *Security Journal* 30, 772–92.

Latour B (2004) 'Why has critique run out of steam?' *Critical Inquiry* 30, 225–48.

Latour B and Woolgar S (1979) *Laboratory Life: The Construction of Scientific Facts.* London: Sage.

Lawson T (1997) *Economics and Reality.* London: Routledge.

Le Lohe, M (1975) 'Participation in elections by Asians in Bradford', in Crewe I (ed.), *The Politics of Race.* London: Croom Helm, pp. 105–17.

Lee S (2021) 'The politics of anti-austerity protest: South Korea in 1997–1998 and Greece in 2009–2010'. *International Journal of Comparative Sociology* 62(1), 32–55.

Leeuw F and Schmeets H (2016) *Empirical Legal Research.* Cheltenham, UK and Northampton, MA, USA: Edward Elgar.

Lincoln D (2020) 'Why ideal gas law is not that ideal'. https://www.wondriumdaily.com/why-ideal-gas-law-is-not-that-ideal/#:~:text=The%20ideal%20gas%20law%20is%20inaccurate%20because%20the%20ideal%20gas,molecular%20interaction%20under%20certain%20conditions (accessed September 2023).

Little D (2005) 'Causal mechanisms in comparative historical sociology'. http://www-personal.umd.umich.edu/~delittle/SSHA%20causal%20essay%20draft%20v3.htm (accessed September 2023).

Little D (2015) 'Mechanisms and method'. *Philosophy of the Social Sciences* 45(4), 462–80.

Loewenberg F (1984). 'Professional ideology, middle range theories and knowledge building for social work practice'. *British Journal of Social Work* 14(4), 309–22.

Lohr S (2019) *Measuring Crime: Behind the Statistics.* Boca Raton, FL: CRC Press.

Lopreato J and Crippen T (1999) *Crisis in Sociology: The Need for Darwin.* New Brunswick, NJ: Transaction Publishers.

Lukács G (1967) *History and Class Consciousness: Studies in Marxist Dialectics.* Cambridge, MA: MIT Press.

Lupyan G and Winter B (2018) 'Language is more abstract than you think, or, why aren't languages more iconic?' *Philosophical Transactions of the Royal Society of London* B 373, 20170137. http://dx.doi.org/10.1098/rstb.2017.0137.

Lynd R and Lynd M (1929) *Middletown: A Study of Modern American Culture.* New York: Harcourt, Brace and Jovanovich.

Lynn P and Elliot D (2000) 'The British Crime Survey: A review of methodology'. National Centre of Social Research. https://www.researchgate.net/publication/242622608_The_British_Crime_Survey_A_Review_of_Methodology (accessed June 2023).

Maehle A (2004) '"Receptive substances": John Newport Langley (1852–1925) and his path to a receptor theory of drug action'. *Medical History* 48(2), 153–74.

Maguire M and McVie S (2017) 'Crime data and criminal statistics: a critical reflection', in Liebling A, Maruna S and McAra L (eds), *The Oxford Handbook of Criminology* (6th edn). Oxford: Oxford University Press, pp. 163–88.

Mahoney J (2012) 'The logic of process tracing tests in the social sciences'. *Sociological Methods & Research* 41(4), 570–97.

Maiz R (2015) 'From structures to processes and mechanisms: the logic of explanation in the work of Charles Tilly'. https://www.academia.edu/30438359/ (accessed May 2023).

Malinowski B (1922) *Argonauts of the Western Pacific.* London: Routledge and Keegan Paul

Manzo G (2009) *The Spiral of Inequalities: School Choices in France and Italy in the 20th Century.* Paris: Presses de l'université Paris Sorbonne.

Maris J (2005) 'The biologic basis for neuroblastoma heterogeneity and risk stratification'. *Current Opinion in Pediatrics* 17(1), 7–13. doi:10.1097/01.mop.0000150631.60571.89.

Marsh H (2014) *Do No Harm: Stories of Life, Death and Brain Surgery.* London: Phoenix.

Marx K (1852) *The Eighteenth Brumaire of Louis Bonaparte.* New York: Die Revolution.

Mason J (2002) *Qualitative Researching.* London: Sage.

Matthews R (2000) 'Storks deliver babies (p = .008)'. *Teaching Statistics* 22(2), 36–8. https://www.researchgate.net/publication/227763292_Storks_Deliver_Babies_p_0008 (accessed June 2023).

Maxwell J (1867) 'On the dynamical theory of gases'. *Philosophical Transactions of the Royal Society of London* 157, 49–88. doi:10.1098/rstl.1867.0004. S2CID 96568430.

McAdam D and Tarrow S (2011) 'Introduction: Dynamics of contention: ten years on'. *Mobilization: An International Quarterly* 16(1), 1–10.

McAdam D, Tarrow S and Tilly C (2001) *Dynamics of Contention.* Cambridge: Cambridge University Press.

McCarthy A, James L, Kennedy J and Middleton L (2005) 'Pharmacogenetics in drug development'. *Philosophical Transactions of the Royal Society of London* B 360, 1579–88. doi:10.1098/rstb.2005.1688.

McCold P. (2000) 'Toward a mid-range theory of restorative criminal justice: a reply to the Maximalist model'. *Contemporary Justice Review* 3(4), 357–414.

McCutchan G, Wood F, Edwards A, Richards R and Brain K (23 December 2015) 'Influences of cancer symptom knowledge, beliefs and barriers on cancer symptom presentation in relation to socioeconomic deprivation: a systematic review'. *BMC Cancer* 15, 1000. doi:10.1186/s12885–015–1972–8.

McElroy K (2016) *Prototyping for Designers*. Sebastopol: O'Reilly Media.

McGavock H (2011) *How Drugs Work: Basic Pharmacology for Healthcare Professionals*. Oxford: Radcliffe.

McIntyre L (2018) *Post-Truth*. Cambridge, MA: MIT Press.

McLennan, G (2014) 'Sociology, cultural studies and the cultural turn', in Holmwood J and Scott J (eds), *The Palgrave Handbook of Sociology in Britain*. London: Palgrave Macmillan. https://doi.org/10.1057/9781137318862_23.

McLuhan M (1964) *Understanding Media: The Extensions of Man*. Cambridge, MA: MIT Press.

McNemar Q (1946) 'Opinion-attitude methodology'. *Psychological Bulletin* 43, 289–374.

Mees H (2016) 'China as the world's factory', in Mees H (ed.), *The Chinese Birdcage*. London: Palgrave Macmillan, pp. 21–32.

Meleis A, Sawyer L, Im E, Hilfinger-Messias D and Schumacher K. (September 2000) 'Experiencing transitions: an emerging middle-range theory'. *Advances in Nursing Science (ANS)* 23(1), 12–28. doi:10.1097/00012272–200009000–00006. PMID: 10970036.

Merton R (1936) 'The unanticipated consequences of purposive social action'. *American Sociological Review* 1(6), 894–904.

Merton R (1968a) 'The Matthew effect in science'. *Science* 159(3810), 56–63.

Merton R (1968b) *Social Theory and Social Structure*. New York: Free Press.

Milgram S (1974) *Obedience to Authority: An Experimental View*. New York: HarperCollins.

Miller R (1987) *Fact and Method: Explanation, Confirmation and Reality in Natural and Social Sciences*. Princeton, NJ: Princeton University Press.

Morgan N, Shaw O, Feist A and Byron C (2016) *Reducing Criminal Opportunity: Vehicle Security and Vehicle Crime*. Research Report 87. Home Office UK. https://www.gov.uk/government/ publications/ reducing -criminal -opportunity -vehicle -security -and -vehicle -crime (accessed May 2023).

Musgrave A and Pigden C (2021 edn) 'Imre Lakatos', *The Stanford Encyclopaedia of Philosophy*. https://plato.stanford.edu/archives/sum2021/entries/lakatos/ (accessed June 2023).

Naess P (2019) '"Demi-regs", probabilism and partly closed systems'. *Journal of Critical Realism* 18(5), 475–86.

Nandi A and Platt L (2018) 'The relationship between political and ethnic identity among UK ethnic minority and majority populations'. *Journal of Ethnic and Migration Studies* 46(5), 957–79.

NatCen (2012) 'British Social Attitudes 28'. https:// www .bsa .natcen .ac .uk/ media/ 38966/bsa28-full-report.pdf (accessed July 2023).

NatCen (2015) 'The benefits of random sampling: lessons from the 2015 General Election.' https://www.bsa.natcen.ac.uk/media/39018/random-sampling.pdf (accessed July 2023).

National Audit Office (2014) *NHS waiting times for elective care in England*. London: The Stationery Office. HC: 964. https://www.nao.org.uk/wp-content/uploads/2014/01/NHS-waiting-times-for-elective-care-in-England.pdf (accessed September 2023).

Neale B (2021) *The Craft of Qualitative Longitudinal Inquiry*. London: Sage.

Neale B and Davies L (2015) 'Becoming a young breadwinner? The education, employment and training trajectories of young fathers'. *Social Policy and Society* 15(1), 85–98.

Neale B and Lau Clayton C (2014) 'Young parenthood and cross generational relationships: the perspectives of young fathers', in Holland J and Edward R (eds), *Understanding Families over Time*. London: Palgrave Macmillan, pp. 69–87.

Neal B and Patrick R (2016) 'Engaged young fathers? Gender, parenthood and the dynamics of relationships'. FYF Working Paper Series no. 1. https://followingfathers.leeds.ac.uk/findings-and-publications/ (accessed July 2023).

NHS Improving Quality (2017) 'Seven ways to no delays'. https:// www .england .nhs.uk/improvement-hub/wp-content/uploads/sites/44/2017/11/Seven-Ways-to-No -Delay.pdf (accessed June 2023).

Nichols T (2017) *The Death of Expertise*. Oxford: Oxford University Press.

Nikolajew V (2013) The new age of Enlightenment: emergence of underlying philosophies of the new civilization of sustainable development. CreateSpace Independent Publishing Platform.

Norton W, Loudon K, Chambers D et al. (2021) 'Designing provider-focused implementation trials with purpose and intent: introducing the PRECIS-2-PS tool'. *Implementation Science* 16, 7.

Oakley A (2002) 'Social science and evidence-based everything: the case of education'. *Educational Review* 54(3), 277–86.

Oppenheim P and Putnam H (1958). 'Unity of science as a working hypothesis'. *Minnesota Studies in the Philosophy of Science* 2, 3–36.

Padial J and De la Riva I (2021) 'A paradigm shift in our view of species drives current trends in biological classification'. *Biological Reviews* 96, 731–51. https://doi.org/10.1111/brv.12676.

Patsopoulos N (2011) 'A pragmatic view on pragmatic trials'. *Dialogues in Clinical Neuroscience* 13(2), 217–24.

Patton M (2002) *Qualitative Research and Evaluation Methods*. Thousand Oaks, CA: Sage.

Paul H and van Veldhuizen A (eds) (2021) *Post-Everything: An Intellectual History of Post-Concepts*. Manchester: Manchester University Press.

Pawson R (1989) *A Measure for Measures: A Manifesto for Empirical Sociology*. London: Routledge.

Pawson R (2000) 'Middle-range realism'. *Archives Européennes de Sociologie* 41(2), 283–325.

Pawson R (2002) 'Does Megan's Law work? A theory-driven systematic review'. ESRC Centre for Evidence Based Policy and Practice Working Paper 7.

Pawson R (2004) 'Mentoring relationships: an explanatory review'. ESRC Centre for Evidence Based Policy and Practice Working Paper 21.

Pawson R (2006) *Evidence-Based Policy: A Realist Approach*. London: Sage.

Pawson R (2008) 'Method mix, technical hex, theory fix', in Bergman M (ed.), *Advances in Mixed Method Research*. London: Sage, pp. 120–39.

Pawson R (2009) 'On the shoulders on Merton: Boudon as the modern guardian of middle-range theory', in Cherkaoui M and Hamilton P (eds), *Raymond Boudon: A Life in Sociology: Essays in Honour of Raymond Boudon*. Oxford: Bardwell Press, pp. 317–34.

Pawson R (2010) 'Middle range theory and program theory evaluation: from prove-
nance to practice', in Vaessen J and Leeuw F (eds), *Mind the Gap: Perspectives on
Policy Evaluation and the Social Sciences*. London: Routledge, pp. 76–96.

Pawson R (2013) *The Science of Evaluation: A Realist Manifesto*. London: Sage.

Pawson R (2018) 'Realist memorabilia', in Emmel N, Greenhalgh J, Manzano A,
Monaghan M, Dalkin S (eds), *Doing Realist Research*. London: Sage, pp. 203–20.

Pawson R (March 2019a) 'The shrinking scope of pragmatic trials: a methodological
reflection on their domain of applicability'. *Journal of Clinical Epidemiology* 107,
71–6.

Pawson R (2019b) 'The "pragmatic trial": an essentially contested concept?' *Journal of
Evaluation in Clinical Practice* 25(6), 943–54.

Pawson R (2019c) 'Pragmatic trials and implementation science: grounds for
divorce?' *BMC Medical Research Methodology* 19, 176.

Pawson R (2021) 'The coronavirus response: boxed in by models'. *Evaluation* 27(2),
149–67. https://doi.org/10.1177/1356389020968579.

Pawson R (2023) 'Do lockdowns work? Evidence from the UK', in Eliadis P,
Naidoo IA and Rist RC (eds), *Policy Evaluation in the Era of COVID-19*. London:
Routledge. https://doi.org/10.4324/9781003376316.

Pawson R and Tilley N (1997) *Realistic Evaluation*. London: Sage.

Pawson R, Owen L and Wong G (2010) 'The Today Programme's contribution to
evidence-based policy'. *Evaluation* 16(2), 211–13.

Pawson R, Owen L and Wong G (2011) 'Known knowns, known unknowns, unknown
unknowns: the predicament of evidence-based policy'. *American Journal of
Evaluation* 32(4), 518–46.

Peirce C (1955) 'The scientific attitude and fallibilism', in Buchler J (ed.), *Philosophical
Writings of Peirce*. New York: Dover, pp. 59–70.

Piaget, J (1971) *Biology and Knowledge*. Chicago, IL: University of Chicago Press.

Pickering M (1993–2009) *Auguste Comte: An Intellectual Biography, vols. 1–3*.
Cambridge: Cambridge University Press.

Polit D and Beck C (2010) 'Generalization in quantitative and qualitative research:
myths and strategies'. *International Journal of Nursing Studies* 47(11), 1451–8.
https://doi.org/10.1016/j.ijnurstu.2010.06.004.

Popper K (1963, reprinted in 1989) *Conjectures and Refutations*. London: Routledge.

Popper K (1972) *Objective Knowledge, An Evolutionary Approach*. Oxford: Oxford
University Press.

Popper K (1976) 'The logic of sciences' in Adorno T et al. (eds), *The Positivist Dispute
in German Sociology*. London: Heinemann.

Popper K (1992) *The Logic of Scientific Discovery* (5th edn). London: Routledge.

Power S (2018). 'How should we respond to the continuing failure of compensatory
education?' *Orbis Scholae* 2. doi:10.14712/23363177.2018.231.

Priest S (2007) *The British Empiricists*. London: Routledge.

Quote Investigator (2014) 'History does not repeat itself, but it rhymes'. https://
quoteinvestigator.com/2014/01/12/history-rhymes/ (accessed September 2023).

Ragin C (1992) '"Casing" and the process of social inquiry', in Ragin C and Becker H,
What Is a Case? Cambridge: Cambridge University Press, pp. 217–26.

Ragin C and Becker H (1992) *What Is a Case?* Cambridge: Cambridge University
Press.

Randall Wray L (2009) 'The rise and fall of money manager capitalism: a Minskian
approach'. *Cambridge Journal of Economics* 33(4), 807–28.

Randell R, Honey S and Alvarado N et al. (2017) 'Factors supporting and constraining the implementation of robot-assisted surgery: a realist interview study'. *BMJ Open* 9, e028635. doi:10.1136/bmjopen-2018–028635.

Rees T (2022) *Women and the Labour Market.* London: Routledge.

Riedl M, Schwemmer C, Ziewiecki S and Ross LM (2021) 'The rise of political influencers – perspectives on a trend towards meaningful content'. *Frontiers in Communication* 6, 752656. doi:10.3389/fcomm.2021.752656.

Ritchie H (2022) 'How many species are there?' *Our World in Data.* https://ourworldindata.org/how-many-species-are-there (accessed July 2023).

Rojek C and Turner B (2000) 'Decorative sociology: towards a critique of the cultural turn'. *The Sociological Review* 48(4), 629–48.

Romer D and Jamieson K (2020) 'Conspiracy theories as barriers to controlling the spread of COVID-19 in the US'. *Social Science & Medicine* 263, 113356. doi:10.1016/j.socscimed.2020.113356.

Runciman W (1966) *Relative Deprivation and Social Justice: A Study of Attitudes to Social Inequality in Twentieth Century England.* London: Routledge and Keegan Paul.

Sackett D (2011) 'Explanatory and pragmatic clinical trials: a primer and application to a recent asthma trial'. *Polish Archives of Internal Medicine* 121(7–8), 259–63.

Sacks H (1963) 'Sociological description'. *Berkeley Journal of Sociology* 8(1), 1–16.

Sanchez R, Heene A and Asan U (eds) (2017) *Mid-Range Management Theory: Competence Perspectives on Modularity and Dynamic Capabilities.* Bingley: Emerald Publishing.

Schagrin M (1963) 'Resistance to Ohm's Law'. *American Journal of Physics* 31(7), 536–47.

Schofield J (2000) 'Increasing the generalizability of qualitative research', in Gomm R, Hammersley M and Foster P (eds), *Case Study Method.* London: Sage, pp. 69–97.

Schwartz D and Lellouch J (1967) 'Explanatory and pragmatic attitudes in therapeutic trials'. *Journal of Chronic Disease* 20, 637–48.

Scott J (2005) 'Sociology and its others: reflections on disciplinary specialisation and fragmentation'. *Sociological Research Online* 10, 1. http://www.socresonline.org.uk/10/1/scott.html (accessed May 2023).

Scott J and Marshall G (eds) (2005) 'Comte, Auguste'. *A Dictionary of Sociology.* Oxford: Oxford University Press.

Scriven M (1961) 'The key property of physical laws: inaccuracy', in Feigl H and Maxwell G (eds), *Current Issues in the Philosophy of Science.* New York; Holt, Rhinehart & Winston, 91–101.

Sedgwick P (2014) 'Explanatory versus pragmatic trials'. *BMJ* 349, g6694.

Segall M, Campbell D and Herskovits M (22 February 1963) 'Cultural differences in the perception of geometric illusions'. *Science* 139(3556), 769–71. doi:10.1126/science.139.3556.769.

Serrano-Gallardo P, Manzano A and Pawson R (2022) 'Non-pharmaceutical interventions during COVID-19 in the UK and Spain: a rapid realist review'. *Open Research Europe* 2, 52. https://doi.org/10.12688/openreseurope.14566.2.

Shapiro B (2000) *A Culture of Fact: England, 1550–1720.* Ithaca, NY: Cornell University Press.

Shedd J and Hershey M (December 1913) 'The history of Ohms Law'. *Popular Science*, 599–614.

Siegel E (2020) 'Earth is spiralling away from the Sun for now, but will eventually crash into it'. *Forbes Newsletters.* https://www.forbes.com/sites/startswithabang/2020/04/

09/earth-is-spiraling-away-from-the-sun-for-now-but-will-eventually-crash-into-it/?sh=4850771a2385 (accessed June 2023).

Smart B (ed.) (2010) *Post-Industrial Society.* London: Sage.

Smith ME (2011) 'Empirical urban theory for archaeologists' *Journal of Archaeological Method and Theory* 18(3), 167–92.

Smith Maguire J (2021) 'Towards a sociology from wine and vina aperta'. *Journal of Cultural Analysis and Social Change* 6(2), 10.

Smith MJ, Liehr P and Carpenter D (eds) (2024) *Middle Range Theory for Nursing* (5th edn). New York: Springer.

Snow CP (1959) *The Two Cultures.* Cambridge: Cambridge University Press.

Sokal A and Bricmont J (2004) 'Defense of a modest scientific realism', in Carrier M, Roggenhofer J, Küppers G, Blanchard, P (eds), *Knowledge and the World: Challenges beyond the Science Wars.* Berlin: Springer, pp. 17–29.

Somers G (1963) 'The foetal toxicity of thalidomide'. *Proceedings of the European Society for the Study of Drug Toxicity* 1, 49–58.

Stacey M (1960) *Tradition and Change: A Study of Banbury.* London: Oxford University Press.

Stake R (1995) *The Art of Case Study Research.* London: Sage.

Stinchcombe A (1968) *Constructing Social Theories.* New York: Harcourt, Brace and World.

Stinchcombe A (2005) *The Logic of Social Research.* Chicago, IL: University of Chicago Press.

Stoltz D (2014) *Diagrams of Theory: Coleman's Boat.* https://www.dustinstoltz.com/blog/2014/01/26/ diagrams -of -theory -james -colemans -boat -bathtub (accessed September 2023).

Stonequist E (1937) *The Marginal Man: A Study in Personality and Culture Conflict.* New York: Scribner, Simon & Schuster.

Stouffer A, Lumsdaine A and Harper-Lumsdaine, M et al. (1949) *The American Soldier* (3 vols). Princeton, NJ: Princeton University Press.

Stroebe W, Gadenne V and Nijstad B (2018). 'Do our psychological laws apply only to college students? External validity revisited'. *Basic and Applied Social Psychology* 40(6), 384–95. https://doi.org/10.1080/01973533.2018.1513362.

Sue V and Ritter L (2007). 'Writing survey questions', in Sue V and Ritter L (eds), *Conducting Online Surveys.* London: Sage, pp. 38–58. https://dx.doi.org/10.4135/9781412983754.n4.

Susen S and Turner B (2021) 'Classics and classicality: JCS after 20 years'. *Journal of Classical Sociology* 21(3–4), 227–44.

Talk: History – Wikiquote (n.d.) https://en.wikiquote.org/wiki/Talk:History#:~:text=This%20is%20very%20often%20attributed,into%20an%20abyss%20of%20skepticism (accessed June 2023).

Tarrant A and Neale B (2017) 'Supporting young fathers in welfare settings: an evidence review of what matters and what helps'. https://followingfathers.leeds.ac.uk/wp-content/uploads/sites/79/2016/06/Evidence-Report.pdf (accessed May 2023).

Tarrow S (2010) 'The strategy of paired comparison: toward a theory of practice'. *Comparative Political Studies* 43(2), 230–59.

Tarrow S (2019). 'Comparison, triangulation, and embedding research in history: a methodological self-analysis'. *Bulletin de Méthodologie Sociologique* 141(1), 7–29. https://doi.org/10.1177/0759106318812786.

Taxonomy (biology) (2023) Wikipedia. https://en.wikipedia.org/wiki/Taxonomy_(biology) (accessed February 2023).

Thaul S (2012) 'How FDA approves drugs and regulates their safety and effectiveness'. *Congressional Research Service* R41983 7–5700. https://www.fas.org/sgp/crs/misc/R41983.pdf (accessed March 2023).

Thomas W (1951) 'Social behavior and personality', in Volkert E (ed.), *Contributions of W I Thomas to Theory and Social Research.* New York: SSRC.

Thomas W and Thomas D (eds.) (1928) *The Child in America: Behavior problems and programs.* New York: Knopf, pp. 571–2.

Tilley N (1993) *Understanding car parks, crime and CCTV.* Police Research Group Crime Prevention Unit Paper 42. London: Home Office.

Tilly C (1984) *Big Structures, Large Processes, Huge Comparisons.* New York: Russell Sage Foundation.

Tilly C (2001) 'Mechanisms in political processes'. *Annual Review of Political Science* 4, 21–41.

Tilly C (2003) *The Politics of Collective Violence.* Cambridge: Cambridge University Press.

Tomlinson J (2007). 'Female part-time workers' experiences of occupational mobility in the UK service industry'. *Women in Management Review* 22(4), 305–18.

Treweek S and Zwarenstein M. (2009) 'Making trials matter: pragmatic and explanatory trials and the problem of applicability'. *Trials* 10, 37. https://doi.org/10.1186/1745-6215-10-37.

Tunis S, Stryer D and Clancy C (2003) 'Practical clinical trials: increasing the value of clinical research for decision making in clinical and health policy'. *JAMA* 290(12), 1624–32.

UK Statistics Authority (2016) Statement on the use of official statistics on contributions to the European Union. https://uksa.statisticsauthority.gov.uk/news/uk-statistics-authority-statement-on-the-use-of-official-statistics-on-contributions-to-the-european-union/ (accessed June 2023).

Unterhalter E, North A, Arnot M, Lloyd C, Moletsane L, Murphy-Graham E, Parkes J and Saito M (2014) 'Interventions to enhance girls' education and gender equality'. Education Rigorous Literature Review. Department for International Development.

Uscinski J and Butler R (2013) 'The epistemology of fact-checking'. *Critical Review* 25(2), 162–80.

Van den Berg A and Jeong T (July 2022) 'Cutting off the branch on which we are sitting? On postpositivism, value neutrality, and the bias paradox'. *Society.* doi:10.1007/s12115–022–00750–8.

Van Dooren W and Hoffmann C (2018) 'Performance management in Europe: an idea whose time has come and gone?', in Ongaro E and Nan Theil S (eds), *The Palgrave Handbook of Public Administration in Europe.* London: Palgrave Macmillan, pp. 207–25.

Vandenberghe F and Fuchs S (2019) 'On the coming end of sociology'. *Canadian Review of Sociology* 56(1), 138–43.

Varadhan R and Seeger J (2013) 'Estimation and reporting of heterogeneity of treatment effects', in Velentgas P, Dreyer N, Nourjah P, Smith S and Torchia M (eds), *Developing a Protocol for Observational Comparative Effectiveness Research: A User's Guide.* Rockville, MD: Agency for Healthcare Research and Quality (US). Ebook at: https://www.ncbi.nlm.nih.gov/books/NBK126188/.

Verme P. 2017. Relative deprivation in the labor market: the choice of reference group crucially determines subjective deprivation and thus affects labor market behavior. *IZA World of Labour.* https://wol.iza.org/uploads/articles/372/pdfs/relative-deprivation-in-the-labor-market.pdf (accessed February 2024).

Wahl-Jorgensen K, Berry M and Cable J et al. (2017) 'Rethinking balance and impartiality in journalism? How the BBC attempted to change the paradigm'. *Journalism* 18(7), 781–800.

Wallis J, Jerath A and Coburn N (2021) 'Association of surgeon-patient concordance with postoperative outcomes'. *JAMA Surg*ery. doi:10.1001/jamasurg.2021.6339.

Ware J and Hamel M (2011) 'Pragmatic trials – guides to better patient care?' *New England Journal of Medicine* 364, 1685–7.

Wethered, F (1898) *Medical Microscopy: A Guide to the Use of the Microscope in Medical Practice.* Philadelphia: Blakiston, Son and Co.

Whyte WF (1943) *Street Corner Society.* Chicago, IL: University of Chicago Press.

Wikipedia (n.d.) Kinetic Theory of Gases. https://en.wikipedia.org/wiki/Kinetic_theory _of_gases.

Williams M (2021) *Realism and Complexity in Social Science.* London: Routledge.

Wilson D and Reuss R (eds) (1999) *Prison(er) Education: Stories of Change and Transformation.* Sherfield-on-Loddon: Waterside Press.

Winfred A, Hagen E and George F (2021) 'The lazy or dishonest respondent'. *Annual Review of Organizational Psychology and Organizational Behavior* 8(1), 105–37.

Wittgenstein L (1953) *Philosophical Investigations.* London: Macmillan.

Wittgenstein L (1958) *The Blue and Brown Books: Preliminary Studies for the 'Philosophical Investigations'.* New York: Harper & Row.

Wright E (1985) *Classes.* London: Verso.

Wright L, Steptoe A and Fancourt D (2022) 'Patterns of compliance with COVID-19 preventive behaviours: a latent class analysis of 20 000 UK adults'. *Journal of Epidemiology & Community Health* 76, 247–53.

Wright Mills C (1959) *The Sociological Imagination.* Oxford: Oxford University Press.

Yin R (2017) *Case Study Research and Applications.* London: Sage.

Ylikoski P (2016) 'Thinking with the Coleman boat'. https://liu.diva-portal.org/smash/ get/diva2:1048216/FULLTEXT02.pdf (accessed September 2023).

Zaborowski H (ed.) (2010) *Natural Moral Law in Contemporary Society.* Washington, DC: Catholic University of America Press.

Zwarenstein M, Treweek S and Loudon K (2017) 'PRECIS-2 helps researchers design more applicable RCTs while CONSORT Extension for pragmatic trials helps knowledge users decide whether to apply them'. *Journal of Clinical Epidemiology* 84, 27–9.

Index

Abbott, A. 22, 153
absolute risk 7, 148
abstraction 15, 34, 165–67, 179–81, 222, 224
academics
    infrastructure 153
    interest 90
acontextuality 194, 196
action of mechanisms 37, 39, 70
active career planners 216, 219, 231
actuality 84
adjudicationist logic 140
adverse reactions 7–8, 12
agency 36–40
    paradoxical consequence of 39
agent-based modelling 77
ambiguity 100, 109, 115, 176–7, 248
analytic sociology 155
animal testing 26, 128
Anstead, N. 116
antagonistic non-members 228, 232
anti-austerity
    movement 80
    protest 78
anti-intellectualism 152
Anwar, M. 194
Archer, M. 39, 42–3, 52–3
arithmetical precision 70
arms-race 46–7
artificial culture medium 25
aspirations 82–4, 99, 210, 231–4, 238
assay development 25
atemporality 194, 196
austerity policies 79, 156
authoritative information 241
autoethnography 107

Bairstow, J. 175
balance/balanced 111–17

impartial observation, empiricist
    myth of 111–18
inquiry, logic of 112
observation 123
Bayesian methods 209–10
Becker, H. 105–106, 207, 241
befriending 239–41
behaviour/behavioural
    change, benefits of 241
    differences, investigation of 13
    generalisation 187
    science 182–8
Bemelmans-Videc, M. -L. 237
Bennett, A. 207
Berger. P. 42–3
Bhaskar, R. 42–3, 53
bias 111–12, 115, 123, 138, 190, 193
    desirability 23–4
    selection 109
Big Brothers Big Sisters of America
    programme 238
big data analytics 111–12
Big Pharma on evidence construction 29
biological process 25, 128
biologic/genetic differences 33
Black, M. 196
blasphemy 4
Blumer, H. 180–81
Boudon, R. 66–8, 93, 195–96, 221
    abstraction 70
    explanatory model hypothesises 67
    research on educational inequality 70
boundary conditions 55–56, 59, 63, 81, 84–85, 180, 252
broadcast news 116, 118
Brownian motion 12
bureaucratic understatement 134
Butler, R. 108–9, 112
Byrne, R. 22, 194, 207, 209

Printed and bound by CPI Group (UK) Ltd, Croydon, CR0 4YY

12/11/2024

14591792-0003